MW01292921

APACHE RECON
Because of the Brave

By MICHAEL L. MOOMEY

authorHOUSE®

AuthorHouse™
1663 Liberty Drive, Suite 200
Bloomington, IN 47403
www.authorhouse.com
Phone: 1-800-839-8640

First published by AuthorHouse 4/12/2010

ISBN: 978-1-4490-8292-5 (e)
ISBN: 978-1-4490-8290-1 (sc)
ISBN: 978-1-4490-8291-8 (hc)

Printed in the United States of America
Bloomington, Indiana

This book is printed on acid-free paper.

INTRODUCTION

People that become combat infantrymen are different, they don't start out different, but after a certain time they evolve into a different mind-set. Soldiers in combat function are on the outer edge of man's emotional and physical capabilities, performing in the swarming hostile environment of battle with their courage, and their concentration, they are alive at an intensity most people never reach. Combat Soldiers cannot deny their fears or needs, while people in more normal existences can slide from day to day, controlled by the routines of job and home, rarely conscious of their own motivations or abilities, combat infantrymen are allowed no such deadened life. In an immediate and primitive way they were forced to meet head on with their own make-up, they would have to live by their wit and live with the amount of fear that greets them each morning as the sun comes up from the East, and make decisions that must be made immediately, that could mean life or death each day. There are no such second chances at some of the decisions you must make; sometimes not making that decision may be worse than making one. You not only have to worry about getting yourself killed, you may also cause the death of someone else, then you would have to live with that the rest of your life, you couldn't do it. You have to learn to kill and feel no remorse for doing such, you can't stop and think about doing it, and you have to do it to stay alive yourself, it's that old saying, kill or be killed, and we had to live with that every day, every second to achieve that goal of going home, alive, while getting the praise I craved. As a young man that had really never experienced what I call anyone telling me what a great job I had done, I didn't understand the rush I felt when ending someone's life, how the reactions of those I served with, when they would pat me on the back and tell me how important I was to keeping them alive, that was what drove me along with my feeling that no one, or no thing was going to take me into death as long as I pushed the button, or trigger, to give me that prestige which I grew to crave more and more as each day passed.

War is neither ethical nor heroic, its purpose is to obtain maximum force in the field and it is ultimately irrelevant to any victim whether he fell from a snipers bullet or was ripped apart by a rocket attack, dead is dead and it's just one to add to the growing list. I feel they, the men out in the jungle had the right to call them selves experts on this subject matter as they saw it. A combat infantryman is someone that sleeps out in the rain, in the mud, scared to death each minute, while others hunt for him, to do him harm. These young men must learn to adapt as soon as possible, on your first visit into Uncle Ho's playground you stand more than 50% of getting yourself killed dead.

There may be differences in what the Army says happened; but I want to put it into the words as those out in the unforgiving jungle saw things, and not everyone out there saw things the same way, but as each of them learned that the war was not a game, but a test to see if under extreme circumstances we could prevail and live another day, until the next test. You can only fail the test once and you would never be able to test again, if you lost, doesn't sound fair, no one will ever tell you war is fair. You never know what a mistake was, until you made it. Then you might not know it then, because you are killed dead, and your loved ones back in the world will have to suffer because you made that mistake. You might see me as being a hostile, barbaric person that would kill without any feelings, and at that time you would be correct in your assumption of me, I only hope I have changed since then, because I am now with you.

ACKNOWLEDGEMENTS

I would like to acknowledge all that I served with, Jon Arnes, Ronnie Baker, Van Brown, S/Sgt Gilbert Mumford, Lt. Leo Hadley, Col Jamie Hendrix, S/Sgt Magwood, Lt J North, Darrell Stewart, Sammy Alewine, Mick Cole, Robert (Chief) Antonio, Mike Faulkner, Ron Brown, Jerry (Pluto), Dempsey, Thornton, Rex Kimbell, Charlie Zollman, Little Beaver, Parrish, Pease, Steve Moore, Galen Cartright, Keith Wynn, Mike Lula, Bill Watkins and some I don't remember your name but you might not remember mine either.

I want to thank my Mother, Wanda G Moomey who had to live through what I went through and worry about me each day I was in country; she was an avid reader and died before this story could be published, for that I'm very sorry.

I also need to thank my wife Kolleen who has put up with me and my PTSD, which made me an asshole at times. I think some of you might have been there also, along with me. I also need to thank my Doctor H. Faruque from the Oklahoma City VA Hospital for helping me with my demons.

CHAPTER ONE - IN COUNTRY

We were out humping the jungle-covered mountains and valleys of the Central Highlands of Viet Nam in August 1967. I was carrying a M60 machinegun while in the second platoon, Company D, 3/12 Inf., 4th Infantry Division, a unit I had just joined. The Point stopped and pointed up into a tree, where we saw 2 legs dangling through the leaves. My Platoon Leader told me to give him a quick burst where I thought the body was. It didn't occur to me at the time that I was about to kill my first human being, but I was about to start what I would continue to do for the next year. I opened up with a burst of 10 or 20, down he came, along with a SKS rifle with a round in the chamber, he didn't scream or yell, didn't even moan, which I thought odd. I went over to look at him, and was surprised to find an adolescent of 13 or 14, with crew-cut hair. One of the bullets had entered his right eye; there was a bloody mash of brains and bone splinters covering his upper-back torso, along with a fist sized exit wound, which revealed that his skull had been cleaned of cerebral matter by the pressure wave of that bullet. He was also hit in the chest and legs but the damage was by that 1 bullet, which ended his short life. I felt some sorrow for him until I went back to my platoon and was greeted as if

I had just scored the winning touch-down, that made my day, as I hadn't really accomplished anything in my short 19 years, and it felt good to get that praise and the slaps on my back as I passed the guys who didn't know what I would do in battle as it was my first day, I was told that I was OK, which finally gave me acceptance, which I devoured and wanted more. Most of the new guys, me included, were ignorant of the ways of battle, as the enemy was treacherous, and sneaky in getting their results, it was nothing like what was taught in the states. It was something you could never learn it all, because it would change every day, sometimes, every hour.

It really wasn't the kill that made my day, but the fact when it happened and I solved the problem by killing these people; I was raised up high enough that I was at last someone special, and on my first day. I figured I had to kill the most, I wasn't going to become just another soldier I had big plans for myself. I was going to remain the Star in my Company and maybe the whole Battalion. After awhile it became apparent that I had to kill and not let it bother me, as I was getting the praise I desired by doing this, I demanded it. In addition, it kept all the others and me alive.

This story I'm telling, is an account of a small group of young men living in a violent new way of existence for them; which went against everything they were told at a young age, that was to kill another, and to feel no remorse for doing so, I didn't like the person I had become, but I relished in the praise I received. It's a hell of a thing to kill someone; you take everything he was or was going to be, you take away sometimes a father, son, brother or husband, sometimes all of them it one person. I couldn't allow myself to feel anything as I killed. But if I didn't kill them then they surely would have killed me, I was not to be killed while there. I was going to kill everything that stood in my way of going back home. I only hope that when or if I get to go home I would no longer go to such extremes, to get my wants. We had to learn to act, and then react to guerilla warfare; which has no rules, or boundaries; each mistake made could cost you

2

and maybe others their lives, or being maimed for life. We are constantly told not to make mistakes then told again. So even the smallest contact could become that one that takes you out of the equation. Tom one of the guys in 2nd Platoon tried to advise me not to run up front each and every time, instead, wait a couple seconds until the rest of the Company can get up there with me. I told him he was someone that didn't understand, why I was jumping up front. I had to have the most points and I couldn't let someone other than me become the top in scoring, I just couldn't. I needed to be number one. I wanted to stay the star as long as I could, I had to, it felt so good to have guys come up after a battle and have them tell me how important I was as far as keeping them all alive. I guess at that time I had a low esteem I felt that if I didn't jump out and begin the killing that someone else might get that praise bestowed on them, then I wouldn't be Number One; I had to be the Star; Always! I started to realize that I might not be in the right frame of mind, but I also felt the rush I received, when I got that slap on the back and was told. I was good. Plus the fact if I killed them, they couldn't kill me. The other machine-gunner Jon, actually had almost as many kills as I, he was back in the middle of our line as we moved through the jungle, which was something, unless you have ever been to a jungle that has out-lived the people that dwell in such, you wouldn't have a clue as to how thick with vines and brush along with the triple canopy, how beautiful it was, and as scary as it got when the sun went down. Darkness was something where the enemy again, had the advantage.

My Platoon Leader tells me I'm doing a good job, jumping up front and firing into the mass of human carnage. Then he tells me be careful one of these times you are going to jump into something that you may not be able to handle." That started bothering me, maybe I was being a little reckless but I still got the praise I wanted. The second kill, didn't seem real to me. Most new guys are naturally innocent when it comes to going out into the jungle, to fight or just look around. While in a Line Company you were to fight; but while on a Reconnaissance patrol, you were there to look around, as I later learned.

During my first ambush, on my third day, it was as if I was in a dream, and I didn't do all the right things, to get the kill. I should have waited until that gook patrol was totally in the kill zone of the ambush so the claymore mines could do the job killing most of them. While on an ambush, most people; even those veterans, are terrified, that there was that chance we could bite off more than we could chew, and have to come up with an alterative course of action, to keep from going belly-up. People don't have the innate ability to kill, and kill with no remorse. However, I needed the praise I got from those in charge and the respect of my peers. After that, it was easier to do and I did it well. I was the gunner that got the most, so I thought I was special. Why the killing didn't bother me was probably because I looked at the enemy as a low life that was trying to take away the praise I needed, and needed to keep. I didn't care how many I got, just as long as I didn't have to put one of my friends in a plastic body bag, I was all right with killing those that wanted to harm my comrades and me. At a point in time my decadent lifestyle began to allow me to feel no remorse while killing those out to kill me, I began to have a grudge against all Vietnamese because, I didn't know the difference between friend and foe, which may seem unfair to those that weren't in that circumstance. I still wanted to be the Star, which was what was important to me at that point in time; I wasn't going to let anything change my stasis. No matter how risky it became, I had to rise for the occasion and kill, kill, kill. I was constantly told not to make a mistake. Most of the time you didn't know what was the correct thing to do, so you could make a mistake and not know it. After a while, the killing starts to wear on you. Especially when you look at the facts, if I didn't kill them they surely would have killed me. I know my Mother would not want to know what I had become, what I did was to kill, with no remorse and someone that wanted to kill more because it fed my ego as being better than anyone else in the Company at doing what we were sent out there to do. That was all, I wasn't doing something that anyone would think I was not quiet right in my approach to my job in the Line Company. I had a E7 tell me that aircraft are fine when employed in battle, but in the final accounting it took infantrymen armored in cloth shirts to clear the ground with blood, sweat, and tears, the infantryman was where the heart and soul of men was found.

It was sometimes difficult to remember that most of those combat soldiers who shouldered the fighting were, but in their late teens and early twenties, just plain American kids who killed because they had to, but who reverted to their basic good nature between the gruesome chores of war. When they came into a village where there was no enemy, the young men shared their food with the little children, without that food, the kids would go to bed hungry, as the NVA had been there and took all of their stored up rice. It just wasn't fair. How can these people take food from the mouths of little starving children and still tell the villagers that they are trying to help those same people?

CHAPTER TWO -
WHY MUST SOME OF US DIE?

We were awaken by the sound of an AK47 being fired in our direction, something that is never a good thing to wake up to, for the first 2 or 3 seconds you try and identify where the crack, crack noise is coming from and more important where it is aimed at. After those few seconds that information is in my head so I open up with a burst of 10 or 12 rounds, at that time the AK shuts down and a couple of the guys from the 4th Platoon head out to where no body was found. Although he hit no one, he did cause most of us to lose the remainder of the sleep for that day; which was so precious and you couldn't recover it. When they fire and run, it makes fear that stays in the back of your brain, not knowing when will be the next time, and will they get you that time?

When daylight comes the jungle can be the prettiest place; with all the green plants and small streams and the tall trees and all of the little animals going about their own way of being a survivor. Then over the radio, we hear that C Company is being attacked and with that information, we were again back into a war torn country where some of us are to die, while others go unhurt through out the entire year. How that works I don't know, it just happens. Sometimes people dieing happens too often.

We were in the IA Drang Valley a place where the First Cav had been in some of the first battles that included the NVA. I've have the honor to meet David W. Storey whose Father S/ SGT Charles W. Storey was killed on November 17 1965 at LZ Albany along the Cambodian border. A place I had visited several times, in 2 years the jungle had swallowed up most of the shell craters, but you still could see signs of the battles. We had to think of those that had fallen in that place of honor. While setting up our perimeter that evening, Jon the other gunner and I have a talk for a few minutes. Jon told me while I was carrying the machinegun I had more responsibilities then a rifleman and that my keeping the gun clean and ready to go at a moments notice was important as it could turn the tide of battle if fired in a way that contained the enemy and allowed us to get the upper hand in a firefight. So I made sure my machinegun was cleaned and ready to go everyday and night, because the enemy had no rules as when or where they would attack or just fire 1 shot at you then blend into the jungle or a village.

I remember my second or third ambush, where Pete my Asst. Gunner was at my left ready to feed my gun as much lead as we could produce; the ammo-barriers had dropped off their cans of ammo. I looked around and saw 15 kids and 2 Adults sitting out in the damp, muggy jungle waiting on some unsuspecting souls to walk into our death trap; where we had set up so we could take their lives. We need to find that illusive hospital that is either here or in the mountains to our North East. We had just had some new guys arrive and for most of them these was to be their cherry ambush and most of them were scared silly, while I was not scared; not because I was any braver than them, it was that I got more praise if I did OK during the battle about to take place. Each man had his own method of overcoming his anxiety before the ambush broke open into a battle for your life. As daylight forces its way into the jungle floor I looked around and could see the tension and nervousness etched into the hard facial features. Some of them chewed gum while others chewed on unlit cigarettes or some were urinating frequently, most of the younger guys seemed to have a motor disorder and jerky movements, while in place. My stomach rebelled at the thought of anything to eat, even gum to chew, my limbs felt like jell-o where I had no way of controlling them. I was nervous because I knew we could run into something that we might not be able to handle, in that case we had to form up a defensive position and fight for our lives, something I would rather not do. This was something all of us feared, biting off more than we could chew.

In such a critical situation I realized what a Godsend it was to have a veteran Platoon Sergeant noticing my fears, he spoke in soothing tones "Just keep taking deep breathes soldier, keep your mind on your machinegun and shoot like you were trained. Listen for my commands; I will look out for you. I will be there with you in the thick of it." During that fight, I encountered my first American death. After I rose up and started to fire into the human mass I heard a bullet fly by and my fellow new comer immediately to my right, an 18 year old from Georgia had been hit, a bullet from an AK47 had hit him and opened his abdomen making his intestines to pour to the ground. I froze, didn't know what to do for him and I couldn't figure out why he was hit and I wasn't? The Platoon SGT told me "to get back at my gun and keep firing it unless I wanted the same for myself? He told me "A medic will be with him in a short time and I had to keep firing into the human fodder to insure the rest of us not to meet his fate." Amid the raging carnage I felt I had to keep firing until the end, whatever end would come of it, I had no idea at that time.

A wounded Gook was running at Pete as he picked up his rifle and struck the Gook in the face with the butt, blood poured from the amorphous mass that at one time had been his face. The Gooks body trembled a little, and then it surrendered its body and fell face down. Amid this raging carnage, I lost all sense of time. I knew there were more of them coming and I was afraid

I would run out of ammo. I was like a machine running on full tilt when the SGT grabbed me and told me "It was all over and all had been killed and that I should take a minute to pull myself back together." My breathing was rapid and my vision was slowly coming back as I wiped the sweat from my eyes and took several deep breathes and I was OK again. That kid from Georgia didn't make it and 3 others were wounded, but I was OK. The smell of gunpowder mixed with the smell of blood and bone, the sight of pain mixed in with a light rain made it a repugnant, acrimonious morning for me, and because I wasn't hurt that was where I first felt invincible; I did some things that a sane person wouldn't attempt. I adopted a nonchalant behavior, which was the ramification of the fact I wasn't injured. We stood our ground and were able to repulse the enemy's advancement towards us. I had laid down a wall of machinegun fire on the enemy, which helped end the fight in our favor. Later that day we went on a little hike into what we were told was a NVA stronghold, where we might run into something big .I didn't at that time know what they meant by Big, except more than I wanted to take the test for. You either had to pass the test or fail; failing was not an option.

I was confused as to how I should act then react to situations that rose up, I needed an answer right then, and I didn't have the luxury of taking time to figure out which would best serve my needs at that time and place. A wrong decision could cost the lives of several of my people or me and no decision could be as bad as the wrong decision. I wondered if while on a patrol and someone popped up in my area, would I react in a timely fashion so that we all might live another day? I couldn't shoot at shadows because it would have given our position away. Nevertheless, I also can't let an enemy walk up to us and cause us causalities. You had to make the correct assessment; your life may be destroyed if you chose wrong. Doing nothing is usually the same as picking the wrong answer. So you are forced into making a decision and living or dieing with that decision. There was no schooling to get you ready for the type of war we were asked to participate in. The every day struggle of life or death out there in that jungle, you were in that struggle 24/7. Every night as you were attempting to fall asleep, your mind won't let you forget where you are and under what circumstances you were in. The everyday stress was more than anyone could endure, but we had to not only endure; but also to excel in the reality that we must kill to preserve our own lives. Each morning as I woke I decided then and there that I wouldn't let myself get killed that day because of some stupid action I either took or failed to take no matter how many I had to kill.

All I wanted to do was go home with all of my fingers and toes. However, at first, I wanted more; more kills more medals, which would grant me more prestige! It was later that I first realized I was carrying a large target on myself and the only way to get it off was to not be so willing to put myself in dangerous spots from then on. Nevertheless, my going up front and keeping the enemy from forming a defensive line kept friends from D Company being on a list to send home telling of their faith. Therefore, I still put my life in harms way by doing so only now I knew what was happening and I was a little more fearful when we were in contact. But I was still a Star among men that were all putting their lives in my hands and I was very proud of myself at that point. I was proud of my actions that gave me the prestige I cherished. It was like winning State Championships. In addition, each day started out as a new road to the Final Four. Some parts of this story someone may have added something they remember that no one else can verify. I reserved the right to add some thoughts to make the story an easier read. Some of the information was taken from After Action Reports from the 101st Airborne, 173rd Airborne, 4th Infantry Div., 6th ARVN Rangers, a couple of A teams" of Special Forces. I may have seen something in one way, while others saw the action as something else. The things I remember are etched into my soul. So many things happened at such a fast pace, everything might have been seen in a different light by another observer; that's what war does to you. I may see an ambush as a way to kill the enemy where others saw it as a way to get themselves killed; all that has to happen is one of them gets off a lucky shot as he is dying or you spring an ambush on a much larger group of enemy than you anticipated. Maybe in a way I also believe that to be true.

I did ambushes; it was one of the many things you must work at to get through it in a safe manner. I even got to the point where I enjoyed pulling ambushes; it gave me more chances to kill. At that point in my life I felt I must kill to stay alive, any of you that don't believe that; you would probably be dead after the first or second firefight. While killing I had to put myself in harms way each time and the law of averages won't let that go on forever. Nor would I be able to keep going on putting myself in harms way, it just doesn't work that way. As I was in country about 6 weeks I started to be able to tell if a soldier was a veteran of combat by the way they traveled, well spread out and wary in all directions, and each soldier seems ready to open fire at the least provocation, unlike the FNG's whom gather together and are more interested in watching the ground instead of looking around and up in the trees along with watching the ground. This was because they were afraid of stepping on a booby-trap, which was a real concern, but after as many soldiers had crossed that way there was almost no chance of them stepping on a booby-trap or a mine. They should look around, because the enemy was more likely to rise up from a well-camouflaged spider-hole and that was something they should had been more concerned with. Some of them would even light up a cigarette while out on patrol and unless a veteran NCO or Officer saw them, they would proceed to march through the jungle giving away their position and possibly their lives.

But in a veteran platoon that cigarette would be snatched from your mouth and when you started to say something about it, you would be quieted down by what ever means it took, that was not a fun thing to do; walking through a wet muggy jungle looking for people that were looking for you, and wanted to end your life. So why make it easier for the enemy to find you? Some of the new guys didn't take us walking around in the dense jungle very seriously; they didn't realize that they could end their lives on that very day

We, as a group were engrossed together, even with the differences of age, race, what part of the country we are from and our place in the financial structure of things. We were in a situation where there is no room for anyone to think of just himself at any time; we needed each other to have half a chance at getting through this mess we were in. I wanted to be that one that everyone relied on, to have the tribute as being that one person everyone would rely on to get them home and in one piece and that became a lot of pressure on me to get them there, which wore on me to a point I was becoming a nervous wreck. However, I acted as if I had nerves of steel; little did anyone know I was scared stiff every time I went up front. Nevertheless, it had to be done for us to make it until the next time. I wasn't the only one to jump up front in times of enemy contact. The Point was first then the Platoon Leader and his RTO then it was I. But I brought up the firepower to keep the enemy from having an advantage. I was lucky we never walked up on a large herd of gooks or a machinegun nest; which would cancel out my gun, and they did have a 7.92 caliber gun, but we had not come across one at that time.

We were all the same out there in Uncle Ho's little playground, where anything from a Sniper shooting to a full-fledged human assault may sit at your doorstep. You didn't know what to expect when that door of opportunity burst open. You had a split second to determine what action to take. There was no second place in that test they called war. It's especially difficult if someone you had just gotten a cigarette from 30 seconds ago, is now a pile of torn and mangled flesh 3 feet from where you and he had begun to return fire. Hero's are still scared, but they do what has to be done when it must be done. I have met several heroes, but they weren't always recognized by the service. This story is about several of them. I don't think myself as one, maybe in someone else's eye. It really doesn't matter at all now, does it?

My first Hot LZ happened in late Sept 1967 riding in helicopters toward the LZ our Lt. Told me that I had to get out and get a line of fire keeping the dinks down, so others can join in on the fight." He didn't want me to have time to think about jumping out first and into what? As I looked out and to our front, I wondered what would this be like? Are we going to run into a much larger unit; one that we can't beat? Maybe it will be one where the enemy has already left the area. There could be a large unit of well-trained NVA or a 3-man patrol of VC or anything in between. When the chopper started its decent to the jungle floor my heart was pounding and I was breathing heavy and someone touched my back and I jumped, I didn't think about the fact we were still 10 feet in the air, or the fact I may not be able to join my Company in the oncoming fight. It was very hot and I had to wipe the sweat from my eyes and I caught a couple gooks that were hidden in spider holes at a spot where if I had jumped when the rest of the guys jumped we could have had ourselves in a crossfire, that is what was their idea. I ended up shooting all 6 of them, and then I had to re-join my platoon, where they were assaulting the tree line. I could hear the crack, crack of someone firing in my direction and see green tracers coming my way. I made up my mind that was not to die today. When I first looked toward the tree line, I saw everything in slow motion. I raised my gun and fired towards the noise I was hearing. My Asst gunner Pete was right at my side making sure my gun was well fed. I first fired to my front then to my left then right. We were only 15 meters from the enemy and I remembered seeing the blood explode from the chests of those little shit-heads as they were screaming and heading towards me. My heart was pounding and my vision was getting cloudy from the sweat creeping into my eyes, but I continued to fire until Pete told me to relax it was over. After a few minutes, we had secured the tree line. The Platoon Leader came over to me and gave me what I wanted. He told me I had done the correct thing in jumping out like that and securing the line. He asked me if I was scared? Of course, I was scared but I didn't have time to think about it until it was over. Then I shook and had trouble breathing. However, when he told me what a great job I had done I felt like I had scored the winning touchdown with no time left on the clock. The heavy breathing stopped and I had a chill run up my back. I was satisfied with my performance on a test, and that's what I felt it was, a test where I got myself points and I had to keep getting the points needed to win. I didn't take that test lightly, because it was a very serious thing, killing those that were out to kill me.

That night it was so dark you couldn't see someone if they walked up on you. For that reason, we had to rely on other senses such as sound and even smell. Because of their food, they had a very different smell to them; they spiced their food with curry. The only problem was that both the enemy and friendly South Vietnamese ate the same food, so they all smelled alike. While waiting for your time on guards to end you have others to worry about, someone could cough or sneeze or even talk in their sleep when that happened you had to wake that person and have him move into a better position. I had to train my-self not to have to grope for the switch to put my gun on Rock N Roll If an enemy patrol walks up on you, you have to decide what action you take. Anything from an open up with all you got, to being very still and letting them pass. With being, still you stand the chance of someone walking on top of you; then you have to open up with all you have and hope there aren't too many of them in this patrol. Opening up on them and controlling the battle I could get more praise, how could I not be hyped? It would be like scoring the winning touchdown in the State Championship Game again and again, you can't ask for more than that. Nevertheless, there always is the fact that someone in your group may get shot-up and maybe a few killed and who's to say it wouldn't be you? You had to understand there always was that chance, Each and every day is like a throw of the dice, and sometimes you lose, losing a little it's all OK and is expected. But if you lose it big or all it could be time to turn in your dice.

The one thing I noticed and thought was great is that there were no bigots in the Rifle Company. White and Black seemed to get along. After a couple weeks, I found that a few of the whites didn't like blacks and a few of the blacks didn't like peckerwoods. But they both had to rely on the other in battle to stay alive, every once in a great while you would run up on a Southern White boy that hated what he called niggers and we had one black guy that didn't like any whites until he was wounded and a white guy drug him to safety, that changed his views. At least while out in the jungle. We weren't going to change hundreds of years of one side distrusting or even hating the other, all we wanted was to be able to work together for just this one year so that we all stand a chance to go home. When morning came, we were out on a patrol then we came up on a fast flowing creek and were told to get some fresh water. Therefore, I with my gun secured the area while the others filled their canteens. Then Jon, the other gunner and I filled ours. We traveled a little further when we hear the crack`, crack of a weapon being fired in our direction. I didn't sound like an AK 47 but more like a SKS, which is a carbine firing 7.62 rounds the same as an AK. The difference is the bang then the sliding of the bolt back ready to fire again.

I ran up front and there was no one to shoot; whoever fired at us had left the building. That was very frustrating to say the lease. It wasn't right to shoot and run. However, that was a fact of life we had to live with every day. You wanted the guy that shot you to be killed by your buddies, you didn't want him to run and hide while putting your scalp on his pole. A term we used for being killed dead another term for dieing from an enemy action.

It just wouldn't be right, but that is the way it happened most of the time. There were a few longer engagements with the enemy but usually that was when they had the best of you by being in a fortified position and we were laid out on the jungle floor trying to hide as best we could. But every once in a while we would have an enemy patrol walk up on us and we controlled the fight and eventfully won the battle, but it was difficult for us to walk up on an enemy patrol because of the noise factor of 150 guys walking around in the thick under brush and tangled vines that made way too much noise.

CHAPTER THREE - FIRE AWAY

I remember one thing my Platoon S/SGT. Brown told me while in Basic; that was in Vietnam it was a matter of seconds to live or inches to die; and Charlie holds the yard stick and stop watch." All you need to do is make that one and final mistake that will get you or someone you know killed. It doesn't have to be a big mistake, just a mistake. Sometimes you don't have to make a mistake to get yourself killed it just happens. We had all types of enemy. We had a Water Buffalo get on my KIA list. He was a formative enemy target assaulting the entire company, and I took care of the problem in the only manner I could. I shot him with 100 rounds to the skull before he succumbed to us. We caught hell over that one. The old man that owned the buffalo wanted to be reimbursed. The CO told him through an interpreter that he would have $100 and some tobacco with some salt tomorrow morning. The interpreter thought the old man didn't understand. We left it at that. That night we were probed by a couple of people and one of them took a shot into our perimeter. We returned fire and they quit their shooting at us. When morning came, we went out to check and see what we could find. We ran into the old man with a M1 Carbine that had been fired. If he would have waited until morning his $100 was on the way plus the tobacco, salt and a couple of chickens for him and another water buffalo on the way. I believed at the time it was just a peasant with the mentality of one that doesn't trust anyone and I could understand his frustration but that doesn't help him now, for that I am sorry.

We were probed the next night while my assistant gunner Pete Graham was out on LP (listening post) for the night. What that was when 3 to 5 guys would go outside of the perimeter and set up a place where they could watch over an avenue for an assault. They are out about 50 to 100 meters and have a radio with them. If they hear, see, or even smell Gook they are to call it in and wait to either be called in or stay out during a possible assault on the perimeter. That was not the safest place to be at during and all out assault. While on LP the enemy has seen where you go because they usually go to the same spot each night if you were at a fire-support area, not a 1 nightstand were we would move the next morning. Our guys could have shot the LP's as they ran in; or artillery being fired around the area might get them. Because I carried the gun, I didn't pull things like that. I was too valuable with my gun to be out there. All you can think of as a gunner and in a firefight is you have 30 seconds to win the battle. If you haven't taken control of the battle then the battle controls you. There always is that factor of a lucky shot by some gook firing into the area while your gun is a blaze. The stress to stay ahead at all times really started to drain me and I could tell that I felt different now than before when I was so Gung Ho, Now I'm a soldier that recognized that I could get killed by doing as I had been for the first 2 months I had been in country. Nevertheless, I didn't know of a better way of keeping alive than, as I had been doing. Getting the kills as fast as possible that is what was keeping me alive. We were being probed that night and all LP's were called inside the perimeter to get ready for an assault.

I watched as Pete and the other 2 guys came running into our line of fire. I recognized Pete so I let him and the other guys

17

come in. Before the last guy could get in a couple gooks joined in on the parade. I opened up the gun right behind the last American and got 3 more KIA's on my growing list. When the bullets hit the first dink, it spun him first in one direction then again in another until he fell to the ground either dead or dieing. The other 2 were wounded and Grizzly let it be known that he wanted a prisoner so he got 2 and was very happy. I got another that a boy because I didn't kill those 2. No one tried to run in on us again that night, but they did keep up sniper fire all night and into early morning. One shot came very close to hitting one of the guys from the 2nd Platoon; missed him by about an inch. The shell hit a sandbag and it was an inch from hitting him in the head. That was too close, so that guy went down into his bunker and didn't come out all night.   We were tired from being up all night and so pumped up and ready for the fight that never came. The gooks were still there and as soon as the sun started rising it started raining. We sat and had a smoke while waiting for the attack. One of the new guys asks what are we going to do if over ran?" The Lt. tells him "don't let them over run our position and you won't have to worry about that." We were told, "If the gooks take the perimeter there is a good chance we won't make it!" During the early hours of the morning, they attacked the other side of the perimeter causing 3 causalities. The enemy attacked a lone bunker with about 50 of their men and after a battle that lasted a couple of minutes, they took the bunker. A young kid from our bunker started to panic he screamed out "we are all going to die today!" We kept him in our bunker so he wouldn't get in the way. The enemy worked their way to the next bunkers to the left and right of the one they took. I told everyone at our bunker "we can't let the enemy take anymore!" So we kept 1 guy looking out to the front of the bunker then 1 guy looking to the rear, with 1 guy looking at both sides and down at the trenches. We can hear the fighting going on the other side of our perimeter. You could hear grenades going off and there were a lot of gunshots going on there. It made us worried that we will be next. We were told that somehow we must stop them at the spot of the first bunker taken. They were funneling more troops into the bunker line at that bunker. A platoon from our Company was going in and to cut off the enemies contact with those outside of the perimeter. Then the CO gets on the horn and wants me to come up to where he is at and to bring Pete and as much ammo as we could carry. What he tells me is I was to get to the bunker right behind the first one taken and stop the enemy from getting more supplies and men into our perimeter. So Pete and I set up behind the bunker about 10 meters away in a command bunker and I open up my machine gun into the area from that bunker out into the jungle stopping them from being supplied with men and ammo. Jon the other gunner in D Company came down to where we were trying to get the battle turned in our favor. He took the bunker to the left and I took the one to the right. Together with the help of a couple guys pitching grenades into that position we retook control of that bunker which gave us control of the entire battle. The enemy had to rise up to shoot in our direction and when they did that, we mowed them down. Pete tells me "we have about 100 more rounds and from the looks of things we will need more ammo." Pete takes off and finds more 7.62 rounds, while he was gone I ran out of ammo but, he showed up 10 seconds later and I quickly put a new belt in and began my rock-n-roll on them again; we proceed to give those attacking from both sides some cover to which they used to gain control of all bunkers in our perimeter. We lose 2 men and we get 12 of them in our growing KIA list. Both Jon and I got a bunch of backslapping when that was over and done with. We along with the rest of D Company stopped the take over and destruction of our Company as well the Battalion TOC that was also there. We also killed several of the little bastards. They counted 25 and Jon and I got 12 on our body count list apiece. Plus we don't know how many of the little shit heads we wounded.

We were all pretty tired after the assault that lasted about 2 hours it really wore us out. Then we had to make sure there were no more of the little shit heads sitting out side of the perimeter to take shots at anyone. After the attack it rained pretty hard for a couple hours, this, added with the heat of the day caused the dead to start stinking up the jungle around us it was nauseating to say the least. We were told that we were going to all leave this perimeter and we started to get things ready. We got on a chopper and headed towards the Oasis; which was a Brigade Firebase and got two days of drinking Korean beer and smoking Cuban cigars. We thought we were in tall cotton those two days. Then we took a chopper to the new Battalion firebase, which was on a small hill overlooking the IA Drang Valley where we were to run missions out of. It rained everyday the first month I was in country and only let up for two days before it started all over again.

I grew up in Southern California and had never experienced so much rain. But the rain makes this a beautiful place it's a very warm area of what looks like forever jungle. As far as you could see, was this green warm adventure waiting for us to explore. If it wasn't for the knowledge that there were several people out in that view that were stinking up the area with their decaying bodies this would have been a perfect day. This would be the perfect vacation spot for me. It's a shame there has to be a war in this beautiful country with its high jungle covered mountains. The people we see in the villages could care less which government is in charge. They catch hell from both and there is no way they could pick sides because if they did and the other side showed up they would have a fight on their hands and these people don't want to fight anyone. All they want is to be able to grow their rice, raise a few chickens, and have some tobacco. See their children grow up and have children of their own. 99% of these people have 0% education and most can not read or write and have to rely on who ever comes in to tell them what they are to do as far as paying taxes with food or their children to military service by either side.

CHAPTER FOUR -
NOT ALL WERE DEAD

Why was I there? I had to think. I was there for a reason; but what reason I didn't know. Maybe I was there to record what I saw or heard or it was just bad luck or maybe I was there just to see some of the beautiful places on this earth? There were thick bamboo areas then the triple canopy made the ground level very dark and cooler in temperature than what it was on the hills around the IA Drang Valley from up in a chopper when you get to an area that wasn't bombed out it's a very pretty sight. It made you think what a great place this would be to visit if it wasn't for this War. Even the monkeys are better mannered there; some of them in the higher trees will pee on you given the chance. You can't shoot at them; it would give your position away, maybe they know that, that might be why they keep doing it? One has never hit me but it sure has come close a few times.

Attacks on American units were usually short and violent and favored the enemy which; left a bad taste in my mouth; them not fighting a longer battle than shoot and run, especially when they hit someone that you knew. We were in an area where mangoes grew and we were told we could eat them but not to eat anything with yellow or white berries. We were also told not to eat any mushrooms and to avoid all plants with thorns and anything that smelled like almonds. If we want to eat something grown out in the jungle watch, what the monkeys eat. Riding in a chopper you get a birds eye view of how pretty the jungle can be and you also see some areas where some Americans had lost their lives and it makes you think; what a waste, there should be an international decree that war isn't healthy for those that become involved in the killing. The door gunner told me guys that had been in country for a while told him common survival advice was to look through the jungle instead of at it. I didn't know what he was saying but to someone it probably made sense.

Most of us were scared 70% of the time and the other 30% of the time you're a Want a-be hero. When you first come to Vietnam, that's usually when you are not in contact with an enemy force. As you get to your unit, you want medals and KIA's but as time passes so do your hero expectations. Most everyone is scared silly after his first or second firefight. That's when you realize you are the target being shot at and you had better find someway to get off the bulls eye. You get an up-close look at someone that has been hit and listen to his screams and see his life slowly bleeding out of his torn and mangled body. After the battle, some of you will see him as he is poured into a plastic body bag, but for some of us this pressure on you to survive makes you a little crazy when you no longer see the enemy as human beings but as Gooks. A Subspecies that causes you to have pain and the only way to rid yourself of the pain is to rid the gooks from their existence and your pain will go away with them or so we thought the pain would go away. However, for some of us it still is lingering in the minds of those affected by the trauma. It is hard to rid yourself of, but we all try.

All of us spent each night in constant fear that the enemy was surely going to attack and maybe you wouldn't make it through the battle that would come at sunup. We all sat up and waited, and the longer you waited the more time you had to think. You started seeing things that might not be there, but can you take that chance? Every one of us had to partake in guard each night it was egalitarian for everyone. We expect the attack to come from the east so the enemy will have the glare of the morning sun to their backs and that would give us a drab place during the first few minutes of battle. If you fire, you could squander your ammo and when the fight starts you have no clue when or how it will end. We received small arms fire during most of the night. We did return fire, but not by the machineguns as we believed, that is what the gooks were waiting for, to know where our guns were. As you sit there, you looked over at the guy next to you and wonder is it his day to die; or is it mine? The gooks left our perimeter by sunup. We thought we would be involved in an all out assault to the death by that time. When nothing happens, we were both relieved and disappointed because you have worked yourself up into frenzy. The CO sent out 10 guys of which I was one, we were searching for any bodies that might have funny papers on their corpse; when rolling these kids we could tell they were well fed and all had clean weapons which told us they were in a strict unit unlike some of the Viet Cong we ran into here in the IA Drang. We might be able to follow them to their hospital that we have been looking for a long time. We found a couple at the East end and a few more hidden in the bushes. I set up my machine gun position to cover the other guys as they were checking the area for dead bodies. A couple gooks were still alive enough to lift their rifles and aim at some of the guys. I yelled out "watch it live gooks" as I opened up on them with the gun and I received 5 more KIA's in the body count! There were body parts flying all around by the impact of the bullets hitting their bodies. I am getting body counts every time we are in any contact with the enemy, so I am regarded as someone that will get his quota of dead gooks each time we were in that contact. I was also told that the CO believes I would stand and fight and not high tail out of a firefight that we could win. Something that I was proud of but also something,

I don't know if I would do today. At age 19, you could convince me that was what to do, but I don't think so now that I have seen what could have happened to me. Maybe I would jump again and put myself in harms way it really would be interesting to see, but it's not really something I want to happen to me again or any of my children.

I knew there were more of them shot-up from the earlier action so we continued the search and we found where they had drug their comrades. The morning fog was lifting to where you might see someone and know for sure they were the enemy. Last night during the firefight, you didn't actually see people that you fired at but instead you fired at the muzzle flashes from their weapons. It was a surreal feeling we got while the fog was rolling in and the gooks were scratching their way towards our bunker line. Now at about 0930 hours when we finished our body count. The body count was what drove Congress and Politicians to keep track of how we were doing and if a battle was worth it to them, not really to us. Nevertheless, the people that were trying to keep score and sell this war to the American Public it's very important. There was no battle ever fought that was worth anyone dying for` especially if you were the one to die. Sure some General could say, we lost 35 men but we took 350 with them" which sounds all right unless you are one of the 35. Then it didn't matter how many of the enemy we sent to hell, the rest of that day should have been pretty restful for us, but still we were so scared that we could not rest for the fear it was going to start up again. Then there is the chance you take with the roll of the dice if you are going to make it or not. Eventually you will lose and you have to be careful when you take that chance, one mistake is all it takes to ruin your day. You could even make a mistake by putting on your boots without first checking for scorpions or snakes. The fire ants will make you crazy if you lie in an area they travel in at night, it's happened to me a couple times, you would not believe how much pain those little bugs can cause, and the worst of it was you would scream in pain and that was something we couldn't allow because it would give away our position. All from a tiny bug.

Now as I was looking out over into the valley below there was some of the most beautiful scenery I have seen in my 19 years of existence. It was October 5, 1967 at 1700 hours. We had been up 36 hours. Everyone was tired and the rain was starting to beat down on us. We put up our poncho's to make a few very small tents and we stayed pretty dry but we were still surrounded by at least 39 dead gooks stinking up the area with that sweet stinky smell that makes you want to heave up all you have, and we had to be there till the next morning. We all hoped we could hold out without eating until we move from that stinky area. The smell of gunpowder and blood mixed with the sounds of pain and the sight of bodies torn apart made it a repugnant, acrimonious morning for me. You just have to do what you are told and you will make it. That's what we were told by numerous people over there. The IA Drang Valley was a tropical paradise if the war wasn't going on. While on patrol we come up on some bomb craters snapping us back to reality, this is still a war zone. How sad that it was that way. However, if there were no war, I probably would not have been there. However, some of the scenic sights are so picturesque; it's like looking at a travel book. Nevertheless, I know we were involved in a war that won't allow such thoughts, I guess you can still think that it was a good place to be but you also had to agree that it was a most dangerous spot on this earth.

We were mostly young and never been in a war before, unlike some of our higher ranking enlisted men, we had an E7 that had been in both WW2 and Korea and he said that this war was the worst of the three, mainly because it was a guerilla war where you had to follow the rules but they didn't. What we have seen at the movies really gives a person a distorted view of how a war should make you feel. What we were taught in school about wars is group A and group B both want the same thing or someone stepped on someone's toes so they have a shoot-em-up until either one or both decide that they have lost enough. John Wayne and Audrey Murphy would always get out of the scraps they get into. Wish it was that easy and no one gets killed, but we weren't in a movie this was real life situations. They never go into how the death of each person affects so many others including those you were serving with in that battle. When you get killed, there will be no next Saturday's episode where you ride off with the fair maiden again. Even John Wayne dies in a couple of his movies. What we needed to do was first decide who was the enemy, then have a full scale attack on them until they were toast, then go to the next one If we make a mistake Xin Loi, shit happens in wars. I'm not saying waste everyone you see, just those that are caring weapons and are not an organized element supposed to be in that area and on our side. I'm not taking the chance. They are Toast. That is the only way to win a guerilla war. Because what they do is hit and run, then hide and hold their hand out to accept welfare from our countrymen. During this time, I started to seek other ways of getting the recognition. There was a trail that was well traveled outside of this village so we are going to set up camp here today, we keep our eye on The Red ball express was what they were calling this trail because it was used a lot. Nothing ugly went on today again, which we are very happy about. But the boys with stars don't like it when we don't call in with body counts. They can't come up with answers that the Press and American people want to hear. Even if it's just one, it's another to add to the list for today. Then comes tomorrow and we should try to get our numbers up. However, that puts you in harms way when you do that. Chances are you will run out of luck if you keep doing these crazy things. We travel a couple hundred meters down the road and come to a spot that looks promising as far as a RON goes. Nothing happens again except it rains really hard last night and every leech in the neighborhood finds us. So far the record, 42 leeches on me at one time and some of them were really bloated which means they were on early and did their job well. Nevertheless, a little bit of salt on them will stop them where they are. When it rains hard, you lose part of your vision and all of your hearing because of the rain. The Gook's like moving in the rain and the harder it rained the better for them.

I enjoyed looking at the different phases of the jungle recapturing the once clearings that were at one time a battle scene of 2 years ago. At that time, I was still pretty much Gung Ho and wanted medals and recognition as a dam good soldier and one you would pick to be on your side if it was dodge ball instead of a war. We had several small firefights while there in the IA Drang; but it was mostly snipers taking 1 to 5 shots at the perimeter then running into a village and waving either an American or South Vietnamese flag getting re-supplied with food, clothing, and even ammo and a weapon if asked for. The sad part is our Government would issue it to them; even show them how to operate the weapon. We will be watching all day and most of the night, if they are sending some high dollar weapons through here we are supposed to catch them in the act and call in all Hell on them. We don't see any movement all day .A day to skate by and not be worried about if we are seen or not. Boy that doesn't happen very often. But I sometimes wonder if the enemy can sleep at night and do some of these things they do to not only us but also to what may be some of their relatives in the South. Do they have dreams where the demons make them sweat at night like it does us? We were involved in a couple small firefights that although didn't last a long time; they still have some of us either killed or wounded.

A guy name Walters; he was shot up real bad. I was in the 2nd platoon with him. That was the first time I can remember seeing a dead American that took all night to die. The kid from Georgia died right away and we didn't have to listen to his screams or watch him as he passed his bowels and choked on his own blood. I mean a mangled, not touched up dead person who pleaded for us to kill him and where body parts were missing and never found. I've seen dead gooks but one of our guys, someone you had coffee with that morning and now he's lying there all chewed up by bullets fired at you and him. He screamed all night, which really worked on our nerves. Then we start thinking one of us could be lying there in his place or next to him both dead, and the question always comes up, why not me?" I didn't think my parents could have handled me coming home like that; all cut up by bullets to a point they would not recognize me. We got into a scrape when we walked into some NVA traveling through this little valley that was thick with bamboo and scrub plants. It hadn't rained all night and into the new day so any tracks we see, they were either last night or early that morning. Our Point Man either didn't see the gooks or was so scared he froze. He won't walk Point again. The second man in line was the Squad Leader; he opened up on the body of enemy soldiers. I was fourth in line right behind the RTO with my machine gun and I cleared the way by eliminating the little bastards. This made my day. I got 14 KIA and 16 weapons captured to my credit. I was the leader in number of kills again. This didn't get me anything except recognition as the top man in the Company for my number of KIA's. Which was my way of equaling what Steve my brother the Jock had done while in High School. At least that's what I thought at that time. I was asked if I was scared while jumping up front by one of the guys. I told him I was more scared I would not get the credit for a kill and I felt one of those little Bastards could not kill me. Nevertheless, deep inside I was scared to death that I would be maimed and not go home with all of my fingers and toes. That would be unacceptable for me. I needed to put myself in harms way as much as possible without paying the price of my being shot up or killed. I don't think it feasible to take that many chances without paying the price. I was very lucky to this point in time and I was worried my number would come up if I kept doing foolish things.

That is when instead of being a hero and just going home alive and well was my new way of thinking even with my still jumping up front. It was so I could control the battle and yes get some plenteous praise but making sure that I wasn't wearing the target all of the time. I felt a little less pressure knowing that I didn't have to save everyone, every time. However, by being out there with the gun in my hand I will always be the target especially if I open up on them. They will then know whom they must take out as soon as possible; it goes with the job.

CHAPTER FIVE - GRENADE

Later that same day we came to our objective; a village where we were to look for weapons, ammo, or extra food. We also have to see if there are a large number of young men in the village. Because the enemy "recruits" all of the young men and women and what they don't take the ARVN's get the rest. Which might make them deserters and they don't wear tags telling you which it is .If you run across some young men you have to make that split second decision right now a no decision could be as bad as a wrong decision and you might not make it to the after action debriefing at the end of the day.

While the riflemen are searching all of the dwellings those of us that carry the machine guns get into a position where we can guard our comrades from any harm from inside the village, When all of a sudden a homemade grenade comes rolling up to me, my whole body stiffens up, I prepare to get as far away as possible the sweat runs from my armpits and forehead so much sweat that for a brief second I lose my vision by the salty liquid running into my eyes. My heart pounding so loud I thought it was going to jump up into my throat I felt that I would surely die from that grenade and although it took but 2 or 3 seconds for it to explode during that time so much went through my mind.

Then when it goes off with about the same power as a cherry bomb. Now I must look up to see where this grenade came from. I wipe the sweat from my eyes and look up to see a little old woman digging frantically into an earthen pot; pulling out her second grenade; or was she? I didn't take the chance, the repercussion might have been that the next one was a real grenade and I couldn't take that chance. So I raised my gun and let her digest 20 rounds to the gut, needless to say the second grenade went off by her feet and her upper torso was lying next to her feet, I had actually cut her in half and I felt really good about doing her like that, really good, had I become a person that enjoys taking another's life? It was a test to me, a test I must pass each day and it is becoming harder to do each day. The law of averages makes each day that much closer to failing the test, then it would be over. The fact I cut her in half will be something each of those villagers would remember and they would either be afraid of the same death? On the other hand, want revenge on me for doing her like that. The grenade that went off didn't have as much power of the first one. I didn't feel ugly towards all Oriental People as a group only those that were trying their best to harm me. I didn't know how to distinguish the good guys from the bad. Because of that, I trusted none of the Vietnamese people that we were in contact with, friend or foe. Then I had to look up and see if anyone is thinking of taking me out. I don't see anyone as brave as the old woman; I really couldn't tell how old she was. Some of these people live hard lives. But to me she appeared old, what the hell I was only 19 at that time so almost everyone that we see in a village is old. All of a sudden 2 shots ring out from an area outside of the village hitting one of the RTO's.

My mind is going a thousand times faster than I can move my body so if I want to do something I have to do it as quickly as possible because my mind has me already doing the next step my body is trying to do the first task and doing what must be done so that I make it through this year. I often wonder would I lose some of these feelings when I get home or will I jump at everyone? I howler out "Is there anyone else that wants to die? Well is there?" Jon comes over to me and tells me "everything is fine." He calms me down from being on the edge of completely freaking out. At that time, I wanted to shoot all of the villagers; but cooler heads prevailed and I was brought down to reality. Jon got the guy that had fired those shots. When someone opens up on you with a weapon and hits a guy you knew, I wanted to kill everyone because I felt that everyone in that village knew the enemy were there but didn't tell us. Because of that, they would be causing someone to die and others to get fucked up pretty bad. We were told that we were to turn our cheek and unless we knew for sure who pulled that trigger we weren't allowed to kill those that might have had something to do with the killing. We find out later this old woman had three grandchildren being held captive by the North Vietnamese and they were to lose their heads if the old woman had not done that to us how could people be so cruel to their own. That was why we never trusted anyone, because anyone may become your enemy at any given time, sometimes they are pushed into doing something they wouldn't do otherwise, and there will be no villagers trusted from our Platoon. We head out heading away from that village. Then we loop around and head back towards the village without being seen we hope.

We set up an ambush not too far from the village in a tree line half looking one way the other half the opposite way. Every 5th man takes a nap for 3 hours then the next guy and on down the line until everyone has had some sleep. The only thing that came down the trail; was a couple very small Asian Deer. They appeared to be not afraid of us so we figure they wouldn't be afraid of the enemy as well, so we can't use them as a way to warn us. We heard some strange noise that night almost as if something was flying from tree to tree and making a thud when hitting the next tree. We were told that there are Flying Lemurs in this jungle and it might be them. The next morning there was no flying anything but we believe these creatures were nocturnal. We are on our way in after a hot cup of coffee and some powdered eggs. It's the best we have I'm sorry to say.

I'm carrying the Gun still right behind the RTO when we run into a couple of khaki clothed enemy and I ran up to the front keeping the shit-heads from forming any kind of a defensive position. I could see the expressions on their faces while they were drowning in their own blood; it was flowing profusely to the ground. I know that sounds like I was some kind of Barbarian, I guess at that point in time we all were. It was a macabre sight, was I going to be able to return to be the person I was before entering that war or am I destine to live out my life with such fear and anger that I can not adjust back to civilian life? The new Point Man opened up before I got to the front, which is what is supposed to happen. In a crisis, he had a certain Sang-Froid that we respected. There were 3 more that ran up to their death when they attempted to out gun us. Bad mistake. That guy walked Point from then on. The guys with M79's and M16's came up and while I was firing at gooks I had seconds to myself up front and firing into their bodies watching them die. It was a good feeling watching my bullets tear into the little skinny yellow skinned asses knowing that me doing that it would and did save someone's life, it wasn't till later when I learned that being the gunner I was first target just in front of the Officer in charge and RTO.

Rice isn't their only food, they also eat a dried fish called Nuoc Mam and it smells like rotten fish. I guess because that's basically what it is. Talk about something to gross you out. If we don't take their extra food from them then the NVA will come in and take it. If we do take it and destroy it that means we are the bad Guys. We end up being just as bad as the NVA is to these people. Big difference the NVA will punish them for helping us even in a very minor way. There are informers in each village that would tell the enemy if someone gave us any information at all. Then the enemy will make an example of that person by killing all of his immediate family in front of him and the whole village then kill him by torture.

It was mid afternoon before we stop to fix us something to eat. The villagers watch and don't understand how we could eat such food? Beans and weenies just don't get to them, as being something someone would actually eat and enjoy. The village will have a shortage of food and our government will give them more rice and the enemy will come and get some of that also. I have no hard feelings for the poor peasants that are trying to live in a lose-lose situation. It was a test, almost a game to me at this point. At times, I had a hard time understanding how some of these people would do some of the things they do to each other. They kill each other without any remorse; we are talking about people that are related to. Have they no shame? Killing brothers and cousins doesn't make sense to me. However, we did they same thing in our Civil War a hundred years ago.

The countryside, which at times was one of the most beautiful sights I had ever seen. What a pity it was to not be able to admire the beauty of this country. We never knew for sure who was who as far as enemy or friend. You have to be sure; the wrong guess could cost you your life. The next morning before we ate and had our coffee I searched the horizon for any wild animal or bird. The jungle is such a quiet and surreal place where all can be so calm of a place to be in. Then to have the gates of Hell opened on you without any warning. It just doesn't seem right. We were on our way; I carried the gun right behind the RTO again. Waiting for what ever comes my way. Hopefully not too much to happen this morning I just didn't feel like shooting anyone that day. Moreover, as luck would have it we didn't run into anyone. Tomorrow is another day that we will probably have to take some lives and maybe lose a couple from our side. I only hope not to lose any of my friends out there. Having friends is not a good thing in battle.

I was trusted by our C.O. to deal with anything that comes our way; also that I won't turn tail and run when met head on with an enemy force. He told me not to worry if there're more of them than expected; he would let me know when to retreat,

He tells me if I see him running away from a battle to be sure to join him as fast as possible. We get going on our mission to find that hospital if possible. After about an hour of our march we run into a small group of Khaki clothed enemy and I ran up front and laid a line of fire that kept these little shit heads from forming any kind of a defensive position. I was proud of my actions while in combat. I was still in the Gung Ho frame of mind! I only hope I know when to lay low instead of jumping up and starting the firefight; one that we couldn't win. I must know the difference if I am to go home all in one piece. We set up an ambush about a klick from our previous location. There is a small party of enemy troops heading into our kill zone. Everyone has a serious look on his or her face and I believe our unit as a whole has become a Company with charisma because of our experiences as of lately where we have scored the most kills lately. As I open up on the enemy, I could see their faces while they were drowning in their own blood. I believe I might have changed into some bloodthirsty animal; I thought so at that point. I did not want to be a mediocre soldier and I realized I might have to be a murderous type of person to get what I craved; I may have had to be the one that was conspicuous. I was told that it might not be healthy for me to enjoy killing as much as I did and that's when I began to realize that I also am a target for those guys and some day they are going to catch up to me and I might not make it home alive. It really opened my eyes to what I had become. A killing machine that had no remorse for the killings I had done. I had become a pernicious part of my team; Company D 3/12 INF. Moreover, I was going to remain as such. It's true it was in a time of war and if I had not been as aggressive in my returning fire, I might not be here writing our story. We had to stay at the sight of our ambush and hope no enemy soldiers come back through this way to get either to that illusive hospital or the Laos border in a couple of hours, it seems that Apache 2, one of the Recon's teams might need us to come to their rescue. They are in contact with a herd or a platoon size element of the 66th Infantry Regiment. We set up an ambush across a trail that is heading toward Laos and it appears the Apache team has run into a large group of enemy troops and is highballing it towards our ambush. A friend of mine Ronnie Baker was in that team. After about 20 minutes, we hear someone racing through the jungle towards us. We prepare for an all out battle when we realize the group headed our way was Apache 2 we let them run through us and 2 minutes latter we have an oversized Platoon of gooks sitting in our little trap. Apache 2 gets through our position and we brace ourselves for the upcoming ambush that we will spring on these enemy soldiers who still think they are chasing the Recon team straight ahead towards Laos. I open up with the machine gun cutting down a good number of them then the Riflemen take care of the rest. The battle only lasted about 3 minutes. When the enemy had enough they, high tailed it out of the area. We lost 1 man and got 15 KIA's to our credit mostly from my gun. At this point I'm beginning to wonder is it the right thing to do, I mean me jumping up front and taking on who ever is there." I felt at that time; maybe I should still lay down a wall of fire into what enemy we run into but maybe I should be more careful about how long I stay uncovered in front of the ambush. Maybe I could stay alive longer if I wasn't so Gung Ho! Once you realize you are in this struggle and will be here for a year or until you are wounded pretty bad or killed. Once you know this, it changes the way you conduct yourself in the jungle and even in a firebase. One time in Sept 67, we found a small waterfall in a creek and a pool of water under the fall. We took turns getting into the water and showering just like back home. We actually washed our hair. It was one of my best days while in D Company.

I enlisted in the Army and wanted to make it a career until I figured out to make any rank you had to brown nose someone and keep it up as long as you want to obtain a higher rank. Vietnam was nothing as if I supposed either. There was no liberating of towns where the people would come out and have a parade as we chased the enemy out of their homes. For the average Grunt there was no behind the lines, there were too many things that could happen to you and about 70% of them were bad news for us. You usually lost your hero ambitions about the time of your second firefight, when you realize you were one of the targets. With me it took a little longer, I guess because I was very lucky and did not get wounded even once charging to the front of the battle each time which made me feel invulnerable, which I had to come to terms with. I can be killed very easily by doing the things I have done. Like running up front and laying down a wall of lead so others can get into the battle with me. Then you get that high as the battle is starting and you lose all thoughts except how are you going to make it out ok.

Also, you discover that you had more instincts about how to stay alive and most of them were how to eliminate the enemy so that you would not perish. When that rush left you; that's when you shivered and shook from the fear that was generated into your body. You felt all the fear that had generated from seeing and hearing and feeling all the pain that is involved in your everyday existence. We then moved on watching all of the usual places where the enemy had a history of hiding and throwing an ambush on us. But we were lucky, One of the older guys that was in the second platoon offered me a bite out of his tobacco, which I figured wouldn't be that bad. We walked on down this finger of a mountain in the 120-degree heat I twisted my ankle and swallowed it all. Now at that point I wished someone would have mercy on me and shoot me. The guy that gave me the chew started laughing out loud and his squad leader got after him for that. I wanted to stop and get something to help me. There is nothing to help I'm told by our Company Medic. I had to throw up twice then keep quiet the rest of the day. Therefore, I suffered until the next morning. I learned my lesson and would never do anything to myself like that again. Actually the 2nd platoon was filled with guys from the South and they all thought it was funny that the guy from the big city got sick from chewing on a plug of "Days Work". Even when most of them couldn't even enunciate my last name because they never finished schooling to which I could have run on them because of their ignorance. The next morning we headed out away from the village looking for any signs of the illusive hospital that they have to have. We split the Company in two and sweep an area where it was thought the hospital would be. We don't find anything and we are back towards the village. But we do run into a Python snake and it had swallowed something about the size of a small dog. We all watched it for a couple minutes and were amazed how big it was. About 12 feet we figured. We left it and walked a little further when we come across a couple guys walking towards us. They don't panic when they see us. So we figure they were villagers heading back to the village. Since they were about 50 years old and had no weapons, we assumed they were villagers and let them go. We called in what we saw and were told to go a couple thousand meters and set up a night position.

We got about 2,000 meters from the village, off any trails to set up our night camp. It was an area surrounded by a couple of thick bamboo clusters and a second layer of trees that kept the ground moist and there were no signs that anyone had been at that spot for a long time. Because of this, we all felt secured that night. Maybe we shouldn't have let our guard down. We were lucky no one probed us that night and when morning came all was peaceful and quiet. That was just luck, if anyone had been in the area we would have been easy pickings. When we left the area, we went by a trail and found no sandal prints or broken branches so we believed no one had been this way for a while. We had our briefing at the start of the day and I did the correct thing by eliminating the old woman yesterday. No one tried to shoot us this night and we didn't catch any in coming. It was pretty much a skate operation for the next 2 days. We walked around several other villages but made no contact with anyone wanting to be cut in half by digesting some lead. The word got around that an old woman did just that after her fatal attempt to waste us. The jungle becomes thicker as we got away from the larger villages. Some places we could hardly get through the thickets of bamboo and scrub brush. We didn't see another soul for 3 days. We spent time looking at the jungle. None of us had ever been in a jungle and the only jungle we knew was from Tarzan movies and this was a different jungle.

I guess everyone heard about what I had done to the old woman? They probably heard us coming and stayed away. We walk in to the firebase.

We relaxed for a couple of days while at the firebase we still ran 1-day missions around the perimeter of the firebase but at night only 6 men went out on an ambush on the finger heading towards our chopper pad. We enjoyed our rest from the war. We were able to come in each night and get a little more sleep than when we were out in the jungle. These were good days where we didn't run into anything looking like trouble. However, we know that unless we started bringing in body counts, we would be put somewhere we could. That gave us the best chance to win medals, but it also put us in harms way. Medals don't mean as much as they used to. They never again mean very much to most of us from this day forward. While out on our next mission we are told there would be some planes flying around dropping chemicals on the jungle, and for us not to worry about it. All it does is kill vegetation and would clear the thick under brush where the gooks hide after a firefight. He was right this stuff was dropped on top of us and it killed the brush and nothing happened to us until 35 years later; Agent Orange is what we call it today. It has harmed thousands of us. There also is a strain called Agent Blue that has the same affect. Even killed a few; Steve Moore was one of them; he died of cancer brought on because of Agent Orange. I have Diabetes 2, which they say was caused by exposure to Agent Orange so they say. A lot of the jungle laid waste to the chemicals and it may have saved a few lives? Nevertheless, the number of dead because of it goes up each year and there is no end in sight for what Agent Orange will do. We went through a period where we found nothing, no enemy troops, ammo or weapons not even any extra rice to report. It was as if the enemy decided to leave this area and cause problems in other areas unknown. As the day's briefing came to an end, we had nothing to discuss to the higher-ups. We thought it was great; no firefights, no chance at getting yourself killed dead. The villages with large amounts of rice stored in earthen pots were keeping their rice. It wasn't just D Company; no one had any real contact. We were to believe that the enemy had bigger plans in other areas; all we had to do was figure out which area. We were being probed every other night and sniped at every evening and even that had come to an end. As I watch, the sun goes down over the tall trees and mountain slopes. Some times during the sunset you hear the animals of the jungle settling down for a night of rest for some and a night of savage hunting for that life you have to end so the animal can devour the other animals as it must be. Survivor for the fittest, that's the law of this war also. We must stay strong if we are to live through this war to grow weak would cause someone to die because of that weakness and not necessary the weak link. You might do something that causes someone else to act or react to the circumstances you caused. When someone dies from something, you had done; it puts so much weight on your shoulders that you never in your lifetime are able to shrug it off. That's as it should be. You don't make mistakes because mistakes can and do cost in some-one's death or disfigurement; would you want to live under that circumstance?

There were other unprotected areas that were having large numbers of fresh NVA Troops sighted. One rumor had us being moved to the DMZ to prepare for an invasion into the North. The NVA had been sighted around a Mike Force Special Forc-es camp at Ben Het. Then another rumor had us going to move south to help out in the Hobo-woods, an area west of Saigon. We really could have just stayed in the IA Drang and be as happy.

Nevertheless, if there were no gooks, we weren't fighting any-one nor capturing anyone. The last rumor had us heading for an area that the 173rd Airborne and 101st Airborne had contact with the 66th, 32nd infantry's and the 40th reinforced Artillery Regiment a group that had run the 173rd off of a hill in June. Why no one went back up that hill called 1338, we might never know the reason behind the decision. We ended up there later. We weren't finding any enemy or weapons so we figured we would have a safe time there in the IA Drang Valley, We were Infantrymen and we were sent to an area known to have a heavy amount of enemy moving into that area. While it seemed like a good thing to stay and keep the Valley clear of enemy activities the Army thought we should be earning our combat pay.

CHAPTER SIX - MOVING NORTH

In October 1967, the 1st brigade of the 4th Inf. Div. Along with a battalion of the 173rd Airborne that was assigned to the 4th, moved up into Kontum Providence, This was being protected by 2 Special Forces A teams. The area around Dakto and Ben Het was an area of very rugged steep mountains overlaid by a triple canopy of thick jungle and the NVA had been running this area for the past year or more. Ben Het was close enough to the borders of Laos and Cambodia that they received howitzer rounds from guns set on rails from an area known as Base Area 609. After they fire the guns, they would roll them back on rails into caves. A metal blast door was closed and it could take everything up to a direct hit. We weren't allowed to go in and destroy them because we had to follow rules while the North Vietnamese didn't! Sometimes I felt we were like moving ducks in a carnival's shooting gallery. Moral always went way down after a fire from the guns that caused someone to lose their life or become a vegetable.

The big battle for our Battalion was for the hill 1338. It happened while I was basking in the sun at the hospital in Cam Ranh Bay

and I feel that I was embarrassed by the fact I had not partici-
pated in that battle. I had an open sore from a leech bite and
by crossing and re-crossing those swollen streams I got what
they called Jungle Rot" on my right leg. They squeezed puss
out of my leg for about 10 days then after another 4 days they
sent me back to Division Headquarters. There I was told I had
been "recruited" to join the Recon Platoon. I found out that while
I was basking in the sun our Battalion was involved in a couple
of big battles. While the Recon Platoon was a safer unit because of the noise factor, there were heavy casualties inflicted
on the noisy maneuver line company units by the NVA and the
disproportionate casualties inflicted by Recon Teams on the
enemy. I believe this was because we fought them as they fight
our line company's as guerilla warfare where we strike then run
and get support from either the Artillery, mortars or a couple
jets to drop a load of bombs or Napalm on their sorry asses.
To increase the chances of our survival, we chose to rely only
on our own skills and instincts. With the frustration of fighting
both the enemy and the rear echelon bureaucrats along with
the confusion and terror of battle, we still had the camaraderie
of men relying on one another in dire circumstances

I pick up a M16 at headquarters and go out to the Chopper Pad
and find out that it's raining too hard up at Dakto for the choppers to fly. Then I'm told there is a convoy heading there in half
an hour and I should be in that convoy. I decide I will wait until
the next day and catch a chopper taking the mail to Dakto. I'm
told that up in the Central Highlands they average 146 inches of
rain during the Monsoon. Sounds like a great place for ducks,
but nothing else. I catch the Mail run chopper and sit and watch
where that convoy I was to take was hit by several RPG's and
there were 4 trucks on the side of the road still burning. I can
look to my left and start to see the mountains of the Central
Highlands. I guess my new home till next August when I would
go home. The area looks like something out of travel brochure;
the hills and lush green valleys looked like someone touched
up a photo to look so dam good. However, as we, all know that
jungle was infested with people that go creepy in the night; a

couple guys went up with me and they told their war-stories and tell 1 or 2 of my own. I was getting close to Dakto my new home with the Recon Platoon. A place where I was told each man was the essence of a fighting man in Vietnam. We were to wear our helmets while in the firebase and a vest but on most missions we wore our Flop Hats and the vest were too heavy and kept you sweating more than you should if you wanted to be OK when you were out and about on those jungle trails that lead to either death or glory.

In October 1967, intelligence reports indicated the 1st NVA Infantry Division (four infantry and one artillery regiment) had occupied the hills near Dakto and were preparing for attacks on Dakto and the near-by camp at Ben Het. Instead of waiting for the assault, the command ordered a spoiling attack by the 4th US Infantry Division, reinforced by the 173rd Airborne Brigade and six ARVN Battalions. The battle began on Nov 3 1967 and lasted 4 days with the 3/12th Infantry attacking hill 1338. Dakto on the map is grid ZB 012 216 about 40 KM North West of Kontum City. It was a Specials Forces camp containing 2, 12 man A" teams and about 200 Montegnard tribe's men who formed a Mike Force or sometimes called a Mobile Reaction Force who's primary goal was to act as a patrol base of operations designed to harass and intercept infiltration from the Ho Chin Mihn trail coming from Laos and Cambodia in the Tri-border area; where the 3 countries come together.

Dakto was situated in a valley tucked amid towering mountains covered with double and triple canopy of jungle. It's location denied the use of the flat jungle floor for the enemy, making it a prime target for attack. After a couple hours, I get on a chopper and head for Hill 1338, also known as Firebase 6. Our people found a hospital that was under ground and it looked like it had been there forever. That might have been the illusive hospital we were looking for. The173rd was ambushed half way up 1338 and they retreated back to Dakto. Why no one went back up, I don't understand. There are 3 guys going up with me. They are turtles and will be going to D Company. I told the big guy he was taking my place carrying the gun. I never did get their names, but why would it matter?

We listen to the choppers radio and B Company is being assaulted by some gooks as they are trying to leave 1338. Our chopper flies over them and the right side door gunner shoots 3 or 4 gooks. He gets the high thumbs up and the door gunner gives one back to the grunts from B Company. This breaks the contact and the rest of B Company fights it's way out to the platoon that was trapped by those gooks that were killed by the door gunner. That was quite a sight seeing the shoot out like it was on TV. Alternatively, in a movie we were actually there. We then landed at the firebase and Ronnie Baker; a guy I was stationed in the states with is there to greet me, we were in C Company 5/31st Inf. at Fort Benning, Ga. before coming to Vietnam; I in August, in September Ronnie came. He was the Company Clerk or mail clerk and was the one that typed up my orders to go to Vietnam; there was no Company Clerks out in the jungle crawling with the Enemy. Ronnie confirms he was the one that put my name in the hat to join the Recon Platoon. For that, I shall always be grateful; carrying a machine gun in a Line Company has a life expectancy of 3 months before you catch a round fired into you. The Recon Platoon was a group of elite soldiers that become that way if they are to survive. They were to find information and hand it over to Intelligence, which could then make a decision as what to do next.

Ronnie introduces me to the rest of the Platoon. I go over to shake hands with S/Sgt. Mumford and he tells me that Ronnie picked me and that he has faith in Ronnie's decisions and that I would become a member of Ronnie's Team. The Recon Platoon lost its Platoon Leader in late November during their attack up on Hill 1338. His name was David Barth. We have heard that we will be getting a First Sergeant to be our Platoon Leader. His name was Johnny Tubberville and he was a red neck from lower Alabama. I didn't get along from the first meeting. He transferred to Recon from somewhere else and I don't know what kind of combat he was in before. He didn't make the cut as far as I was concerned. I guess that's because I had a run in with him when a certain soldier didn't wake me for my guard and he tells Tubberville that he had me awake before he went back to sleep. I felt the reason he would say that was the guy that was supposed to wake me was a black man and Tubberville didn't want on his record that he was prejudice against blacks. Anyhow, we had an intense argument for about an hour where he tells me he's going to kill me next firefight we are in. That causes the hair on my neck to stand straight up. I get over it because this guy won't be out here long; he has made a few enemies in the first week he was here. Things happen out in the jungle that no one can explain.

We then wait about an hour to get our orders as where to go and when. Before that happened I was to unpack then re-pack my rucksack. The first thing to make sure I have at least 20 magazines with 18 rounds apiece. Then I'm told to carry as many frag grenades that I can carry. We not only use them to separate us from the enemy we also set-up booby-traps with them. I decide to carry 8. I also get 2 smoke. Then a large knife and 2 Willy peter grenades. They take out my poncho and let me keep the liner but the poncho shines at night when wet and makes a noise when rain hits it. I also leave my writing paper and envelopes at whatever firebase we are working out of. I only carry 2 canteens because of the weight; and right now in the Monsoon, we find fresh running water everyday. The water we cannot let go below half a canteen because it splashes as you move. So once it gets that low you either get some more or you pour some out.

The only problem about using that water is the villager's use running creeks as a way to wipe their ass. You can catch so many diseases, on top of it sounds awful that we would do that. I also get 10 boxes of M-16 ammo not in magazines but to reload if I run out of the 20 magazines. We all believe you can't carry too much ammo. I being the New Guy I carry the extra battery for the PRC. 25 radio. The guys then tell me to only carry the C-rations that I will eat there's no reason to carry something you won't eat same as in a line company. I also get an extra pair of socks; which turns out being the best thing to carry besides ammo you don't want your feet staying dirty and wet all the time. Now I know why they call us Grunts as I lift the rucksack on my back. A man can get old quick caring it on his back everyday.

We head out that morning on a 5-day mission to find certain trail that the enemy has been using to bring in supplies and ammo along with recruits out there in the mighty jungle. We sit and wait at the Bus stop for a chopper and after an hour, it comes by. Nothing like being on time, but we find he was rescuing some wounded off a hill that the 173rd was engaged with the enemy. The guys tell me to relax you can only die once but you can go on these missions forever" A chopper picks us up and with in 10 minutes we are dropped off, you are down and still alive, now run for the tree line, No! Not that one over there. We catch hell as soon as we hit this tree line. We don't know where the gooks are. We only know the general direction from their burst of fire comes from. The gooks could be but 5 meters away and you wouldn't know unless they opened up on you, then you're dead, more than not they have shot what they had then they ran off somewhere safe Charlie yells at me guess what? That green snake that wrapped around your leg when you first got off the chopper, it's called a Bamboo Viper a very deadly snake. Charlie tells me I could tell that you didn't know what it was by the way you grabbed it and flung it away. You either are one of the bravest asshole I know or you didn't know what it was. I don't say a word; let him think what he wants. It will never happen again. The gooks that fired at us when we were dropped off have left or at least have quit firing at us.

We scout around for a few minutes; we make no noise, no wise cracks no Coughing, unlike with a line company where there is so much confusion especially if you get some turtles that are all assigned to your unit. Ronnie tells us to get some rest; we probably will get no rest tonight. We head out for a nice spot where we can rest for about 3 hours. Ronnie says he will take the first guard and in 45 minutes, he's to wake me then on down the line until Van is to wake us all. We are to continue our mission, it could get very ugly if what they think will be coming down this trail actually comes. They are expecting some heavy machine guns and maybe a small artillery piece that it would be great to destroy one of them for our KIA and weapons count. I just have to remember body count isn't as important here in Recon. What we want is lives saved because of our actions. There is no way to calculate how many or whose life we may save, but we feel pride in doing that as we know some ones baby boy isn't shot tomorrow because of our action. It gave me a greater pride than when I was killing to get the praise.

When nightfall comes, we are ready watching down into a valley on a steep ridgeline and to our surprise, there is some one walking around down in a valley with flashlights on .Not anyone we know would be caring a flashlight not turned on anyway. Not that many anyway we count 12 lights and we don't know if everyone has a light or it's every 10 or 100. We call this information in to Mumford. It would mean they have no idea we are in the area. We call in artillery on that spot and half way thru the fire mission the Artillery boys want to know if we are in contact. Ronnie tells them no, so they say the 173rd Airborne is in heavy contact about 15 Klicks southeast of us. They get the artillery that they need more than we do at this time. As much firing as we hear from over there, one of them either the 173rd or the gooks are running out of ammo very soon. Maybe both. We listen to the radio but we must also keep an ear open in our area. The enemy may very well be on their way to where we are and if we get so engrossed in what is happening there we could be in deep do-do. We keep one guy watching to see where the flashlights are heading. It appears they have re-entered into the triple canopy and we can't see the lights. Nevertheless, we keep someone watching incase they reappear. From all the firing over on that hill, all 5 of us are glad we aren't the ones there. We can actually see the artillery, mortars and rockets landing on that hill where the 173rd was. We pull our regular guards that night and when the daylight comes we are told to stay where we are because if it had not been for that all night battle southeast of us. We would have gotten all of their attention. We call in one shot of H.E. and it lands right in the middle of that clearing so we tell the Artillery boys to mark that spot that we will be calling it in tonight in the event we spot them again and don't have time to start from the beginning to get help quickly. The battle that took all the artillery action last night appears to be over. We haven't heard an artillery round go off all morning, hopefully they will be able to get their wounded out and to a hospital. We listen to the radio and it's telling us that perhaps the gooks that attacked that unit thru the night might be heading towards us. Maybe they will go thru the valley we are watching or maybe just walk up here and ask us to dance the afternoon away. It's real quiet now and we are watching the valley and watching the trail that comes up here that gives one of us a chance to catch some Z's. I'm really tired and this action that we might be in the middle of has really drained me.

We get a call from Mumford and he tells us to head back to the firebase and to keep an extra eye open for any enemy that might be wounded and heading for that hospital we know they have to have. They had a 20- bed hospital in a tunnel system on hill 1338; where our unit had a big battle and we know they have to have another to replace it. We travel at a safe speed so we won't run into anyone carelessly. It starts raining again and that slows us down, we can't climb as easily as when it's not raining as hard as it is. We listen to the 173rd and they are still on that hill and it appears the Gooks have come back and might have the upper hand at this point of the fight. So all attention is going to them, as they need it to get healthy again. It was about noon when we run into a 3-man gook recon team. Lucky for us we spotted them before they saw us. Mick was walking point and. His initial burst wounded all three and his second zapped them all. We were only about 300 meters away from our perimeter so we figure those gooks were out on Recon missions of their own, where they try to gather information about our firebases. We collect their maps that show where the big guns are, machine gun nest, and the TOC. We are pretty proud of ourselves finding and stopping the gooks from attacking this time. But there may be other teams out, checking out the Perimeter. We also capture two AK 47s and one SKS carbine with several magazines full of 7.62 ammo. Along with some grenades that looked hand made. It looked like the one that old woman threw at me awhile back. They had some things on that map that had changed in the last couple of days. The big guns have been moved facing the chopper pad, incase the gooks decided to attack that way. That tells us they have been here before and have come back for a second or third time. We figure the gooks have decided to abandon their attack for a few more days. However, we also recognize that we are the prime Target and they will be coming after us real soon. They guys on the perimeter change a couple 50 Caliber machine gun positions, the big guns and mortars are too difficult and heavy to keep moving. We come in after 2 more days of nothing more found, but the thought that someone might be there is always racing through your already distressed mind. We get to sleep for as long as we want when we come in, because while out on a mission we get very little sleep. The border and the sanctuary it afforded were among the enemy's greatest weapons. They could shoot one of my friends then hightail across border and we can't follow them, we can't even shoot across the border, legally but I know at least 1 time when artillery was shot across it, to eliminate an artillery piece that was causing havoc on D company while I was there with them.

On our next mission, I get to walk point, which is a great honor. These other 4 men are saying to me that they trust me with their lives by letting me walk point. I read the map correctly and stop and listen quiet a few times .I'm learning what they call the Laws of the Jungle." The only thing I didn't like about walking Point was Point is the first guy to run into "wait-a-minute vines"! What they are is vines that grow near a lot of trees and when you walk close to one, it reaches out and grabs you. Then you have to "wait-a-minute" to get the vines off your flesh or if you keep going the vines will rip some of your flesh off of you, then you will have an area exposed to the bacteria that are out in this jungle causing your great discomfort.

I didn't run into any enemy soldiers and I took us up the right finger coming down off the mountain to set up. I didn't realize everything about walking point. First you have to go to a safe place, then you can't be heard or seen coming up on the enemy. We had to blend into the surroundings and gain information on the enemy and if given the chance call some artillery on them. Then there are the booby traps you can't fall prey to, then the snakes and wait-a-minute vines, the ant nest that are up about head level for us. Plus you have to be aware of your surround-ings, is that a bunker complex up on that ridgeline? Or is it just a shadow? You have to know the difference, if you think it's just a shadow when in reality it is a well-secured enemy bunker system that is full of gooks. Which would be the death to us all, and you have to know the difference right then! It does push you to your edge; but you can't let it consume you. There also is the fact the enemy can and did use some chicanery when it came to hiding booby traps as well as their bunker complexes. As a member of a Recon Team you can't be boondoggled in your every day routine, as it could become that final mistake none of us wants to take, it also could cost you all if you or anyone in the team acts in an impetuous or haphazard way while out by yourselves in the ever-dangerous Uncle Ho's neighborhood.

On the second day the regular point Robert Antonio takes over, which was a relief for me. There was a lot of pressure when 4 other men rely on you to keep them alive. But I find out it's that way on a 5 man team no matter which position you are in, the other 4 men rely on you doing your part, there are no skate jobs on a 5 man team. You should be able to do each man's job. When we bring in the AK47's, a guy on another team wants to know if he can carry one of the AK's out on missions?

Mike Lula informs us there are over 2,000 rounds for the AK at our ammo dump but he gets a M14 instead. He can get his ammo from the boxes that Machine gun ammo comes in. His has a selector switch so he can put it on rock-n-roll and have more of a punch than a M16 it's a little heavier than an M 16; packs more of a punch, fires a bigger round. Actually, I wouldn't mind having one to carry. But I will stick to my M16 it hasn't failed me yet, I some times took a Savage 12 gauge Shot Gun with me if I'm walking Point it's a pump that holds 5 shells total and is easy to reload which is important to me.

Our next three missions were pretty ho-hum, but you need ho-hum missions to keep your sanity if nothing else. We still have to climb up and down these jungle-covered hills and always be the lookout for the enemy. You always have the potential of running into a large group of gooks; anytime you come back with no contact it's a good thing, a really good thing. Some officers want rank so bad that they put themselves plus another 150 men in real bad circumstances just so they get a shot at a medal. Most officers and NCOs won't admit to such but we down at this level know better. It's close to Christmas we've been told. The only date we all know is the date we get to go home. What else could be as important as the day you leave your own little piece of hell? Anyway, Santa Claus don't do the Boonies; some REMF might get a tree and the whole box of goodies that I have read about in the Stars and Stripes paper we get monthly. Nevertheless, that stuff has its way of getting into the black market. Like the guys that get to see Bob Hope and Ann Margaret, they don't pull us in to watch such a thing, but tell everyone that they are entertaining the troops, but I guess if they pulled us from the field, who would take our place? We very rarely see stuff like that. It would make us too soft and might take away our thought process of staying alive. But it might show us what we are fighting for. The rear guys give us nebulous reasons why we don't get any of the frosting from the cake; but we have learned to live with or without it. However, who among those at Division Base camps would be able to come out to the jungle and stay alive or even go on a mission without being seen. Anyway that's the excuse we are told when we ask for our share. So maybe it's a good thing. Another thing that makes us think of REMF and the way that they put a thumbscrew on us. I would have loved to take a couple of them on a LP some night just to hear them squirm and cry like a little girl. The scariest thing you can have happen to you is to be out on LP and have the gooks attack from your side of the perimeter so you have no chance of getting in side the perimeter because the guys on the bunker will be almost as scared as you are when you come bursting in on top of them. The REMF may get mortared some day and one of the rounds may land close to where they are hiding in their bunker, but it's nothing like being one on one with an adversary who wants nothing less than you totally scraped from the face of this planet. Because of that action, the REMF may believe they were in a battle. We would shrug that off as nothing happened.

Then there is the feeling you get from killing the enemy. It feels so good and when you get to love it. Not really, the fact you took a life away from maybe some young kid that was forced to be there with you. It isn't for the praise anymore. Now it's because we might have kept some Mother's Son from riding home in a plastic bag. That is the important thing for us along with any information we can bring in that might save a few to many. You don't get to set the boundaries, no one does. Some guys go a whole year with out ever seeing neither a gook nor a dead American. I don't know how they do it; it would be impossible to go a whole week with out seeing such let alone a whole year. Nevertheless, not everyone has the same war as the next guy. Most of the dead gooks you had a part to play in each and every one of those deaths. But we can't dwell on what we can't control. There were a whole lot that was way beyond your control. You had to learn how to adjust some of the bad things that you will find and hopefully it won't be too late to adjust to what ever you must. We get aboard our chopper and that's when Ronnie tells us we should have a pretty good skate job on this mission.

When we leaped out of the chopper we headed down that finger off the ridgeline, we ran into some very thick fog. The area was very dark and dank which made it a miserable place to stay at. This was not a good thing to have happen to us. We slow down and call in our position and are asked; why did we slow down? When we tell, Mumford why we have slowed down he said he agreed with what our decision was and to be as safe as we can, but still finish the mission. The fog starts to lift and then you have the smoldering sun to deal with. It gets to 120 degrees we were told and it's a very humid 120. The jungle in this area looks as if no one has ever trampled through. It is thick underbrush and bamboo. Everything seems to all grow into each other and you can't tell where one clump of bamboo starts or finishes. There is no way we can get through this thicket and make it to our destination. We call in and tell of our problem and we are told to try to go around the thicket. If we busted through the bamboo, we would make so much noise and might walk into an ambush ourselves. We get around the thicket which we figure was about 100 meters thick and it only took 30 minutes to circle around it. We take more time to move around but we usually aren't found and therefore we don't get into unwanted contact as often as a Line Company. That is how I am going to live through this mess they call a War; I couldn't explain how a person feels or how a person is supposed to feel when your world comes crashing down on you. In a Line Company some are always going to be too fastidious to roughing it out in the jungle infested mountains of the Central Highlands, others can adapt to what ever comes to them without a loss of either mind or body. There are those that were considered daunt-less in their approach to the fighting, which makes it easier for those that were devastated by it to a point where they will also survive. We are alerted that someone is moving on this trail and they are headed straight toward us. We try not to travel on trails but if we travel in total darkness, we would have to, as the enemy did. We have 9 Claymore mines set up in a fan shaped kill-zone. In addition, we have 5 weapons aimed into the zone. Whoever is coming is moving at almost a running pace; they need to get somewhere very quickly.

When Mick clicks his plungers three times, each the ambush begins. The glare from the exploding mines let you see the expression on their faces as they meet death head-on. Their bodies are all turned to hamburger meat and bone splinters causing all to have quick deaths. We were fortunate that there were only 5 of them and we were able to get all five in the kill zone all together.

My throat was completely dry and I must swallow. I hacked and finally got enough spit to be able to swallow, but until that, I thought I might die. The three guys went out to check for funny papers while Mick and myself stand guard so no one can creep up on us; and adding to the fertilizer already left by those 5. After going through the pockets of those and all we found was a whistle to blow commands while attacking and about 300 dong in their money. However, we don't find any maps or anything that looks like a set of orders. Now it starts raining pretty hard and we ask for permission to get as far away as we can from that ambush sight because the noise that the claymores and rifles alerted any enemy troops within 5 klicks away that an American unit has just killed some of their own. Nevertheless, before we leave we must try to destroy their weapons. We take out the bolts and fling them into the jungle and then try to bend the barrels as much as possible, it doesn't take much to make them inoperable. We had to leave as soon as possible. There is no time to waste; we must get to be somewhere else and quick. We set up for that night about a klick away from our ambush and set up another and wait and see what pops up in our area tonight. We set up and nothing happens that night which is a very good thing. However, while you are on guard, you still hear and see things that aren't there. It takes a lot out of you to set up and see movement in the dark; which turn out to be nothing more than a bush being moved by the wind. You always have that fear that it is an enemy moving towards you because he knows where you are. You have to be able to determine what it is and live or die by that decision. If it is an enemy, he probably doesn't really know where you were so you have a chance to get another bead on him with your weapon and hope there aren't too many behind him. If you are lucky you notice no one is there and you can relax until the next shadow appears, then you get to go through it again and again. One of these times there will be someone there and you will have to deal with it, right then and there.

CHAPTER SEVEN - MCCOY

Our mission would always be to Recon an area and report back so that a Line Company or Artillery will take care of any enemy force that we could stay away from. If we get into a tight spot, where as the enemy is in contact with us there will be every chance there is to get us out of that scrape with the minimal loss? We can and do call in support, anything from a couple mortars fired our way to an Arc light of 3, B52 Bombers. Nevertheless, we were the Eyes, and Ears of the Battalion; we were not a fighting unit, but we would fight as a unit if the need arises. The gooks usually have 2 or 3 of their recon teams searching around one of our fire support bases to make maps of the area in case they decide to attack with a human assault or fire a couple shots then run and hide for harassment to the guys inside the perimeter. Before an all-out attack, they always get an up to date map showing, which way the artillery pieces are aimed and how many mortar tubes are there. They also put on their maps where the 50 cal. Machine guns were. The enemy is pretty scared of the 50, I guess I understand because I had 1 fired at me once, and it's like a cannon being fired rapidly at you. One hit and you could bleed to death before someone gets you to a medic and that might not be enough help, you probably would need to have some blood and our medics had none.

We listen in on a conversation between someone from Intelligence and someone named McCoy, I ask who was McCoy and was told; He is a guy that is on his 3rd or 4th tour here in the Central Highlands. He won't speak to you and can be your worst nightmare if provoked. He dresses in a Loincloth and carries an AK47 and only 2 magazines full of ammo. If he needs more he will take it from the gooks." I got the chance one morning to see him when he came in for a briefing with the Intelligence Officer and he had something around his neck. Ronnie tells me "it's all left ears from the gooks that he has killed." I thought it would be against some law or rule in the Army to have them. Then I was told "he wears them only when he was told when some Officer won't run into him with his ears." I could hardily believe that story so I got as close to that guy as I could. Which was about 2 meters and they sure looked like what I thought some ears would look like if you hung them from your neck. At that time, I said "HI" to him; he looked at me and mumbled something at me. I was told that when he went out on missions he only carried 2 magazines for his AK 47 and if he needed more he would start a fire and cook some rice; then when someone showed up to see if they could eat as well, McCoy would jump out behind the fire and start shooting until they were either all dead or those still alive would run away from him. It sounded fishy to me, but I did see his ears and he did wear only a loincloth and that was all. He must lack some of the basic hygiene that we in an organized unit get, such as insect repellant and toothpaste. I was told there was another guy named Kelly; Tom Kelly that was in recon and he got scared almost to death and now works at Quarter Master for the Recon Platoon. No one remembers what happened to make him that way, but it must have been pretty scary. I've only met him once, he didn't appear to me to be injured but his problems were in his mind and those can really screw you up as many others and I were to find out in 30 or more years. McCoy most differently was laconic in his speaking to you and he most definitely was not mediocre in his tactics while out in the jungle.

We were then on a new mission and so far it has been a good mission with little chance of us running into some gooks. That was because this area had been bombed by B52's just yesterday. The bombs cleared a path about 50 meters wide and 400 meters long. It was a very impressive sight to see. Made me glad I was on this side of getting bombed. The B-52's fly so high you don't see or hear them coming all you hear and see are the bombs blowing up; then it's too late to do anything about. The closest I have been to such an ordeal was about 500 meters and it almost knocked me off my feet and caused my ears to ring. We are going in to see if we could spot anything that was either damaged or destroyed. There was nothing to report, we didn't see anything, but we had to cut our stay short as we hear someone talking in a real low tone; it has to be gooks, because if there were any friendly in the area we would have been notified. We run into a platoon-sized unit of NVA. There are twelve of them and all are carrying AK47's, so they have a lot of firepower on their side, we decide to not take these guys on in a battle we could lose. The Gooks must have smelled us, because all of a sudden they took off running towards us, but not firing their weapons. We run as fast as we can go and these guys were hot on our trail. We stopped at one point and opened up on them with everything we had. Most of our actions while fleeing an enemy were off the cuff; there was no one way to achieve our goal of getting separation; sometimes we had to fight then flee, sometimes we just sit and hide from a much larger force, we very seldom sit and fought to the end, because with just 5, we could be the end, just long enough for Ronnie to get our bearing and call in some artillery to put space between them and us, then we changed direction and headed east away from the Fire Support Base, a direction we believed would be the last that they would look for us we still are not out of hot water, next thing we had to do was get back on course to finish our mission, and without them finding us again, we had to travel a little faster than normal to get back on course and arrive before the Artillery barrage began. They had already planned the barrage ahead of time and we need to either get to our objective and be safe or abort the mission and await new orders. We get out our map and the fastest way to our objective would be to follow this trail for about 1,000 meters. This goes against our training and what we have hammered into our thick skulls, but it is the only way we can make it in time. We still have 500 meters to go before we reach the trail so; we are off. We have good luck and don't see or hear anything that would be enemy troops. We do stop and check out the scenery if just for a second or two. This part of the jungle may never have seen a human being or at least not for many years. We finally get to the trail and look for any signs of movement recently done there. It all looks clear and we head out to our objective and we have 3 hours until they start shooting up the area around the hill we are to be at. Chief is running point, there is no walking as we normally would, we had a little over 2 hours to get to the objective and by running this 1,000 meters we should have made it in time for the fire works show. It didn't take long to run the 1,000 or so meters to get back on track as to how we wanted to approach our objective. We sit and listen for 2 or 3 minutes and we hear nothing to cause us anything to worry about. We also needed the rest from running with that pack on your back. We were in pretty good shape to be able to run that distance; for I was exhausted as I assumed the other guys were also. But we must get going after about 7 minutes break to catch our breath. Just to be on the safe side Grizzly gets on the phone and tells us he has 2 Navy jets coming by to say hey" to us. Then tells us they were on a mission and it was scrubbed, and since they can't take their bombs back to the carrier, they will drop them where we need them. It gives us about 4 minutes to secure an area for us to stop at, until they drop their arsenal on the valley leading to our place to be tonight. That was a good thing. The Navy had 2, 250lb bombs apiece and a couple of Napalm each. We find a place about 100 meters away from the place the bombs will be dropped and wait about 2 minutes; then the Navy jets show up and first they both drop 2 bombs each in the area that will make it safe for us to run in. First pass came from the south and finished with the Flyboys flying over us after dropping their bombs. Then they come over us and drop their Napalm in the narrow valley they had just blown to hell. There was a roaring ball of fire that not only covered that valley but the sides leading up the 2 fingers leading up to the ridgelines. Everything that was alive in that area is now toast and we should have no problem getting to our objective for this evening. We were surprised to find seven broiled bodies in that area we had just fried. There also were some funny papers in a canvas bag showing where some tunnels were. I looked at the funny papers and they believe are from the K25 NVA Engineer Battalion that's what the Battalion Interrupter tells us. If those flyboys had not dropped those bombs and Napalm we might have walked into a serious situation; hell we probably would have been killed. Once we get to the summit of this knoll that will become our residence for this evening, we call in about the funny papers. We were told to put the funny papers in with our maps in the plastic sheets to keep it from turning into rotten paper. The jungle is not some place you would want to leave anything with the lid off it. Anything would grow mold after a couple hours of that heat and moisture. We had to move to our destination without being seen nor heard.

The use of hand-signals keeps you on your toes watching the Team Leader to see what and where you do things at all times plus looking out yourself for any signs of enemy movement in that area. The signals are pretty basic, Stop, Go, Left, Right, or Get down. If someone fires at you then you had better know what to do and get it done right then and now! Sometimes someone will take a single shot at you then run that's when you had to make a decision and either ride it out or have the courage to change your mind in a fraction of a second. A second too late and that's what it is; Too late. We get to use these hand signals as we walk into a group of gooks headed towards our left. We stop, look and make the decision to call in Artillery on them after they had left our sighting. The Artillery pushes them back toward us, which could be a bad thing. However, as luck would have it there were only 6 of them forced back at us. We pitched grenades at them, and then opened up with our rifles. Killing all 6, which adds to the Battalion's body count list, we then go down and search for anything that may be important for our side to know, size of units, location of supplies, a hospital or a staging area, anything to help the cause. We of course don't read Vietnamese so anything we find we turn in hopping it will be enough to slow down or stop the War. When we read off what is written an officer from Division translates it and tells us if we are to keep it or dispose of it. About an hour after the shoot out, we are shot at from a bamboo thicket 25 meters away. It's impossible to get through the bamboo to reach this person and one of the guys is carrying a M-79 grenade launcher, which looks like a sawed off 40 mm shotgun. He fires several shots that land close to where the shots came from; After waiting a couple minutes we didn't hear or see anything in that direction so we head that way. When we arrived there, we found no one, no cigar; we couldn't find anything except 3 spent casings. If the gook had hit someone and then vanished, that is what was so frustrating about that war. You hardly ever get the chance to fire at someone that had just killed a buddy of yours. That's the main reason you have very few buddies. Nevertheless, you have to have someone that will be there for you when the time comes for you to need someone to cry on his shoulder. You try and pick someone that will be safe till either you or he goes home. You don't want to receive a letter from one of the guys left behind that someone you knew was now gone. It leaves a void place in your mind that can never be replaced. We run into an area that is heavily congested with scrub bushes and some bamboo, there also is a large flower looking thing that is red with a yellow center. I had seen one before while in D Company there was a guy that was a Teacher of science at the High School level I asked him what it was and he knew it was called a Rafflesia; that it's a parasite that feeds on the root system of certain tropical trees. It is always interesting for me to learn of the differences out in Uncle Ho's playground.

There are some very beautiful scenes that I had seen while there. I remember waking up at sun-up in time to catch a glimpse of a group of small deer down at the rivers edge getting their morning drink. Then looking up in the trees to see the monkeys first giving breast milk to their young and taking their morning piss. If you are below them, they get a kick out of hitting you with their piss. You can't even shoot him out of the tree because it would give your position away. The dam monkeys would sit up in a tree and piss on you and chatter and laugh till you moved away. They almost got me that first morning but, lucky for me I saw it coming and I moved out of the way in time to keep from being soaked in monkey piss. Talking about something that will stink until a good rain comes and washes your stinky ass; I wouldn't be surprised if the monkeys would throw their crap at you given the chance, monkey crap stinks pretty badly. , It would take a hell of a rain to wash fresh monkey crap out of your hair, and it has been raining a lot every day the last 2 weeks, but I still think it would be discussing to have them throw runny crap on you, just something else to worry about.

We move out looking for someone to shoot, just to make the day a profitable one, we found some propaganda that the enemy had left for us to read. The first one tells blacks that no Viet Cong ever called him nigger, the second one talks about how we were fighting so the French could have control of their country again and that the French would again enslave them. Then one tells about how Jody is home with your wife or girl friend and you are over there fighting so some rich man can become richer, and I'm sorry to say all three may be the truth or at least enough of what could be happening that you question yourself about what the hell were we doing there? Because there was, no support from home you may have felt in some ways that what the gooks were saying was at least half-truths. However, if you dwelled on that, you surely would have perished. What we did was to put our-self in a way that we are going to go home and in one piece and you will do whatever it takes to do so. While sitting up on guard, that night I listened to a LRRP Team in contact with a company sized unit of NVA and one of their members is wounded. As I listened to what was going on, I felt that we might get into a similar circumstance and what would we do when it happens. We didn't go out as far as the LRRP's did, but we do some of the same missions as they do. Therefore, we listen to hear how they get out of their predicament and how we could do the same as needed. They ended up jumping up and high tailing it away from the enemy. They were lucky that they weren't followed by any of the gooks. They then called artillery behind them in case anyone was trying to follow them. They had called in a plot of where to fire the artillery at and they had to outrun the artillery. Then they were extracted within 10 minutes of the escape.

It started to rain at about 0500 hours and it was 1 hour till sun-up and we all wanted to be awake as the sun comes up from the east. This is because at sun-up the enemy likes to put the sun to their rear and come screaming in their bullhorns and firing on full automatic as they come in. Die! Yankee! Die! And spraying the area with 7.62 rounds to keep your head down until they get up to the hole you are in then drop a grenade in the hole and there's 4 more KIA for them. But none of this happens and you are still so worked up over what might happen that when it doesn't, you are kind of disappointed and until the adrenalin wears off; you were all strung out waiting for that big battle that doesn't happen it takes a toll on you and then when it does happen that takes a much larger toll on you. I can remember nights where we got zero sleep because the gooks were probing our team out in the dark jungle, it's like they know you are there, they just don't know exactly where. We make a game out of being able to hide from these little bastards as they make a game out of us finding them. Either way the ones that lose, lose there is no second place out there. You either win or you lose; if you lose, you are out of the game and will not be a factor in what happens the next hour. So you try to cheat fate and get out of the predicament as best you can. There is no second place in this arena in that jungle. Sometimes you got hurt even in first place. The only rule is there are no rules and you can't take anything for granted. Each and every minute out of each day, you will either keep on your toes or you might lose, losing means the ultimate price is paid for your mistake or shortcoming, which you would have to live with the rest of your life. As morning comes, there is a quiet that is serial and as the fog lifts from the jungle's rivers and the birds start looking from now. It is so beautiful that you sometimes can't believe there is a vicious struggle going on day and night. There were some snub-nosed monkeys up and raising hell because we were there. We also saw a small deer getting its morning drink at the creek. Then the phone asks what are you doing and for you to go to a new location 2,000 meters north of where you stopped to rest while the valley was being fried. We can look at our map and go to this place described to us. We travel back through the valley that was burnt to the ground yesterday. There is the sweet sickly smell of burnt human flesh that reaches down into your bowels and no matter what you thought; everyone threw up till their guts hurt with the pain of rupturing a gut, it is such a sickening sweet smell that seems to get stronger as time goes by. You would think we could get some Commanders in Chief out here from all sides and have them smell this sickening smell this type of war would cease and quick.

We get by that area and come to the point where we were to leave and head in the direction we were told to. Ronnie wants me to polish my skill at walking point. That was a great honor; for these 4 guys are putting their lives in my hands and I didn't let them down. I need to use hand signals to let those following me to know what is or is not going on at the Point position. I go through the first 2 hours without saying a word. We come up on some fresh sandal tracks and I motion for Ronnie to come up and see what I see. All I said was look here" Ronnie calls the team to come up front and we needed to decide what course of action we would go through. We call in our information and are told to follow the tracks at a "safe" distance and keep them in constant radio contact in case we need to be extracted at some point. We follow those tracks until we come to a point where 2 more have joined in on their parade. We figure they must be Trail Watchers reporting in what they have or have not seen.

We were told that we must stop following them and for us to call in artillery on where we believe they were at that time. We get a secondary explosion and were told to set up camp tonight and go first thing in the morning to check out what exploded. I read the map, recognized where we were at all times and Ronnie had me call in some mortars that evening. I felt like I was one of the members of a 5 man recon team and I was accepted as such by my peers. My brother Steve would be proud. There were no higher honors than that. I do a pretty good job of calling in the mortars and I get them called at the correct spot incase we would need to use them. I fall asleep early tonight because I'm worn out. When it comes my turn for guard, I sit up and listen to the radio. I have the volume turned way low so no one else could have heard it. Apache 5 was getting probed and the gooks are getting very close to walking up on them. That is the scariest thing because; you must remain quiet and low to the ground. You know that the enemy knows where you are but not exactly. If you lie still and don't get stepped on, they may not find you, no matter how close they come to you. As it gets closer to daylight, you want the gooks to give up and go away. Steve Moore who was the Team Leader he called in artillery and mortars on top of himself to clear the hill of gooks .It apparently worked because the gooks put their tail between their legs and left the area. Apache 2 was going to head East in the morning so they called in mortars to their West then East and left the area making sure they stopped and listened incase the enemy had set an ambush for them. They shot up the area to the West hopeful that the enemy would think that was the area they headed out for.

The Apache team was lucky there were no ambushes set for them. We head out for our area to occupy for that evening. We don't find any new signs of movement so we do feel a little safer on this mission. Nevertheless, we must stay focused on what could have happened. We are at an area that has a perfect LZ in the middle of some of the taller trees in the area. Most of these trees had what we called buttress root systems so it gives a person a place to hide from artillery or even a patrol out looking for them. We set up at the edge of the grassy area and set up our claymore mines to cover the entire LZ. We settle down and as the sun is setting over the mountains to our West. This should be a pretty good place to pull an ambush if the occasion arises. I pull 1st guard so I have the first 2 hours and I have something small moving around up on the trail about at the spot we had our dinner last night. I wake up Ronnie it's his time to pull guard and I point out the critter moving amongst our discarded cans. He tells me it's probably a rat, not to worry about it. Guard goes on until Mick pulls the last shift. Mick sets up and is looking away from the LZ when he hears a twig snap on the other side of that LZ. He waits to make sure it's not some animal coming to graze on the grass.

What Mick sees is 2 NVA looking through the LZ to see if they see someone where we are. As soon as they start across the clearing Mick pulls at the plungers of the Claymores and as we, all jump up prepared to do battle we find a couple gooks wandering around spilling their blood over the grassy area like they are lost. Mick did well at pulling off the ambush. He couldn't wake us up because he might have been seen or heard while doing so. The remaining gooks try to race across the clearing and overrun us. We don't let that happen, we call in artillery to a spot where it did drive the gooks into us. We had 2 more Claymores set up in case we did get rushed. Ronnie plunges them and we knock down 15 men during the firefight and get credit for such. Even when the artillery got most of them, we might have gotten the 6 and the artillery boys the 9.I don't know how to explain how it feels to have a much larger than you group assaulting you. What went through my mind is we had to kill them quick not giving them the chance to have overwhelming firepower on us. We also find some funny papers on those guys, we figure they were on a scouting patrol looking to find a way to cause havoc to an American position. By either firing into the position with rifles or a recoilless rifle a couple of times, just to make sure we were awake and ready to rumble.

We put a stop to that and call in for an extraction from this LZ. There were a lot more gooks behind those we killed and they appear to be gathering to push for another assault on us. However, before we can get lifted out, we must clear the LZ of unfriendly people. We start out by calling in mortars surrounding us because that is what the gooks were doing. If we can't get the gooks to leave this area, we can't be picked up and that would be the end of us. Grizzly gets on the phone and asked where the enemies were? Ronnie tells him they are trying to surround us and if we could get a couple gun-ships to come in and spray the area with some 7.62 maybe a chopper could get in long enough for us to dash to it and hop in. We are told there is a chopper pilot that is willing to do that but he can't wait for us to climb in; we must all 5 leaps in one motion. We ask for 1 more volley of artillery before the chopper comes in. We are told there will be 6 shots at the clearing then the chopper will be down to lift us to safety. Here came the artillery and after the 6th, one we head out to the LZ and the chopper arrives just as the gooks. We are in a firefight as we jump into the chopper and head away from that spot. No one is wounded in that escape and we were very lucky and good at what we do to make it. When we are about 10 feet in the air, 2 gun-ships open up on that LZ with their mini-guns and spray the whole area causing several more to add to their KIA list. As the chopper was rising to get away, we took several machine gun blast through the bottom of the chopper, but no one was hurt and as soon as the gun-ships and we were out of the way, artillery cleared that hilltop of anything alive. We get back to the Firebase and were told we will have 2 days off until we go back out. We decide to gather any beer left over from the artillery guys and have a party, it sounded so good to use terms we used while civilians.

There are no Military terms for a party, just not in their books. At times of rest, which were while at a forward firebase I wondered what it was like to be an average NVA soldier? Was he there because he wanted to be, or because the American Imperialist were invading his country, or was, he forced to fight? Was he a communist, or was he some poor sap that was forced to be there? I probably will never know that answer; but the question runs through my head whenever I feel safe enough for my mind to wonder from trying to stay alive. We walk in and are greeted by Tubberville; I'm learning to accept him as our leader; I guess because it's not going to change in the near future. He and I are not friendly however we do speak to each other when the need arises, I guess maybe I was a little harsh towards him, we started out on a bad foot and it took awhile for it to heal so we could stand each other. Which was a good thing.

CHAPTER EIGHT - STORIES

We each get 3 beers and go to the biggest bunker that faces the chopper pad. There are enough guys not wanting to drink that can pull guard on that bunker. We get pretty drunk on 2 beers and have the 3rd to carry us through the night. Even when the beers and any sodas we might get have all lost their effervescent quality. We start out telling war stories. Festus tells us about Bill Watkins and the time he called in that he was being surrounded and he needed artillery support, after they shot up the area he was in the movement stopped. All that could be found was a couple dead monkeys. So from that point on Bill was known as the Eyes, Ears and imagination of the Battalion."

There was another story about Reb" as Bill was known, the first mission that he was the Team Leader he was woke up by the guy on guard and told to look a few meters away that there was someone standing over there puffing on a cigarette. Bill watched for about 30 minutes and the puffing continued, so Bill went around to the back of this guy and before he could attack this guy. Bill found that it was a tree stump that was hit by Willy Peter and when the wind would hit it, it would glow like someone was puffing on a cigarette. Mick brings up when they were assaulting 1338 Ronnie was attacked by 3 or 4 gooks that wrestled his gun away; Ronnie was a captive. This lasted about 2 minutes and Ronnie fought his way back to where the rest of Recon was. I throw my 2 cents in and tell of the time there was a Water Buffalo attacking me while in a line company; this mammoth Buffalo was snorting and throwing his head from side to side and was about 20 meters from taking some of us out when he finally fell after I pumped 100 rounds to his skull. He turned out to be a very formidable enemy. The old man that owned the Buffalo wanted us to pay for it. We told him there would be someone bringing him $100 and some tobacco and a little salt. The old man either didn't understand or thought his Buffalo was worth more. Later that evening we were probed and someone shot into our perimeter, so we opened up on that spot, and the rest of that night was pretty calm. Next morning we go out to check and that old man was who had fired at us. Why he hadn't waited, it's such a sad thing. Part of our problem is the different culture than them. I have one more story to tell and these guys have heard everyone else's story over and over. My next story is when I was in a line company I was involved in a search of a village down on the shores of the IA Drang River. We were looking in a hooch for anything that would be a weapon or ammo. I stayed outside and kept my machinegun aimed out into the group of people standing out in a circle. When I get a grenade rolling on the ground next to me. I panic and turn to run when it goes off with about the same power as a cherry bomb. Rocky stops me and asked "so you were the one that cut that poor old woman in half with your machinegun?" I told him "yes I was" "well I want you to know, that was a sight I wished I had seen." I guess everyone had heard that story before, so all I added was when I went up to look at her face and she had a Mona Lisa smile etched on her face, that was the last story for me that night. Because of the beer I was tired and crawled off to my bunker and fell right to sleep .I don't remember if I had a dream that night, but it was the best sleep I can remember having while out in the jungle. I woke up about 30 minutes before I was to pull the last guard of the night. It was still dark and I told Chief he could go back to sleep a little earlier, I was up and awake; so off to sleep he went. As luck would have it, we get probed about the time my regular guard would take place. I have to wake the guys in the bunker to get ready for what might not come; we must be ready in case it does. After the guys are awake and looking out of the bunker into the dark jungle we could hear some movement to our front then there were some people to our left. We have a pot of hot water brewing some instant coffee and we really don't want anyone disturbing us while we enjoy it. Because of the enemy movement, we don't go to the mess tent to get some real coffee. When gooks decide to attack while we are in, makes us wish we were back out in the jungle where we were in charge as what we were to do or not do. This way we have to go with the flow and Line Companies usually have 10% of their troops green. Never been in a battle and are scared, as they should be. Nevertheless, they have a history at fucking up and pissing on themselves. We all have been there and there isn't anything to be ashamed of, nothing comes at sun-up, but we still had to be ready incase they were coming. The next day was spent resting up for the next mission, after staying alert all morning because we thought that was when they were going to attack, but that is what they call physical terrorism, where you are kept on the edge 24/7 and not allowed to get any rest from the thoughts of dieing, it keeps working on your mind and will wear you out. The enemy would much rather fight you when you are worn out from lack of sleep with the added feeling that you were scared silly and might give away your position, which could get you killed dead. Then that night we pulled our normal guard. Nothing is really normal out in the boonies, we again hear that the Gooks may be making ready for a full-sized attack on the perimeter that night, and again nothing happens, but you have to alert and ready to go if an assault does come. We again leave the perimeter and head out into the jungle that might have someone looking for us again. After neither five days and nights, of nothing seen nor heard we head back to Firebase 13.

CHAPTER NINE -
AN ASSAULT WHILE WE WERE IN

While in a firebase, we pull guard at the bunker facing the chopper pad. Most of the time 3 to 5 of the guys would sit up looking out into the darkness that has creped up on us, looking for any signs of an enemy approaching toward the pad. What they want to do was to bury a bomb of some sort in the chopper pad then blow a chopper to hell; maybe one with Grizzly on it. We watched and never saw anything until when we heard the digging. Now what do we do? If we go out there and they decide to blow the thing while we are on the dam thing; that would get a telegram ready to go to mom, we sure didn't want that to happen, we decide to contact the L.P.'s and inform them what is going on and assure them they are not in an unsafe spot yet. But they need to watch incase the gooks run that way.

What we decided to do was roll a couple grenades towards the noise of the digging and go from there, we tell the L.P.'s what we were going to do, and tell them to watch for anything running their way. Charles, Mike and my-self pitch a grenade apiece towards the noise and wait a couple seconds, which seemed a lot longer. When the grenades went, off we could see the 2 diggers and immediately shot the hell out of them, the grenades probably did the job, but we wanted to make sure. The L.P.'s call in to tell us there are several dinks down there coming our way. It looks like this was a for real assault on our perimeter and that was the only time we wish we were out in the bush. We were in to rest a couple days before going back out into the depths of the jungle where we could hide. However, being in that firebase there is nowhere to hide nowhere to run, the last time we were here we had visitors also. On the other side of the perimeter a trip flare goes off and the soldiers on that bunker open up on 6 or 7 gooks that they could see. It doesn't take long before we saw enemies to our front; the enemy escalated their attack at our bunker. Ronnie tells us to hold our fire until we got a good shot off and to fire in burst of 3, we don't know how long this would last and running out of ammo means getting out of the bunker or trench line and heading for the ammo dump while exposing your self while doing so. We do send Mike Faulkner to get as many M-16 rounds and frag grenades as he can carry and to hurry back because he didn't want to get caught out in the open when they start mortaring us. Which takes place about the same time as he got back; he hands out the extra ammo and sets the grenades on the opening to our front. If an assault is to take place, we first blow our Claymores, then shoot at whatever moves plus in the event that we are getting an assault to our front we will pitch those grenades out to halt the assault when it comes. As we sat in our bunker only seconds away from the gooks being hurled into combat against us, I could see the grim faces of those in that bunker with me, all knowing that unless we repel the assaulting gooks our troops could be in the spot they would never leave alive. Nevertheless, we quickly had to scrub that notion out of their minds and tell them over and over again that we had to rise up and defeat those that were trying to rid themselves of us. After a couple minutes we see 10 NVA out to our front and several more to our left and right, they were going to try and rush us and take over the bunkers 1 at a time we start receiving small arms fire and Ronnie gives the OK to blow two of the Claymores to our right because that is where the firing was coming from. One of the Claymores had been turned around and it fired up at the bunker to our right. It didn't cause anything but fright when it was fired. Ronnie tells everyone to duck if we fire a Claymore because it appears Charlie has turned some of the mines around to face us, I look up then out into the jungle that has a lot of smoke from trip flares and from them firing at us. They are firing at full automatic we figure to get us to return with the same, they wanted us to get low on ammo then push forward with a larger assault than the first one. I open up with my burst of 3 and hit one of them and spin him around so he was not facing me, I hit him with another burst of 3 and he goes down, I was looking out to my right and there were about 20 of those little bastards crawling up towards that bunker so I pitch a couple grenades at them then I look back to in front of us and there were a couple carrying long pieces of bamboo. We were taught in AIT at Fort Gordon that those are called Bangalor-Torpedoes, they are loaded with an explosive and they are used to destroy a barbed wire around the perimeter that protect us. I shoot at him and hit him in the face with my burst of 3. He goes down and his device explodes killing another that was trying to put it under our wire. Now the mortars start; they are being fired from the next ridgeline from a clearing that we can see. We call in to Artillery and give them a grid to fire at. A fire mission of 3 rounds hit that area and stops the mortaring, that was some good shooting and a well-placed call giving them a target that only we could see.

Then we had to look to the right then left, nothing at this time but they were coming up in front of us screaming into their bull-horns and firing into the front of our bunker. During this attack dust along with splinters of steel and flying chunks of earth were flying towards us. I ducked into the bunker helpless as a child. I assumed the fetal position and sat there knowing I should rise up and meet the oncoming enemy head-on and rid myself of their ugliness. I rose and opened up on a group of 5 to my left. They fell backward as my firing entered at their face level and jolted them back, tearing their cheekbones into splinters. It was at this time and in this environment as a youth of nineteen, I lost another bit of my innocence. I was determined not to sell my life so cheap; to get me some panicked enemy would have to get off a lucky shot maybe one not directed towards me. I decided then that I would stay up and fight off any that rose to assault me. We were developing into Extraordinary Professionals. We kept our nerve while others succumbed to panic. We used our rifles as surgical weapons with deadly precision. We had the feel for battle; we knew the rhythm of defense, cover, and attack. Our lack of fear of injury or death amounted to a state of mind that one might call bravery, or was it?

It was one strange thing about war, that a few soldiers appear invulnerable to serious injury or death. I felt I was one of those. I go out the right side into the trench line and Ronnie goes to the left. We take some grenades with us and pitch them towards the large force attacking our bunker. This act turns the tide of battle in our favor, we look out and don't see another enemy at that time but we were told not to get too relaxed, shit could start up again and it could even be a stronger herd of gooks than last time." Ronnie yells out "there was a large group down about 20 meters from our bunker." We had to find a way of stopping them from assaulting us right now. The bunker just behind us had a 50 Cal. Machine gun and it appears there was no one to fire it. So a couple of us went and retrieved the gun and 5 boxes of ammo. We are still hearing movement to our front. We believe the gooks are going to try another assault across the chopper pad and into our happy home. Van gets behind the 50 and Mike gets it loaded and ready to rock n roll. We could only take so much then it starts working on your head, how long could we hold this bunker then the perimeter if the whole thing goes to hell? When an enemy force knocks you off a hill, it usually means at least a 40% loss of manpower. At about 0730 hours, the sun was up and our bunker faced the East so that's where we expect the attack to come from. Within the hour, we saw a very large number of enemy troops gathering about 50 meters down from the chopper pad. All of a sudden, we receive 20 rounds from a mortar crew on the next ridgeline. This keeps our heads down for a few minutes then we have to force ourselves to peek out to where the charge was coming from. There is a large herd of gooks coming up toward the pad and we don't know if we will be able to repel them. The enemies strident screaming was enough to scare you to death. But once you learn that is the purpose of the screaming it no longer ruffles our feathers. Van gets up and fires the 50 cal. Machinegun into the mass of humans. That put a stop on their assault for a couple minutes until they regrouped. Van shot most of them in the legs, but a 50 will cut your legs off. There now are about 15 people down the way with their legs missing, it stops them from attacking us and would make someone near them decide not to come our way. We get a call from Battalion 6 telling he was going to fire some canister rounds right on top of our bunker and for us to wait until the 3rd round is fired before we raise up to continue the battle if need be. Van and Ronnie rejoin us inside the bunker while the canister rounds are fired. The canister rounds are fired and we look up just in time to catch the 15 or so enemy that had ducked when the Artillery was fired at them. Ronnie and Van go out to secure the 50 and the rest of us begin firing at the gooks coming at us full force and screaming something in those dam bullhorns. The enemy was then stopped. That battle lasted until 0930 hours then the enemy ran away from the siege and we walked out to the front of our bunker to make sure all had left and there were no stragglers. We get to the apex of this knoll and look down to the path that the retreating gooks went down.

We don't see anything that would make us think any enemy was still around. Darrel sends me back to tell the others the area is free of any little bastards. However, we are now going to see if we can at least find blood trails that might lead us to their Mayo Clinic. We will need to be very quiet and beware of any signs of that herd that left us but 6 hours ago. I then realized that I was not alone in my feelings of invulnerably; there were a lot more of us than I had realized until that moment. We were told to follow those that were wounded and maybe we will find the hospital? We get about 250 meters down into the area we were following their retreat when we start hearing moans and an occasional scream. There might be someone wounded left behind. We need to get to them before they perish. They have become very valuable; because they can tell us where that hospital is or any other sight that they use for their wounded. We get to within 100 meters of the moans and discover that there are about 20 of the enemy wounded. Some were nearer to death than others. We secure the area of any weapons that these people might have on them. Then we call in and tell Grizzly what we had found.

He calls up 2 choppers to take the 10 that were in the best shape and left the remaining Gooks up to us to deal with. Lucky for us those that were in the worst shape passed away before the 2 choppers got there for the pick up. Otherwise, we would have to administer the coup de grace to them. Now we have to continue our search for the remainder of the gooks before they get to the border. We get almost to the border known as the fence after the enemy had already crossed it, so there was nothing that could be done. We call in and tell what has transpired and ask for further instructions. We were told to set up an ambush incase anyone was coming back to bring in those wounded.

We fix our meals lay out our Claymore mines and get set up for what ever comes our way. We take turns getting an hour or two of sleep. We need some sleep or we really shouldn't be moving at sun up without any sleep. Nothing happens during the night; when morning comes, we pick up our Claymores and head out on our mission; we travel about 2 K's and set up another happy home away from home. We all get to take turns at sleeping a couple of hours apiece we set up another ambush but still no action. We do hear over the radio that D Company is being probed by approximately 25 to 30 gooks, which are firing one or two shots then moving to a new location. They do that hoping this they do most of the day and into the evening. They continued through out the night not allowing anyone inside that perimeter to get any sleep. Just as the sun is coming up from the east so was the enemy. They kept you awake all night then attack as soon as the blinding sun is to their back. They came screaming into their bullhorns and are chanting Yankee die. D Company repels them away from their perimeter but not without a price. They lose 5 men wounded but no KIA's .D Company felt that they were lucky when they lost no more than those wounded. But when you hear plus see a large number of enemy that is when you suck your under wear up inside of yourself and work at getting out of the mess you've found yourself in. We listened to D Companies battle and hope all goes well for them. That was my old unit and I still had friends in that Company. The firefight goes on for about 2 hours and still there are no KIA's in D Company at that point of battle. They now have 9 wounded and 3 seriously. Then Griz-zly gets on the phone and tells D Company 6 that there are 3 B52's headed to our area and for him to give what grid he wants them to start dropping their arsenal of bombs. The bombers will be here within the hour so D 6 needs to give a grid then hide until the Arc Light is finished. The area called in almost touches the outer perimeter of D Company but it was far enough away that the only thing that happened to the American Company was ringing in their ears. The closest bomb was well off the perimeter by at least 300 meters. Nevertheless, there was so much destruction that the enemy had to vacate the assault and leave the area heading for the fence. D Company is still on alert because a few of the enemy stayed and are taking sniper shots into the perimeter. What we had at our site was a large group of monkeys chattering up in the treetops. The monkeys don't harm you unless peeing on you causes harm, but they make too much noise; so as soon as it's daylight we decide to move a little down this embankment. First, we check each other for leeches. There are some on each of us, a morning same as any other morning out there, It's overcast again and it looks like early morning most of the day, until the sun melts through the fog. We call in., We are told to come back to the FSB only come up about 100 meters from where we went coming this way. That way if we missed some thing, maybe we'll find it. Also, if some gooks were following us we might run into them. Either way it makes for a productive afternoon. You know body count. There will be no sun today because of it being overcast and foggy; so it will be cooler today, probably in the 80's. We hear some SKS being fired as a single shot weapon you hear the Pow clang of a SKS. The Pow is when the round is fired and the Chang is when it reloads it's self; so this guy is taking pot shots and the people in that FSB are a little jumpy as far as being alert. If we screw up, these guys from the line company guarding the perimeter might open up on us or shoot off their Claymore mines. This could end up being a non-productive mission for us. B Company is involved in a major battle to our west. We listen in on the radio as to what was going down. It appears that B Company was being over run by a large body of enemy soldiers, we listen and it sounds as if there were more NVA than what they first reported. It's 3 Company's of Infantry supported by a platoon of mortars. Then a major assault at 0700 hours and the enemy really hit them hard and caused a lot of causalities, not many killed but up to 40% wounded. Why the enemy didn't follow up after the attack no one knows but they could have destroyed an American Company if they had, they would have had a titanic force out numbering B Company 10 to 1 at that point in the battle. B Company was very lucky; it would have taken another 35 to 40 minutes for them to be reinforced by another company. That amount of time is enough that the enemy could have completely wiped out B Company. But that didn't happen for what reason, that was a mistake on the part of the enemy; they could have done major damage to our morale, like we were told; don't make a mistake and that goes for the enemy also.

CHAPTER TEN - TIGER?

We are back at a FSB and would run missions out of there till we get to move to the next one. All of our teams are in now waiting. Battalion 6 has called in Puff the Magic Dragon to fire around our position because we are getting probed every night and it was believed that the enemy had Spider holes all over in the area just outside of the perimeter. The next morning we are going out on a sweep around our area to check on what damage was done .Now; this little goings on pretty much spent a whole lot of cash. We better come up with a large body count. We circle the bridge area and come up with 15 bodies. The line company that is at Ben Het reports 80 KIA .We get on the phone; ours in at 52 bodies, plus several drag marks. That gives us 132 KIA plus several dozen drag marks. Also we have 14 AK47's, 10 SKS's, 2 Tokaren TT34's pistols, 6 Chicom Type 56 assault rifles (.an AK47 with a collapsible stock is the only difference). G2 is happy, Grizzly is happy so everybody is happy. I wondered if the gooks had to call in a body count to Uncle Ho? More than not, they had to call in an action report that shows they either caused property damage or physical damage. Now we had to watch our every step if the gooks are building up still then we haven't stopped them from their idea of destroying us all. Tomorrow we are all going out into the jungle; we were getting soft being here at the Bridge site.

We still have our First Sergeant; and I still don't like him; but I'm learning to tolerate him and his Korean War tactics. He tells me I will never see any rank in this Army. All I said to him was this won't be a problem for me, when my time is up, I will be done with this Man's Army. I didn't mean to be a troublemaker but a spade is still a spade. He had threatened that would maybe get me next time we are in a firefight. Why was this happening to me? This guy won't go on a mission with us; he's basically a REFM out at a firebase. We were told a rumor that we would be getting a second Lt. To take Tubberville's place; some guy from A Company that was in a hospital from being wounded. We are off on another mission and the only person we had to call was Mumford so we got the straight story as to what is to happen to us. Mumford tells us we are to stay at the bridge and part of B Company was coming to join us. But for right now, we have to worry about this hill we are climbing in the rain.

We were calling in Artillery in advance to us climbing this hill. We want to make sure there is no one there to greet us. We were climbing as the last of the artillery has been shot we listen and watched for another half hour and we were happy, it appears there were no enemy troops on this hilltop unless they are really dug in deep or dead. We slowly climb to the top and first thing, we notice there is so much bamboo up here; no one will be able to sneak up on us. Because if you go moving bamboo it is very noisy, it also it would be very difficult for us to sneak away in darkness that soon will be there. I walk out about fifty meters along this trail that appears to be used a lot and set up a trip flare to warn us of coming danger. I get this funny feeling like someone was watching my every move. I also catch a whiff of some smell that I should know what it is but not right now. When I return, I have about thirty-five minutes to cook a meal if I want it hot. I pick out Ham & Lima's for my meal. While eating I tell the guys of the smell that was about fifty or more meters down this trail. It smelt like an old wet dog. Ronnie gets on the phone and inquires if there are any wolves in Viet Nam? We are told no, but there are Tigers out here, but more likely, we have a village dog that is lost. As the night continues, the smell becomes stronger again. It is strong enough that we are all awakened by it. We all now know this is a Tiger and no village dog. The smell is way too strong and every once in awhile we hear it purr. I guess it's happy it has found a free meal and is getting ready to pounce upon us at anytime now. There is no way we can move fast enough to get away from it. We all sit in a circle facing out and we begin telling each other we are sorry if the Tiger jumps you but it must get one of us if it attacks. We decide Xin Loi for the guy that the Tiger gets but the rest of us are going to have to kill this Tiger before it gets anyone else.

While we are sitting here T" tells us He hopes this Tiger is one that only likes white meat; this strikes the four of us who are white very funny. It's enough to take the edge off of the fear and after a couple minutes of each of us laughing Out loud, which is dangerous. Some gooks were not too far away from us that they heard us laugh and tripped the trip flare. We immediately called in our artillery and mortars; which caused damage to the assaulting Gooks and the Tiger as well. When morning comes, we find seven dead Gooks and one dead Tiger. We are told to come in and cut our mission short we have seven KIA's and one Tiger as Body Count. These guys had SKS' which fire the same round as an AK but it doesn't go on Rock N Roll; so there isn't as much fire power as an AK does but it still will get the job done. We took the bolts out and threw the rifles in a creek that was pretty deep. We felt pretty good for a couple of hillbillies and a Hippie. We are told that Tigers run in pairs and this one should have a partner out in this same area. Everyone wants to know how scared were you when we knew it was a Tiger after you? We tell everyone of them if they go that way there are five pairs of pants all full of shit if they really want to know if we were scared or not. Because of that Tiger, we got a nickname that lasted about 2 missions as Rama of the jungle from an old TV show. Finally, everyone decided was enough calling us Rama's and we went back to being an Apache team. Having a Tiger probe you for most of a night is more than what we signed on for. All of us were frightened pretty badly when we discovered it was a Tiger, even more than if it had been a couple of Gooks, at least with the Gooks we would have known how to handle it.

CHAPTER ELEVEN - DAK-POKO BRIDGE

The 2nd Platoon of B Company 3/12th was lifted from Firebase Twenty-Five to the 1st Brigade base at Dakto 2. They were moved to the rear because the 40% casualties suffered which rendered them under-strength and had been declared Combat Ineffective until sufficient replacements were received. Several days later, the 2nd Platoon became OPCON to Battalion and was deployed to the bridge crossing the Dak Poko River on the highway 512 that ran from Dakto west to Ben Het, which was near the Cambodian and Laotian borders. The rest of B Company moved on to Firebase 13, closer to Ben Het. B Company's C.O., Captain Robert H. Morton, had been one of their WIA and they were waiting for a replacement. 2nd Platoon replaced a unit that had been occupying positions on the Dak To side of the Dak Poko river bridge. Our Recon Platoon was deployed on the Ben Het side of the river as a security force for both the bridge and a 155-SP artillery unit. The platoon that Lt Joe relieved left as he arrived, so 2nd platoon's C.O. a 2nd Lt. Named Joe Jones went to see the Recon Platoon Leader James Tubberville to get briefed on their new situation and discovered that he was an E-8 and Lt. Joe, as a 2Lt, and now was the new security force commander. The defensive perimeter had an awkward layout. On the Dakto side, 2nd Platoon's perimeter stretched from upstream opposite the firebase, straddled the road about 80 yards east of the bridge, and met the river again about 30 yards downstream of the bridge. On the other side, our perimeter began beyond rather than opposite of the 2nd Platoon upstream, outlined the firebase back to the road, and then followed the road back to the bridge. Deep erosion ditches on the downstream side of the road made extension of Recon's perimeter to the river downstream of the bridge not impossible but tactically ill advised. Twice while at the bridge, the NVA fired RPG or recoilless rifle rounds into the perimeter from the low ridge that overlooked the firebase from downstream on our side of the river. Both times the artillery responded immediately with direct fire against the ridge with their 155 mm guns. As a result, the attacks were short-lived and resulted in no U.S. casualties. One of these occasions found the artillery's mess sergeant in his shower when the first enemy rounds were fired. He was seen streaking nude, except for the trailing of soapsuds, across the perimeter into the protection of his bunker. A sight that none of us ever want to see again. Too bad the fog had lifted everyone saw it bright and clear it wasn't a pretty sight. But he was uninjured while running for his life.

The NVA attempted to blow the bridge three times, and the USAF didn't miss it much one day, putting in a B-52 strike close enough that we heard their bombs whooshing through the air as they fell but didn't know what we were hearing until the ground began shaking, the noise of explosion reached us, and the valley erupted in dust and smoke. Could not have been a full kilometer from the bridge. A small hill just outside our perimeter helped keeping the sound and shock of the explosions from affecting us too much.

The NVA also attempted to mortar the bridge one day while a convoy was stopped at our location. They dismounted and parked almost bumper-to-bumper; the convoy stretched the full limits of the perimeter. Lt. Joe and his RTO were standing by the second platoon CP bunker, the highest point in the perimeter, when we heard the first round leave the tube but were not positive we had heard a mortar until the round impacted. We heard the second round leave the tube, and the guys from 2nd platoon countered with an M-60 from the top of their bunker because they could hear the tube downstream and saw an individual in an open field adjacent the river in the vicinity we suspected the mortar to be located. They followed the first two rounds with a rapid six or eight more from a single tube, but all impacted in the river about 100 feet downstream of the bridge. The convoy had cleared the bridge, maybe even the perimeter before the last round hit. Transportation that day was moving as soon as the second round hit. The convoy had to get away from each other to cut down their chances of getting hit by mortars, I guess 82mm exploding in the river and an M-60 shooting over their heads was a little much for the mortar team we found down on the shores of the Dak Poko River.

All other attempts to blow the bridge were made at night against our end of the bridge. Our end provided an easier access to the NVA because it was outside the perimeter. The first attempt, 2nd Platoon's squad downstream of the bridge a Sgt Stinogle positively detected movement across the river and put some M-16 fire and a couple of M-79 rounds into the west bank. We called for and received artillery illumination, and the rest of that night was quiet. The flares made it so we could see but it also showed the enemy where we were. After the first attempt, Battalion ordered that an LP be placed on the west bank. Recon and 2nd Platoon alternated nights. The second attempt resulted in grenades and/or a satchel charge being thrown in on Recon's LP, causing several casualties mostly damage to their inner ear because of the explosion. Battalion cancelled the LP and sent us a tank each night thereafter. The first night a tank without a Xenon searchlight showed up, but Battalion had that corrected within 24 hours. Each night we had the tank park at the river in the old pontoon bridge road cut so he was inside the

2nd Platoon's perimeter but could illuminate the underside of the bridge and the west bank on call I don't remember whose idea it was for that location or if that's where Battalion ordered the tank be located, but it saved the bridge.

The third attempt was almost successful. Both Recon and 2nd Platoon's squad downstream of the bridge detected movement. B Co's Sgt Stinogle was fairly certain he had heard something across the river, but not positive. I insisted there had been movement near or under the bridge. I opened up on what I thought was someone walking in that river and I was correct. This guy about 30 and well fed and had 2 satchels around his waist and I got a that a boy" for taking him out. Darrell Curtis and Lt. Joe managed to wake up the tankers, they always came in dead tired from a day of convoy escort, had a six-pack and went to sleep, and had them sweep the underpinnings of the bridge with their Xenon light while Lt. Joe inspected through field glasses. Curtis and he determined that at least two pilings at the west end of the bridge had explosives attached. Lt. Joe told Curtis to have the tank kill the light and radio Recon about the explosives and to get someone under the bridge to remove them; also that Lt. Joe was coming across the bridge; don't shoot him. There was no direct route to the bridge from their bunkers. The engineer cut through the bluff on their side of the river; made it necessary to move away from the river almost to the perimeter until level with the road, then over to the road, then back to the river; almost 100 yards of running in the dark just to get to their end of the bridge. The other possibility was down the bluff to the river, past the tank's location in the engineer cut, then climb up to the east end of the bridge. Never a fast runner, Lt. Joe calculated this route was quicker, fell most of the way down the bluff, almost got shot by a startled tanker who had just cut off his Xenon and didn't have his night vision back, climbed back to the bridge and made the best 40 yard dash of his life, wondering if he would get across before it blew. The Recon Platoon Leader SGT Tubberville met him at his bunker, where they discussed what must be done, if that explosive charge was set on a timer, they had better get it removed quickly.

Sgt. Pease from Recon went under the bridge with Lt. Joe, moved past the charges and crouched next to a downstream bridge piling, prepared to engage the enemy. They were well within lethal range of the explosives had they detonated while they were under the bridge - they very knowingly and deliberately risked their lives to save that bridge that night. The 2 men pulled all that TNT out, Lt. Joe stopped at the first charge, discovered it was attached with commo wire, U.S. of course, they couldn't see, smell or hear a burning fuse; Oh Shit" he says they have a detonator, can't just pull the fuse, fleeting mental vision of a smiling NVA clicking a claymore detonator; he felt for wire lead coming to the satchel charge, found it; The knife he had wouldn't cut it fast enough; No time to saw this stuff, remembering the fingernail clippers in his pocket, He snipped the lead handily, moved to #2, found and cut lead, searched for more leads, never trust a Commie, couldn't find any more and found no more charges, cut the two charges from the pilings and they carried them up to the Recon Platoon Leader's bunker. I think that each consisted of 24 half-Kilo blocks of TNT.

During our stay at the bridge, we were mortared several times, had several rockets fired at our general direction from the ridgeline just about 200 meters to our south. One evening we had guest that weren't invited to our sunset observation of the monkeys swinging from limb to limb of large trees. These guys that went under the bridge were both Hero's as far as we were concerned, but nothing will happen for some reason or two they never received any recognition for what was done. Welcome to Vietnam! Not all heroes are recognized by our services; if they were, there would be a lot larger list of heroes.

CHAPTER TWELVE - SKULL

We are out again and are set up at the base of this finger and to report any movement that we find. If at all possible, we are not to engage in a firefight unless we are spotted, other wise we call in a grid and hurry away as best we can. While we were out and about, we run into a skull of a human being, the first real one I have ever seen. Mick put it in his rucksack, and when we get back to the perimeter after an uneventful trip we show the skull to everyone, and Festus wants to put it on his bunker but first I get a couple pictures of it on my shoulders, with my head in the shirt, at the time, we thought it was funny. Festus would sit it on a pole at night and light a cigarette and stick it in his mouth. About once a night, someone from outside the perimeter would take a shot at it. Then Festus would fire back with his M16, Festus got his name because he looks like the guy on the Gun smoke television show. He's always into something like Festus also. Not anything really wrong but not quiet right if you know what I mean. Every time Festus pulled guard, he would light up a cigarette then stuck into the mouth of that skull and some time during that guard, he would catch someone taking a shot at it. We don't know what happened to it. We came off a mission and Festus didn't have the skull any more. No one said anything about it being gone, it was just gone. Those guys we captured up by the fence of our perimeter turned out to be NVA want to bee's they were going to map out the perimeter and give it to some NVA that came into their village at nighttime. We figure we can set up an ambush just before you get to that village. Sure enough about an hour after dark, these three gooks dressed in their starched uniforms show up at the north entrance to the village. We shout out for them to give up but they aren't in the mood to take a helicopter ride tonight. Which is a bad thing for them; we have to waste them before they get into the village. Now the villagers are worried that the reminder of these gooks outfit will blame them for their comrades being killed dead. We offer to send some of the MACV cowboys down to their village to arm them with M1 Carbines and 45 cal. Grease Guns, maybe a Thompson or 2, that's the last time we were near that village we heard the gooks came in and there were some informers in the village that dropped a dime on them. Xang Loi about that. But that is the reason most of the villagers won't tell on the intruders in their village. We go back to our firebase and get ready for another mission this one is going due west almost over the fence but not quiet. We are about 200 meters from the fence when we have contact with approximately 10 NVA who were on their way back to safety when we stepped up to the plate and hit a home run by spotting them and assaulting which we then caught by surprise. I could see the look of surprise on their faces as the ambushed started, then there was nothing, all fell to the ground, and besides some nervous movements the battle was won. We had to be careful here this close to the fence. If they had any friends close by they could capture us, they would like to show us around before they either send us up north to spend a few years as their guest or cut our throats. Neither one sounds like any fun to us so we call in a jet to drop bombs and Napalm both in front and behind us. We still got small arms fire from in front of us. We have to have one more pass by a jet and we are good to go. When he dropped his first a bomb then on his second pass he drops napalm. As soon as the smoke clears, we head into where he dropped his load and after we get there, we run through it to the other side where we are safe and sound. We see a couple of dead gooks as we pass through the bomb craters and where the napalm was dropped. After we get through that mess, we call in with all the good news. Every one of us is unharmed and we got a few of them. We're asked how many? We say we counted three or four so that makes five. We get as far away from that place as we could. We call in and are told that we are to sweep through this small valley then come on home. Sounded good to us, we all wish we were going home after that mission. When we got back, we have some Turtles that have come home to us. Some will have no names for a while. Some people skated the whole year over there then some of us paid the ultimate price. I can't figure out how that works, but it happens.

North Vietnamese were so much more dedicated to that war than any of us were. We wanted to go home in one piece and they want to save their nation from the people that want to enslave them. That's what the French did and we wanted to give them back to the French. I guess they were being attacked by a nation that wanted to see them enslaved again. All I wanted was; what each of us wants; and that is to go home in one piece. If I state my beliefs it's called treason, And I thought that was what we always fight for is the right to disagree with what our government does. I guess only if it goes along with what the party in control says. I didn't have time to think about that then. I was too busy trying to stay alive along with some very good friends of mine. We went on a mission, going back down 1338 and into the valley south of Dakto again, it seems someone believes that there is someone running around down there causing havoc with the villages that are on the side of the South's government. So we are trying to sweep the gooks away from these villages. The villagers didn't have much of a chance, we came in give them food and supplies along with weapons and then the NVA came in and told them if they won't fight us then they must be against them. They drag out anyone that speaks out for us and murder their families in front of them and tell everyone else in the village that's what will happen to them if they side with the South government. Now which would you do? Me I didn't care if we won that war or not. I just wanted to go home and in one piece, but I didn't see that happening. I had a feeling that everyone gets when they didn't have a whole lot of time left. I was going to do my job and hopefully come home and live happily ever after. We don't run into any one down in that valley this time, but it sure beat humping in the soaking wet, muddy mountains, but it ends after four days.

We don't run into anything so there must not have been anything down there, they sent us back up into the mountains South West of Ben Het again to see if we can get some contact and body count that way. We found signs that someone had been traveling at night through the valleys below and coming up into the hills to rest during the day we set up an ambush half way up one of these well-traveled hills and sure enough we have a small platoon of young men wearing their starched uniforms and carrying new SKS's. We set off the claymores and open up with rifle fire and with a few well-placed grenades pitched; we have our body count along with a rough drawing of the firebase at Ben Het. I was elated we go back to the Firebase and get in a couple games of horseshoes before we get news we will be going out very early the next morning. The gooks started hitting the chopper pad with mortars so we had to stop playing horseshoes. We were behind anyway so it was to our advantage to stop when we did, we went to supper then went to a movie, no shit at this fire support base there is a large bunker maybe holding 25 to 30 people and they show a movie every other night. We went and saw Bonnie & Clyde, The movie was a fake to us because we knew no one could get into so many bad circumstances and come out OK. But I guess that's what sells tickets, but there was no popcorn, which doesn't sound right. After the movie, we went to bed. It was 0300 hours when Mumford came in to wake us. That was the reason we had all of our gear out and ready to move at a moments notice even if it was 3 am. Gilbert Mumford tells us we are going to be inserted into an area that has had several reports that someone is moving around and they want to insert us in while dark, then we are to find somewhere to hide until sun up then we will get orders on what to do. We were flying about twenty feet above the tree level and when we got to where they were to dump us, we repelled out of the chopper which I don't do well, then we got together and moved about 500 meters further west. We think that would be rude of them to greet us with some small arms fire. I fell the last 10 feet of the repelling; I guess it wasn't something I was good at. This was another disappointment for me. After we have gotten far enough away from the drop sight to sit and rest till daylight. It's raining again only this time we found a place that gives us shelter from the rain. It's a place dug into the dirt under a rock that overhung above it. We can't start a fire but all 5 of us could fit in that cave. It sure made sleeping a lot easier and you could see quite a distance on 3 sides. The gooks must have known of this place. There are all kinds of bloody bandages on the ground. We keep an eye out for any wounded or half-dead gooks. We call in and tell Battalion 6 what we have found and he gave us an order to see if in the morning we can pick up a trail that might lead us to the hospital they have in this area. Then we call in mortars about 200 meters from our little cave. After four rounds hit in that area we call it a night and when the sun comes up it stops raining so after a cup of hot instant coffee Grizzly calls and has us call in some artillery until when we decide there weren't any enemy hanging around. Also, any trail left by the wounded had washed away. We didn't find anything that would interest Battalion so we call in artillery very close to us, and then give the Mortar crew a grid for them to fire if we have to run right on top of where we were sleeping. We spend another night at the cave waiting for some wounded gooks to show up. But no one shows up and we now are going to a hilltop not too far from where we were so we could go slow and carefully. We go very slowly climbing this first little knoll; which is very muddy because of all the rain last night. We finally get to the top and sit for a couple minutes to see what we can. There is a finger from this knoll leading up to the hill we are to spend the night at. We only have about 500 meters to climb up to the top. First thing we do is preparing something to eat. We have a quick meal then head out up that finger till we get almost to the top. Ronnie waits until we are all up to the top then he shows us where we were to set up our camp for the night. After we get set up we get a call from Battalion letting us know a large element of NVA were spotted by a small plane about 1500 meters to our west and heading our way. We were advised not to try and take them on because there is a herd of them. We can call in Artillery, mortars and even jets after they have moved close to us. Because they were so close at that time, we couldn't be extracted from our position. Not real good news, but if we can stay hidden until they move through the area, we should be all right. We sit and watch as 50 or more of them come out of the jungle and head down the path. We have to decide what we will do if spotted and attacked by a large number of these shit heads. We planed on heading straight down the finger to the left of us and had already given the artillery guys the grid we wanted shot at. After getting a hundred meters from the enemy, we planned to stop and hold our ground to give Grizzly time to give us a way out of that circumstance. But as it never comes, we decide to set up a night position and put out our trip-flares and Claymore mines.

The darkness came and we could still hear a large body of people moving in from our west. We had set up places to call our support in. So we call up the Artillery guy's and told them who we were and to fire green five HE rounds and wait for further requests. Green being the code for where we want the HE rounds to hit, if we had called for Red that would have been on top of us, which would be if we were about to be found or overran. Then it sounds as if the noise of bamboo being cut has changed directions and could be heading straight in our direction. We don't call anything that might drive them into our path. After an hour, the Gooks start something that I had never been through before. The gooks did what was called Recon by fire. What they hope was we were still around and would return fire that would give our position away then it's all over. Even if we were still there, we could not return fire no matter what's going through your little head is that they know where you are. They don't. It's a risky thing if they did know where you were then they will attack and probably kill you and if you fire back, you will come to the same faith. There also is the fact that they like us have a smell all to ourselves because of the food we eat. There is no deodorant out in the jungle; if we had it, they could smell it better than our normal sweat smell. We are in an area where monkeys go to take a crap so that smell all though nauseating; it keeps the little bastards from smelling our normal body smells. When they fire close to you, and you don't fire back and they don't know where you are they have wasted several hundred rounds of ammo that has to come down the trail to resupply them. More times than not, they don't know where you are exactly. Just in the basic area by listening in on your radio transmissions and by trail watchers that you may have walked by while traveling out in the jungle. We sit still and listen, as it appeared the enemy was heading south of us. We hoped they thought we were in that direction and kept looking in that area. It starting to rain and with it comes the cold air. Not what someone from Minnesota would call cold, but out here a 40-degree drop is cold 110 to 70. At daybreak we decided to move even further away from our drop zone and go up the finger of this ridge What we are told is that by the size of the recon by fire that the Gooks used last night to try and locate us there must be a Battalion of infantry here. We are told that there isn't a LZ with in 2 klicks from us. That's the reason we were inserted the way we were. Also we can't go toward the firebase; it was being attacked right then and the 5 of us wouldn't make that much of a difference so we head in the opposite direction. We need to get to that point before the gooks that were still following us do, and we bet they had already left for that spot. We must be very careful we were now the hunted, and it's not a good feeling. As our luck would have it our LZ was west of us meaning, we had to go towards the enemy to be rescued. So off we went heading into the pits of Hell is the best way we described it. We didn't know for sure what or where we were to go and do to get away safely. It's very dark now and we really don't like moving in an unknown area where there might be gooks that know this area and have ambushes set up that we might run into. We can hear shooting from the West of us, it sounds like maybe 3 or 4 clicks away. We can't tell by the sound how many or what types of weapons are being fired the sound we hear is from far and away, which is the best way to listen to a firefight. After about half an hour, the shooting stops and we hear artillery being shot into the area around the unit that was being attacked. We must brace ourselves because that enemy unit is heading right at us, and we've been told there was a whole herd of them. Not something, you wanted to hear while out and away from any friendly forces. We get set up for an artillery barrage to drive them away from us, while killing some of them, sort of like getting two birds with the one stone. As the enemy got closer, we realize there were more of them than we suspected, and they appear to have sidestepped the artillery aimed to keep them from crawling up our backs. We try and redirect the cannon fire, but we were so close to being found that we couldn't risk being heard while re-adjusting fire. What we decided to do was to lie still and hope not to be found. I guess that was a moment we didn't make that mistake everyone talks about. As we lie down flat on the ground and pull some of the tall grass over us, we get the uneasy feeling you get when you first sit in a Dentist chair, not a good feeling. We really can't see each other so if someone jumps up and starts firing into the searching enemy we might have a problem. They looked around for about 20 minutes, and then we thought they gave up. I was the first to raise my self-up and I was the first to be jumped on by one of those that sat and waited for us to make a move. That first guy I shot with a burst of 3, and then another one headed right at me. I fired into his face and the blood erupted from his head and the bone splinters along with the blood went everywhere, then one of them tosses a grenade in amongst us, and when it went off with very little powder in it but Ronnie was wounded in his back. So there we were the 5 of us with 1 wounded and the enemy still crawling around in the area we were still trying to hide at. I lie down and pitch 2 grenades towards the direction I believed they were coming from, and as luck would have it, they turned and went down the finger leading to the valley floor. Ronnie is hurting and I'm not in the best of shape, I'm wore out from all the tension and firing but the others were able to get him patched up and ready to head towards our LZ, which was about a klick and a half away. I ran into a piece of bamboo and caused a cut on my good knee. The bleeding on my knee was slowed down by Van putting a pad on my wound, it wasn't really that painful, but I was still afraid of infection if we had to cross any creeks or small rivers, Ronnie is holding out pretty good himself, We were quite fortunate to drive the remaining forces back down the other side of that finger, we weren't in the best shape if we had to run and shoot, we waited just 5 minutes before a chopper swooped down and took the 5 of us to safety. I was taken to the emergency aide station at Dakto along with my friend Ronnie, where we were both treated and after a 3-day stay, we were sent back to the jungle. My right leg was sewed up, Ronnie had the shrapnel removed then sewed up and he was given light duty for 14 days. We stayed at the bunker facing the chopper pad and pulled 4 hours a piece at guard at night on that bunker, the only reason I didn't go out was because I already had an infection in my other leg and an infection was so easy to get out in the moist and muggy jungle so we weren't sent out in the jungle for that time, but we still had to pull guard each night for those 14 days, and although we were probed on 6 of those nights we never had a sniper shoot at us nor an assault during that time frame, When we were back in the jungle, where we felt more secure in that atmosphere, where we could feel free and able to transcend our way through the jungle with out being detected by the enemy. We felt we were back and happy to be so; it's funny that we would feel safer out in the jungle where we were usually out number most of the time, but we could fight if needed and hide when it wouldn't be to our advantage to take on a much larger unit, but sometimes you aren't afforded that luxury. That is when it gets a little hairy to spend a day or two moving about to keep from our scalps being taken.

While out we hear that our First Sergeant has moved on, back to a base camp job; probably the best for all concerned. We now are getting a LT. from A Company. He is now out of the hospital and reporting back to Battalion and like myself he is recruited" to join the Recon Platoon. His name is Hadley and his father was a Lifer in the Army. For Hadley's action, while in A Company he earned a Silver Star and a Purple Heart. When he comes to Recon, he gives a little speech on how he will not have us do anything he wouldn't do. He also wrote a letter to his parents where he told them he saw the Recon Platoon as an elite group of well trained soldiers and how he felt it was because we were in five man groups that were together most of the tour of South East Asia. The fact we knew what could happen when 5 goes up against so many, we had to know how and when to use any of our many support groups, the Artillery, Mortars, and Air Support to get us out of jams that we seem to get into, we also had to know when to expose ourselves by fighting our way out of trouble.

CHAPTER THIRDTEEN - FIREBASE UNDER ATTACK

Apache 2 is in a firefight with a platoon size element of the 66th NVA Infantry Regiment. No one was injured yet, but the gooks are acting as if they are holding their position until they get some relief. Not a good thing to happen. Apache 2 calls in some big guns, 155 howitzers and calls in on top of them. They get 5 rounds HE (high explosives) and if it weren't for the fact they were in amongst some pretty big fallen trees they might have been killed as 17 gooks were. All Apache 2 had wrong with them is the never ending ringing in their ears. I guess I could live with that for a couple of days. Little did I know it would last the rest of our lives. We are headed for a different LZ than the one we were told is the closest to us. This one was in a different direction and maybe the gooks wouldn't head to this one. We get on the horn and tell Battalion 6 RTO that they are to abort that LZ and to wait for further instructions when we figure what we are to do. Playing this cat and mouse game wasn't fair. The gooks got to listen in on our radio frequency but we didn't theirs so that is their advantage. We are west of hill 830 and we don't want to run there. Too many war stories have come out of this area. We sure don't want to be another one. Our best way to go was towards the southwest to hill 855 but that would mean being with out food for two to three days. However, it would put us way out of range for anyone trying to capture us? We call in and tell FSB 16 that he is Chicago and we are headed for St. Louis and we will be there five minutes before bedtime. What I have told him is that south west of his position and to find something on the map that ends in a 55 minutes. It comes up being hill 855 and we will call as we get there. We set up another night position and pull our regular guard and the thing we do differently than normal is we wait a couple of hours in case there our gooks close by that they will either be seen or heard. Then we would deal with it. For the next two days, we walk around trying to locate that group of gooks that is supposed to be in this AO. We have the same scary moments as we always have. Running into a large herd of gooks or stepping on a mine, it's one of theirs, the French or ours. Either way you end up screwed for life, which may not be very long after blowing parts of your body all over the jungle. We didn't see nor hear a hide or hair of them. Maybe they have given up looking for us? One can only hope. The next day we are at the ridge that runs up to hill 855 so we call in as to who we are and that we are 400 meters from pick up point one. The chopper flies over spots us then flies around us to make sure there isn't a surprise party for the both of us. He doesn't receive any ground fire and swoops down to our LZ and we jump in and we are off. We then start receiving small arms fire from the next hilltop. They were still-hunting us and were only two hours away when we were rescued. We get in and the first place we head for is the mess tent that is on this firebase. They really won't serve lunch for another hour but we talk our way into a ham and cheese sandwich each. In addition, a tall beer from our rations couldn't have a better meal if I say so myself. These narrow escapes are getting to happen too often now. We need to start having some Skate Missions. This firebase will be closing down in the next couple of days so we need to find away to the FSB that the recon platoon is on. We are headed that way on a chopper bringing in the mail. We check the mail and we all five have mail from the world. It was always a good thing to get mail. Every once in awhile some poor son would get a Dear John letter that will ruin a good day at a F.S.B. Out among the enemy you can't let personal stuff get to you. It's a good way to get one of your buddies killed dead.

We arrive at the firebase and are told to sit here and be quiet until Battalion 6 decides what we are going to be doing. We aren't a big enough unit to attack as a line company. There have been so many sightings that we would not be effective out in five man teams. We might go on one or two day missions but nothing like we were used to do. Grizzly tells us we are too valuable of an asset to lose. We all feel good about that decision Jan. 20 1968 at 0625 hours we are listening on the horn to a battle that is on its second day. It's an unusual thing for the enemy to hold contact pass a day. So this might be something big happening? It appears that D Company was being probed during the night then some sniper fire well into the morning then at about dusk of last night they were hit by a platoon size attack to their west side. Now they are in contact with a much larger force. We listen to the horn telling what has happened and what needs to happen to make every mother's son safe and secure. C Company was to move out on down and into the ridge and when they came to grid YB 874 295 they were to try to recover the bodies of six men killed dead the day before in the afternoon. A Company was airlifted to F.S.B. 25 to join C Company during the night of Jan. 19-20. The artillery and mortar positions at Ben Het received an attack resulting in seven casualties. Body count for this day and the previous day was 21 KIA NVA. Many drag marks, 1 US KIA, 28 WIA, and 6 MIA from B Company 3/12. 1 US casualty KIA Battery 6/29 a FO. On the morning of Jan 20th following two air strikes, artillery, and mortar preparation along the ridge. C Company followed by A Company left the base camp at 1007 hours. Approximately 200 meters out C Company drew heavy small arms and heavy weapons fire along with hand grenades from dug in positions to their front and flank. The bulk of the enemy force was located on the steep knoll known as hill 800. With snipers dispersed in trees and spider holes along the flanks of approach. C Company immediately sustained casualties from extremely accurate mortar fire and rifle grenades .Due to the proximity of the enemy and the wounded, contact could positions of the not be broken. A Company was ordered to establish and hold a corridor between C Company's position and the fire base perimeter to keep that avenue open incase if they had to retreat into the firebase. This is the reason we were given all of those lectures on what the NVA were doing and Why. At 1135 hours after extracting the wounded and as many of the dead as possible, C Company under heavy sniper fire returned to the firebase then A Company follows them in.

The enemy continues sniper fire. We were at this firebase on the other side of the perimeter where we saw nothing out to our front but they're sure was a lot of shooting going on at the other side of this perimeter. One of the guys on the other side of the perimeter saw one of the snipers and while standing on shell torn ground and taking the time to aim, that soldier with his M16 strikes a classic pose of a combat infantryman in battle, unafraid, taking care to score his kill. We were scared that the enemy would take over the other side of the perimeter and eventually come to us. We watch to our front and saw nothing. At 1138 hours, an air strike was called in on enemy positions followed by six more through out the day. I got a M79 grenade launcher and some HE rounds. I started firing far out hopefully killing anyone at a staging area preparing to attack this side of the perimeter. Through out these air strikes the enemy continued to direct a heavy volume of automatic weapons fire at the Air Force fighters and periodically placed sniper fire into the firebase. This was to keep our heads down and to keep in our heads that we aren't safe in any circumstances. The enemy force is estimated to be a battalion-sized element of the 66th NVA Regiment. They were capable of sitting through the air strikes and artillery fire in relative safety while the trail watchers observe FSB 25. High-speed approaches enable them to reach the fighting positions as soon as the jets leave. Through out the afternoon D Company located at Ben Het received a heavy volume of 82 mm mortar and 75 mm recoilless rifle fire. Results for the day were 11 NVA KIA body count, 8 US WIA, A Company 3/12, 2 US WIA B Company 3/12, 17 US WIA C Company 3/12, 5 US MIA C Company 3/12 and 1 US WIA HHC 3/12. Jan. 21st between 0730 and 0930 hours, five TAC air strikes were placed on and around hill 800. During each strike, the aircraft received heavy automatic fire from at least 4 positions along the ridge. The last air strike was followed by heavy artillery and mortar fire preparing the area for an assault by A Company heading towards the NVA and delivered an attack designed to draw the gooks out of their fortified positions to the point of contact. All this time we are on the other side of the perimeter drawing sniper fire every time we stick our heads out to make sure no one was coming in at our front. It had to be done. Some of the time, we wished we were out on a mission instead of sitting in a perimeter waiting for something ugly to happen to us. At least while out on a mission we could leave the area and hide so we weren't found but here in this perimeter we have to sit and wait. It takes what little control we had away from us and we are then waiting for something to happen. A Company was immediately engaged by snipers but continued to a predetermined point 75 meters out and returned quickly to the firebase at 1025 hours. At 1030 hours, a 15-minute artillery and mortar barrage impacted on the enemy positions, 15 minutes later another barrage of fire. The contact area was being kept under a constant artillery and mortar attack for the rest of the day. Only 2 NVA were seen killed but many more suspected. D Company again received a weapons attack. C Company their way back into the firebase leaving some of their dead behind. We were called up to go out and retrieve the bodies left behind. We are given a grid of YB 885 291. We worked our way up to that position very slowly and sure enough there were 5 bodies missing from C Company and 2 of them had bullets to the back of the head. They must have been alive after the attack then they were murdered. That was why we sometimes took no prisoners and didn't feel bad about blowing away some guy on his hands and knees begging, I guess for his life. I have never been in a chopper when this was done but I have been on the Razor back where I saw a gook fly out of a highflying chopper and this happened so the whole valley and both ranges running next to the valley could see it happen. They dropped this guy with his arms and legs swinging and screaming his last on the way down. Every swinging dick saw that happen. I don't know for sure that he was thrown out or jumped. Either way, it made a deep impression in my minds eye. I imagine it did so to the gooks that saw it also. Back at the Dak Poko Bridge where A Company is watching both sides of the bridge, the enemy has launched a couple RPG's into that perimeter. A Company pulled out and a unit from the 2nd/22 inf. took its place. On the morning of Jan. 23rd 1968 we were sent up to the firebase to run a mission out where we were receiving rocket and recoil-less rifle A & C, Companies continued the operation to clear the ridge north west of FSB 25 to hill 800. At 1230 hours with A Company leading, they received small arms fire, hand grenades, and 60mm Mortar rounds, C Company received light sniper fire from their west. At 1315 hours, A Company received such intense small arms and heavy automatic weapons fire that they became pinned down except for their first platoon, which continued to move against the enemy positions on hill 800. They eliminated a machine gun, which was responsible for pinning down the rest of the company. Continuing the assault A Company reached the forward enemy position at 1400 hours only to run into a solid wall of 60mm and 82mm mortar fired at them. Suffering numerous casualties the two companies withdrew into the firebase, followed by the intense mortar fire. The withering fire hailed onto the tops of the bunkers at the firebase causing several more causalities and secondary explosions to which a great fire raged treating to detonate over 2,000 rounds of 4.2-inch Mortar rounds. I went out and helped to put out the fire. There were 3 of us in the ammo dump when the Willy Pete rounds hit it. We had very little water to try to put out not the Willy Pete but the wooden crates holding the ammo. It took us about 15 minutes of shoveling dirt onto the burning crates. I don't know how we did it. However, the fire was put out after another 45 minutes. I was overcome by the smoke and was sent to the hospital for 1 day to make sure I hadn't damaged my lungs. Results for Jan. 23rd 1968 were 5 NVA KIA, 1 US KIA HHC 3/12, 2 US WIA HHC 3/12, 5 US KIA A 3/12, 19 US WIA C 3/12, 1 US KIA C 3/12, 3 US WIA C 3/12, 3 US WIA E 3/12 of which I was one. I woke up in the bottom of a group of guys that were screaming, crying, and bleeding on me. I had been knocked out because of the smoke but I wasn't as bad off as these guys were, or as bad as I thought I was, not that I knew that at that time. When I woke up I had blood all over me plus it hurt to breathe, I just knew I was dieing. Nevertheless, after they washed out my eyes and told me I was OK. I understood how the poor souls that were mangled had a much rougher row to plow than I had, for that I was thankful, I wasn't missing any body parts and now I can breathe and see again. While in the hospital I learn that a Navy ship, the USS Pueblo was captured by the North Koreans, what were they thinking? Do the commies want another war? Do we want another war? It was hard for me to realize it really happened, I could only imagine how the crew felt.

I was kept over night then sent back to my unit. It was good to be back, I was gone about 14 hours then I came back with a clean set of clothing that fit and three pairs of new socks. Before I got in the chopper for the ride back, I ran into a Quartermaster clerk that decided I would appreciate some fine cigars. Therefore, I agreed that it would be a good thing to have in my position and I loaded up an empty sandbag and sneaked them into my ruck when I returned to the FSB. These were better than the King Edwards we got in our sundae packet along with cigarettes and writing paper with envelopes.

At 0800 hours 26 Jan. 68 heavy artillery and mortar preparations were fired on hill 800 and the Peanut as well as hills 750 & 900. At 0829 hours, simultaneously D Company followed by C Company left the firebase to attack hill 800 and the first helicopters landed on hill 750. At 0917 hours, 100 meters short of their objective, D Company received small arms fire and automatic weapons fire from the front and both flanks. D Company maneuvered 2 platoons on line to gain fire superiority and sent 1 platoon to the left to flank the objective. Snipers appeared in trees and spider holes on both flanks and sent to a devastating volume of fire into the friendly ranks, halting the lead company. C company sent 2 platoons forward to protect D company's flanks, allowing them to continue the assault. Using hand grenades and close combat, D company breached the enemy forward positions and methodically destroyed each bunker. Air strikes and mortar fire reduced additional enemy fortified positions continued on the northwest crest of the objective, while D company continued the methodical assault and finally seized the objective. C Company joined in the consolidation at 1335 hours, a search of the battle area resulted in the recovery of 3 KIA's from C Company, previously listed as missing in action. The 6th ARVN ABN Battalion made contact with an estimated NVA battalion shortly after the assault. Heavy fighting throughout the day and night of 26-27 January occurred. However, the ARVN unit gained and held hill 900. Hill 900 is covered with tall grass and some bamboo on the south and west sides. It will be a good place for the enemy to be driven off and defended for they didn't have any place to hide behind and were easily shot with artillery and mortars, the 4.2 mortars. Mumford tells everyone that an officer that had his cigars stolen, and is out looking for them, I of course had given one to Mumford; he gave a chuckle when he told us that. That was his way of warning me of this officer looking for who-ever took his high-dollar cigars. The officer is a REMF so no one out here cares for him. The cigars were pretty good, too good to have him to smoke them. I didn't care they were mine and no one was going to take them away from me. The next day I was back at my day job. I share my cigars with the guys on my team, they all looked at me knowing I was the one that swiped the cigars and I was told it made them taste better. They smoked great but someone was telling us these things are worth two bucks apiece, not on our pay. Everyone that smoked a cigar knew it was stolen but they thought it was great to get over on a REMF. We were going out again, but this time we were going to circle the perimeter of this F.S.B. and see if we can't catch who ever it is that is popping mortars into our fire base camp. After an hour out, we hear someone moving on the other side of these trees in front of us. We are too close to where the noise is coming from to get on the radio and inform the firebase what is going on. We figure just before we open up on these guys we will call in telling everyone what is going on so no one on the perimeter will blast their Claymores on us. We don't make contact on our terms unless by accident when we run into a group of these savages. Getting wounded plays more on my mind than actually being dead, that I could feel OK about but if my parents and brothers had to get that telegram from the Department of Defense. I didn't want them to feel that pain, and that was more important to me right then. If I'm dead, I probably won't know about it. On Jan. 25, the TOC came down with the order for every one to keep their boots on. That is telling us we might be in for an assault that we might not be able to repel. It is obvious to us that the terrain north west of FSB 25 was advantageous to the gooks in their defensive stance and his containment of our Battalion unless a successful assault on hill 800 could be made. A coordinated attack with the 6th ARVN Airborne Battalion would make an air assault on hill 750 grid YB 884 310 and then seize hill 900 YB 874 316. They would continue the attack on Jan. 27th moving south from hill 900 and passing west of the Peanut toward Ben Het. Company D 3/12 was air lifted to FSB 25 to lead the attack. At 0800 hours Jan. 27th, heavy artillery and mortar fire was fired on hill 800, the Peanut and hills 750 and 900. At 0829 hours, simultaneously D Company followed by C Company left the firebase to attack hill 800. The first choppers landed on hill 750 at 0917 hours 100 meters short of their objective. D Company received small arms and automatic weapons fire from the front and both flanks. D company maneuvered 2 platoons on line to gain fire superiority and sent 1 platoon to the left to flank the objective. Snipers appeared in trees and spider holes on both flanks and sent a devastating volume of fire into the ranks of C and D Companies. C Company sent 2 platoons forward to protect D Company's flanks, allowing them to continue the assault. Using hand grenades and close combat D company breached the enemy forward positions and methodically destroyed each bunker. Air strikes and mortar fire reduced additional enemy fortified positions on the northwest crest of the objective. D Company continued the assault and finally seized the objective. C Company joined in the consolidation at 1335 hours. A search of the area resulted in the recovery of 3 KIA's from C Company previously listed as MIA. I guess it is a good thing that we found those bodies but we would like to find them alive and in good health. All we really want is to leave this place in 1 piece and sane. The latter is harder to obtain than you would ever guess. One of those guys had a bullet hole in the back of his head. When that happens it makes it easier to not take prisoners when we come across someone that fights up to where we have them beat then they want to go to a POW prison. It won't happen. Not after what we had seen done to our Brothers. That's why you don't make friends. It's too hard on you when you lose one. We were out on another mission that was a good and peaceful one. I pulled last guard and watched as the sun come up over the horizon and living things in the jungle began to move about. The monkeys were breast-feeding their young while the orangutan are finishing their breakfast and are starting to notice that we are there. As the sun begins to climb into the sky, you notice the wet leaves shining from last nights slow but steady all night rain. I grab the can that I ate the fruit cocktail out of last night and begin to warm up some water. First, I make sure that my very small C4 fire won't attract any unfriendly people to join us. As the water is getting hot a couple of the guys wake up and start their own fires to make coffee. I pour the instant coffee into the can and prepare for the treat of fruit flavored coffee and it isn't half-bad. For just a second or two you actually forget you are away from home and engulfed in a major war in a far off place. It is so peaceful; if that would only last until mid-afternoon that would be great. Then reality sinks in and I realized I was still out here in this jungle that was infested with those little yellow-skinned bastards that want nothing less than to send you home half a man, than what you came to country with. Ronnie, Neilson and I talked about how we felt while waiting for something to happen while we were on an ambush. Ronnie tells how he wished that no one fell into our trap and I some what agreed. I would like 3 enemies to walk into our kill zone and for us to spring the ambush and lose no one in the process. Nevertheless, we really have no control and that bothers me. I can't decide if or if not we spring an ambush on what ever comes our way. That can be dangerous if the force is larger than we had anticipated. We have before ambushed the lead platoon of a regiment size force heading towards Cambodia, but they didn't want to fight. All they wanted was to cross that fence and be safe from any of us. We were lucky that time, if they had all decided to fight it out, we would be in serious trouble.

The 6th ARVN Airborne Battalion had heavy contact with an estimated NVA Infantry Battalion. There was heavy fighting through out the day and night of Jan. 26-27 occurred, but the ARVN unit gained and held hill 900. Results were 17 KIA NVA. 4 US KIA D 3/12, 11 US WIA D 3/12, during the night of 26-27 Jan. 68 the 6th ARVN was subjected to a massive mortar and rocket attack. At 0645, the NVA launched a Battalion sized attack against hill 900. Both forces suffered heavy casualties although the ARVN defense was successful, it was recognized that to continue the ARVN mission was to abandon key terrain. The decision was made to hold hill 900 until additional units could be brought in. Our attack against the Peanut was also set back 24 hours in order to continue with a coordinated attack making the gooks fight in separate areas. D and C Companies had moved from hill 800 and were ordered to establish a defensive perimeter on the hilltop at YB 876 293. At this location, the bodies of 2 men of B Company were found. These were the men that had been killed in action near the Peanut during the battle on Jan.19. How their bodies got there we don't know, they may had been prisoners until the Gooks couldn't move fast enough, so they had to kill them, I supposed we would do the same, but it doesn't make it easier to think what they might have gone through before they were killed. During the night of Jan. 27-28, FSB 25 received a weapons attack, and the ARVN position was heavily probed through out the night. Trip flares and sniper shots kept the ARVN's on their toes all night. On the morning of Jan. 28 A and C Companies 1/8, inf. were air lifted to hill 900. The ARVN's attacked south to seize the grid YB 871 304 which was a small hilltop; C Company began their assault to seize the Peanut deploying 3 platoons on line in the saddle between these 2 hilltops. Moving forward at 0930 hours the center platoon received a heavy volume of small arms and automatic weapons fire from parallel trenches across the top of the objective, causing immediate casualties. The 2 flanked platoons maneuvered against the enemy by alternated bounds and forced the NVA to constantly shift firing, relieving the pressure on the center platoon. At 0950 hours the right platoon breached the enemy position and began to clear the trench lines just like in the movie Sgt. York" starring Gary Cooper. However, none of them got a Congressional Medal of Honor for their effort, but big Thanks from the ones that were pinned down, which meant more to them than a CMH at the time. Heavy resistance was continually met from fortified positions, but by 1130 hours, the Peanut was secured. The 2 trench lines were extremely well constructed and had connected bunkers, which had 10 to 12 feet of overhead cover. Only 1 NVA KIA was found, while C Company had 8 WIA, 3 more bodies were recovered from B Company that were missing since Jan. 19. The body of the 6th man was never found; he was presumed killed dead. During the night of Jan. 28-29 a weapons attack harassed the 1/8 inf. on hill 900 and the ARVN on hill 848, as well as C Company 3/12 inf. Position at the Peanut and FSB 25 was also hit with small arms fire which was enough to keep them from getting any sleep that night, and no way to make up for that lack of. The next morning the ARVN were air lifted to the city of Than Canh east of Dakto 1 and a Tet truce began at 1800 hours that same day, at 1946 hours the gooks violated their short-term truce, by rocketing and shelling with mortars against the Peanut. Hill 900 was probed most of the night. We as a reconnaissance platoon were going back to being a recon unit. No more holding down a defensive position at a FSB. It's Tet and we plan on 4 or 5 days to rest up and recoup from the long nights of the month passed. We were briefed last night at 1930 hours; we will be going into the valley and each of our teams will be set up in 5 different villages. The villages will be west of Dakto and along hwy 512 that goes to the Special Forces compound at Ben Het. We will be looking at any signs of enemy movement into the area around Dakto. Intelligence has been listening to gooks on a captured radio and they are planning several attacks big and small. We are to help the leader of these villages hold down the fort, we hope the truce will last, because it gives us one more day each day of not being hurt, but again it didn't happen, it appears the whole of South Vietnam is in an up roar; Even the American Embassy in Saigon was overrun by the NVA. The Tet Offensive was timed to the Presidential election, and to clearly relegate the political scene in America to a secondary place in the Commie strategy. General Gaip routinely praised the U.S. anti-war movement for its sympathy and support, yet he emphasized that the decisive arena was the South where the Commie suggestion hinged on changing the balance of power in their favor. Similarly, he dismissed our election as merely a reshuffle in the hierarchy of the Capitalist ruling class, which would not alter the nature of American Aggressive Imperialism. Between 1710 and 2210 hours Jan. 30, FSB 25 received more than 60 rounds of 82mm mortar and 20 120mm recoilless rifle fire, which resulted in 8 casualties. At 1845 hours, 34 rounds hit the Peanut and hill 900. Jan. 31st the Peanut was abandoned and both A and D Companies were moved down to the Dak Poko river to deny the gooks a crossing sight into the Dakto airbase, leaving C Company on FSB 25, and B Company at FSB 13 as a reaction force to Ben Het, and convoys on highway 512. At 1145 hours, a convoy was ambushed on highway 512 between FSB 13 and

Ben Het. Grizzly took a bird up to direct artillery fire and air strikes, destroying the ambush and collecting 12 KIA NVA for himself, the ambush was pushed aside and only one person was wounded and no one killed, which was some good news, it could have been worse.

The rest of the day was pretty calm until 1745 hours when C Company at FSB 25 reported a trip flare going off about 150 meters away from their perimeter, although we weren't up front we decided to go to the bunker we thought was most vulnerable; staying alive is number 1 on our list of something to do day after day, we expect some action during the day and night, at 1834 hours 8 rounds of 82mm mortars and 10 rounds of 120mm recoilless rifle shots hit inside the perimeter. During the next hour more than 50 rounds hit, our bunker received a direct hit by a 82mm mortar, a little dirt fell on us, but what we were worried about was a sizable ground assault. If we kept our heads down then the heavy foot attack would overwhelm us and surely kill or capture us all. Sure enough after about 10 minutes, some gooks were spotted about 50 meters out side of the wire. Every one opened up on them. M16's, M79's, M60's, and hand grenades every swinging dick took a shot at them. That changed their minds for the time being then we started getting hit with World War2 rifle grenades, and although they weren't very powerful, they still ended up wounding 3 guys. But at 2055 hours they fired 25 RPG's at the 4 bunkers facing the chopper pad, everyone had the same fear; the gooks were getting ready to partake in a sizable ground assault at those 4 bunkers. We just happen to hold 1 of these positions; there were 5 of us in that bunker and we got 2 more from HHC 3/12, the cooks. Nevertheless, we might need them if the gooks try to breach this trench line then destroying the 4 bunkers and every one in them. We could see a bunch of gooks moving around like they are getting into some sort of attack formation, as the attack starts my heart jumps into my throat and was pumping so hard that I believe the gooks could hear it, I look at the others in that bunker none of them looked at ease, everyone was biting their lips or sucking in air in anticipation of the assault about to take place. We had to remember the gooks would not attack unless they felt they had the advantage, so it didn't look good for us, some of us might die.

There must have been a couple hundred of them. All screaming and firing in our direction, blowing those dam horns and whistles they tried to perform what is known as the Hugging Movement, that's where they get so close to the American perimeter that the Americans can't use their artillery and air support without the possibility of maiming or even killing their own people, which gives them the edge. In addition, the fact we are in a triple canopy jungle with cloudy skies and its midnight so the only people we see were the ones that were illuminated from our fire. Which is O.K., if we were firing at the right people; now and then, we get a flare that helps. However, it also lets them see us behind our safe places. Sometimes it isn't an equal trade off if we have to crawl out of our safety to keep a watch on the enemy crawling their way towards us in an attempt to send us to Hell. We can't let that happen, so we creep out of the bunker and watch about 20 NVA crawling towards us, so I grab 3 Claymores and Ronnie grabs the another 3 and we push our plungers 3 times each and blow those twenty to hell, now we have 6 more Claymore mines in front of us. It makes you wonder did those first few gooks draw the fire of the Claymores so we wouldn't have any left?

We had twelve Claymore mines not six pointing toward the enemy and the rear of each was up against the wall of a tree stump so that when we knew the gooks were right there we would blow them straight to hell again, and they will have to deal with what's on the other side, probably not a place I would want to be. The enemy appeared to believe that those first six Claymores were all we had because they rose up and headed straight towards the other six we had. Ronnie again pressed the plungers three times each and that knocked down a sizeable force. We didn't know if that was all of them on this side of the perimeter or not? On the other side of our perimeter, a platoon-sized group of NVA was probing them. From all intelligence reports, they were from the 32nd Infantry Regiment. We can expect to be attacked on all sides before that night was over, on our side next to the chopper pad, we are all up and ready for the mass of humans that we knew would be coming. I laid out my magazines. Rex tells me to keep them in the bandolieers in-case we have to relocate very fast. I agree and put them across my chest. I did put three grenades out of nine to heave for when they attack again. We have already used up our claymores and that was their plan. They could afford to lose 50 men as long as they get us to explode the claymores. Charlie tells us he has 2 more claymores and he can rest them up against the sides of the bunker to give them hell one more time. The LP's were lucky on our side and came in once they were told it was safe for them to come in. I bet those guys sucked some underwear up when the battle began. We were all pretty scared; but the cherries are worst off, because they have never been in this large of an attack and for some this is will be their last assault. We know that we should keep our heads down to keep from getting it shot off, But if you didn't rise up and take some sort of an aim you were not going to stop them from running up to you and Tag you're it; or better known to us as killed dead. As we were up and firing at targets, we see this light behind us, we then hear the roar of the cannon, Battalion 6 had ordered 3 canister rounds fired at chest level. They were filled with little darts called flechette and they do the trick, if they hit you, they will go through you and the fins will stick inside your body while the sharp darts will stick to trees or other people, it makes a real ugly-wonderful scene. When these rounds are fired, it puts a stop to the ground attack for a few minutes. We could see the gooks off in the distance getting ready for another assault. This time Grizzly calls for 3 rounds HE (high explosive) directly at the formation of gooks in the near distance. The three ex-plosions were so loud we couldn't hear anything but that dam buzzing noise that we still hear today. Most of the gooks were either dead or wounded and what few that were not have left the hilltop for safety. Grizzly then calls for a gun ship to mop up the remaining gooks. We received small arms fire the rest of the night. It kept you on edge every minute and every time they would shoot into the perimeter, you woke up and about the time you were drifting; back to sleep they would shoot again. They did that to keep you on edge because some times they would probe your perimeter while shooting. I could barely keep my eyes open, I was afraid that I might drift off to sleep never to wake again. You can push your body only so far. Lucky for me I stayed awake and was alert when enemy movement was detected at daybreak again out in front of the chopper pad. Grizzly again ordered direct fire into the mass of human flesh to be torn apart and scattered all over this hill that will consume their every drop. This stopped the gooks in their tracks at least until 1 gook by him self comes out of the jungle with a tripod to which he sits on the pad, he goes back into the jungle and returns a few minutes later with some boxes of ammo, this guy is amazing to watch. He again goes back into the jungle to return with a Type 24 7.920mm heavy machine gun. Everyone figures this guy to be high on something, something strong, he sits down behind the gun pulls the lever to lock and load when every one watching this opens up on this poor guy. His body was spread all over the pad and no one came out to claim the machinegun that he left on the pad. He is either the dumbest, or bravest man I have ever seen. Maybe he has some dew in him? Something wasn't right about this guy. It had to be drugs! It was Feb 1st not April Fools day, he had to be brain washed or on drugs, or completely devoted to what ever cause he had, we respected him for that, we didn't want to think he was just goofy, although goofy gets my vote.

We were told a couple jets were to fly over and drop some bombs on an area we were to give them, when the jets flew over our area they received small arms fire, then they dropped their load of Napalm on them. Then everything stopped; we had to get in our bunkers and not look out with this napalm was being dropped just 30 meters from our bunker and the trench line. There was a large orange then white glow coming into our shooting positions. Then you felt the heat and smelled the gut wrenching smell of burning flesh. We must look up as soon as the flame had dissipated, to verify that the assault has been terminated. There is nothing alive for at least 100 meters. All that could be seen was charred. When we pulled our usual guard that night we heard moans and an occasional scream in pain as the NVA woke from their deep sleep. There was the never-ending smell and ungodly screams and the thought that not all of these bodies are wounded to a point that they cannot execute a successful shot at one of us. Watching to see his weapon move or his head rises to get that shot off. During my turn at guard, we were given an order to pitch a grenade out into the mass of disfigured and burning flesh. We did this not to save these dammed heathens from there suffering but to give us a better feel about the guard we were pulling. We have heard of several enemy had been out among the dead and dieing and when nighttime came, they finish the attack, so a grenade thrown out there will wound or kill whoever is out there. It also works on your mind if a bunch of them are out there crying, and screaming in pain, after listening to that all day and into the night it's a wonder more people from our side didn't go a little wacky. Of course, the members of our bunkers that was sound asleep when we threw out the grenades they all jumped up and gazed out over the smoldering bodies. When we tell them what was happening, they really were a little pissed at the fact they were scared to death when all 40 of the bunkers pitched one or two HE grenades into the Human carnage. Besides the moaning and occasional scream in pain, it was an uneventful night. It started to rain and we didn't know if there was anyone out there in the battlefield that was willing to start the battle up again. A sweep of the area the next morning produced a large amount of weapons and 7.62 ammo, 26 SKS and 14 AK47's plus that 7.92mm machinegun.

We received a couple well-placed mortar rounds inside the perimeter while we were out checking things out. We braced our selves as best we could. We might have been out when the gooks attacked again, that was not what we wanted. However, if it came there was little we could do about it. There were so many drag marks you can't tell how many; because they run into each other and you can't tell if there's 1 or 3 drag marks. Last night was a real narrow escape, an estimated reinforced infantry battalion had attacked FSB 25, and the gooks had successfully breached the wire and succeeded in reaching a point 5 meters from the bunker line before their attack was broken. The results from this firefight were 64 NVA KIA, 3 US KIA HHC 3/12, 8 US WIA C 3/12 from those few well-placed mortar rounds. Now I know for a fact that when they shot those darts at the gooks there were more than 20 of them then. Nevertheless, they want to only count the bodies that they see in the morning. Well hell I count 42 of them in front of our bunker. Therefore, we get a better count and there are over 160 dead gooks around the perimeter. We don't see a live gook for the next couple of days but we catch hold of 46, 60mm and 82mm mortar rounds plus 12, 75mm recoilless rifle well directed rounds hitting inside the perimeter. We got very little sleep that night, but what were you supposed to do? I felt that if I was to fall asleep I might never wake up. Those mortar and rockets might have been used to soften up the perimeter before a large scaled assault on the perimeter, so you had to stay awake and on top of what was going on, no way could you sleep. Feb.12 0830 hours A and D Companies seize the hilltop known as hill 886. We continue reconnaissance operations to locate an enemy base camp and underground hospital that we know is in our AO. We don't know where it is, but there has to be a hospital somewhere in these mountains. The area we were at now drops off straight down maybe a couple hundred feet or so. Therefore, that's one direction we don't have to worry about protecting tonight. However, we also can't use it as a way to run and hide. People that have never been in a life or death struggle have no idea what it feels like to sit and wait for something ugly to happen to you or your buddy next to you or even the son-of-a-bitch that caused you problems; you still don't want them to get added to the KIA list. The relief that is there when you wake up and you are not only alive, but also all in one piece! Back to the firebase, out for 3 to 5 days then in for a couple days or a couple hours then back out to some area where someone has seen or heard some enemy movement, so each mission might be that one where you get cashed in.

We are to go out that morning and see what we can. There were several dragging marks and we need to get a more detailed account of enemy deaths. We were unofficially told to add another 25% for the people upstairs, which mean the Generals ECT. The first day out we didn't find any new bodies; but instead several makeshift stretchers that were covered in blood. I pick one up and fold it under my rucksack it'll make a great hammock if I can get some of the blood off it. Anything to keep the land leeches off me. The next morning comes I have no leeches to count and that is great, some of the other guys have 3 or 4 on them. Out on a patrol someone has to watch while the rest eat. We make enough coffee so the guy pulling guard will get something for breakfast. We then head out like every other day we are out here at first walking into the jungle, which while there are no enemy sighted the jungle is magnificent. There isn't a prettier sight in the entire world until some ass-hole opens up with an AK 47, then the jungle transforms it's self into the worst place on earth for you to be at. This may last 5 minutes, or a lifetime if you are killed dead. All we need to do is cause a group of birds or monkeys to start up, that's a sure sign that something is moving around on the jungle floor. The gooks know this, so many times, they wait to see if any birds or monkeys are, disturbed then they head out in that general direction and try to ambush who ever they run into. If they are out numbered they usually don't attack until they have an advantage, then they go at it full blast, that's guerilla warfare. I agree that if the battle would last 4 minutes or more we would have the upper hand. However, that's not the way a guerilla war is fought. 60 to 90 seconds is a long engagement as far as hit and run tactics, it doesn't give you enough time to think, what do I do? It's all instinct that carries you through a battle. I know I've said some bad things about my Country; don't get me wrong I love this country of ours. I just don't agree with each decision that is made that concerns how and when I might die.

We come to this cliff, which is a couple hundred feet up, we look over the side and there right in front of us is the Garden of Eden, a lush valley that is covered with triple canopy of trees with brush below, add a river and a couple creeks, this would be an ideal spot to build a home and live off the land if it weren't for the thousands of gooks crossing through here almost every day. I wonder what they think of when they go through that valley? I'm for sure not every gook out there is a gung-ho die-hard commie, some of them have to wonder if they could be happy living in a place like this? From the spot we are at, we can see several clearings. That is what we are supposed to watch, along with the three ways there is to get to our spot. This little part of the countryside would be hard to recon by air. Gooks moving around down there could hear an airplane or a chopper flying low enough to spot them, all the gooks would have to do is step back into the triple canopy, until the aircraft moves on. Where we can see the clearings without being seen by them from below. The Big Guys think the gooks are building up to attack in the Central Highlands. That's what the higher ranked think, as they sip their brandy and smoke their fine cigars, in between telling war stories trying to out do each other in their brave acts. Hell, some of them even got Bronze and Silver Stars while shooting at no one. Not all officers are this way but tiny groups of them are; and that makes you wonder. I don't know why I feel this way, maybe because I have seen it happen more than once, I know when I say something like this to someone that is a strict conservative they label me a traitor, sissy and someone that doesn't know what he is saying, but trust me on this one. Now Grizzly earned his as a Platoon Leader during the Korean War. I imagine most officers got it the hard way. It shouldn't bother me; but I look at a Combat Infantry Badge being as a Badge of Honor. I feel it is along with the CMH to be worn with pride. Those that don't have one wish they did, because it is looked up on through out the services. We are again out on an ambush site hoping that we are visited only by a very few NVA we don't want a large size ambush that can only go sour on us. The rain is coming down in blinding sheets where we couldn't hear or see an enemy soldier if they walked up on us, it is making a t my feet, so I feel I should move to be more comfortable. We also lost our sense of smell and couldn't smell their curry smell. Therefore, we couldn't tell if an enemy soldier or a group of them was heading toward us. As our good luck comes, the rain slows down to a drizzle when we spot 13 young NVA heading down this trail. It had to be new recruits because they showed no caution when it came to walking toward us. Just before they were spotted, I had awakened the other guys so we were all set up and ready for the ambush to begin. As soon as the 13 of them are in the Kill Zone, I press the Claymore mine plungers 3 times and they all go off at once claiming all 13 as kills. Ronnie and Van both tossed grenades into the group making the ambush a complete success as none of us were even scratched. Now the five of us have to sit and be quiet so we can hear any movement behind those boys. Boys that were probably cherries as far as firefights were concerned. The young are sent attacking first then the more seasoned troops come up after you had spent all of your claymores and some of you rifle ammo. There was a group of them behind the boys, and we opened up on them with our rifles and tossed some grenades into the cluster of human fodder, they were also young and probably were supposed to be together with that first group. We figure either they were replacements coming from some village there in the South, or they were transcending from the North to begin their military careers, which we put an abrupt end to. After they attack, we open up with all we have and repel them back into the safety of the jungle. We were scared there might be even more and had to decide if we were to run and to which direction do we head out in? First, we first check the bodies for any maps then we start out to finish our mission, which was to go out on this finger of this hill and sit and watch for anything we could use as good news, we all like to hear good news. The rain stopped and we were now walking next to a trail when all of a sudden Mick stops and points toward some sandal prints that were not filled with water so these tracks had to be made within the last

10 minutes. We called in the prints and told to be very careful; but to follow these to maybe that long sought after hospital and resting spot the enemy has somewhere in these mountains. We are soon called in because the higher ups think an attack is emanated and they need us to find out where and when. Unless we can find some high ranking enemy Officer we won't be finding out any information because the higher up officers in the Gook Army don't tell their privates any thing about what is going to happen until that morning. Kind of like our Army, isn't it? You do as you are told then if all goes right you might get to go home in one piece and sane. Make too many mistakes and you become a part of history; a part you don't want. You will be fitted with a green plastic bag and sent home, if they find all of the pieces.

CHAPTER FOURTEEN - THE 173RD

We will be watching all day and most of the night, if they are sending some high dollar weapons through here, we are supposed to catch them in the act and call in all Hell on them. We don't see any movement all day, a day to skate by, and not be worried about if we are seen or not. Boy that doesn't happen very often. Ronnie tells us to get some rest; we probably will get no rest tonight. Nothing happens that night and on the way, we ran into a couple snakes and a few monkeys but nothing harmful.

Once we are in Van and I challenge two guys from artillery for a game of horseshoes. Van was very good at playing Horseshoes, without him I doubt we would win most of the ones we did, we win the first game and were ahead when we catch a couple mortars hitting at the chopper pad. We don't stop playing because 2 is all we get; just like a sniper attack every once in a while we would get mortars dropped on us. Van is ready to pitch when a rocket flies past him at chest height and landed outside the perimeter. The look on Vans' face when that rocket whizzed by was something out of a horror movie, his eyes were wide open as his mouth and he had the look of terror that is hard to describe. That ends our playing, and we are back to watching from inside our bunker. The artillery guys located where the rockets were coming from and zeroed in on them; the artillery leveled the ridgeline the bastards were firing from. Maybe they got them; maybe not. When nightfall comes, Apache 3 was watching down in a valley and to their surprise, there was some one walking around down there with flashlights. No one we know would be caring a flashlight; not one turned on anyway. Not that many anyway they count 12 lights and they don't know if everyone has a light or it's every 10 or 100. They call this information in and they are told to call in artillery and mortars into that area Gooks with lights on would mean they have no idea they are in the area. They call in artillery on that spot and half way thru the fire mission the Artillery boys want to know if they are in contact. Zollman tells them no, so they say the 173rd Airborne is in heavy contact about 15 klicks southeast of us.

They get the artillery that they need, more than we do at this time. I have some good friends that went to the 173rd after jump school at Ft. Benning before I screwed up my left knee and was told that my knee might never allow me to run again. I was transferred to a unit at Benning where we were used as enemy troops at the Ranger School. We were in Company C 5/31st Inf. of the 197th Infantry. There are several guys that I went to Jump School with over on that hill right now. O'Connor, Stewart and several others whom I not know their first names or I never knew their last names either. As much firing, as we hear from over there, one of them, either the 173rd or the gooks are running out of ammo very soon. Maybe both? I have talked to both O'Connor and Stewart when the three of us met at Dakto Fire Support Base; they gave me what actually happened during this battle I also got this from Karl Schmidt of A company 2/503 173rd Airborne. I was told there was a total of 50 to 75 Enemy soldiers killed while the Army said 500 or so. It really doesn't matter to us. I guess it makes Ma and Pa feel better to know little Johnny took 30 of them with him. He still is Dead!

We are getting ready to go back out after having 6 hours sleep and we were told to be very alert. Where they were sending us was an area where we had been told several NVA companies have formed into a Battalion of Infantry. We took it as us being out again on another lovely walk through Uncle Ho's little playground. We learn of a couple Officers from Base Camp going up in a chopper and firing into the jungle. Maybe they saw Ho Chi Mihn crawling around on the jungle floor?

Enough of that I don't know any of this to be fact. It's rumor and you can't tell yea from not. No officer is ever going to admit that they might have received a medal without merit or that they knew of such a thing. But a spade is still a spade.

We pull our regular guards that night, and when the daylight comes, we were told to stay where we were, because if it had not been for that all night battle southeast of them, we would have gotten all of their attention. Charlie calls in one shot of H.E. and it lands right in the middle of that clearing so he tells the Artillery boys to mark that spot that he will be calling it in tonight. The battle that took all the artillery action last night appears to be over. We haven't heard an artillery round go off all morning, hopefully they will be able to get their wounded out and to a hospital. That was the one thing we liked while out in a battle, you always were 15 to 30 minutes from a hospital as long as they can get a Dust-off to carry you. We listen to the radio and it's telling us that perhaps the gooks that attacked that unit thru the night might be heading towards Apache 2. Maybe they will go thru the valley they were watching or maybe just walk up there and ask them to dance the afternoon away. It's real quiet, and they were watching the valley, and watching the trail that comes up there that gives one of them a chance to catch some Z's. They were really tired and that action that might come our way had really drained them. They make it through the night and come in for a days rest.

We run only day light operations hoping to run into a gook recon team with their maps. What we found were indications showing a build up south of Dakto in an attempt to attack and destroy the artillery support as well as any choppers on the ground. The gooks fighting as a guerrilla-fighting unit would not seek out a must win to a minimum. Because the NVA has told every village that, they are to take the American air base at Dakto and that this didn't happen to save face they must destroy an American unit out in the field. We believe it to be either Ben Het or FSB 13. Apache 2 found papers on a dead gook that confirmed this and both places were put on alert to watch for signs of a large enemy build up in their collective areas. The papers were found in an area in between the 2 American strongholds. These papers show where elements of the 66th NVA infantry regiment were in the area and were making contact with the different villages in the immediate area. A and B Companies conducted heliborne assaults in an attempt to locate these enemy units, but nothing turned up. D Company is moved to FSB 25 while C Company along with our recon platoon was moved to FSB 13. A Company along with B Company were preparing for a heliborne assault on suspected locations of the 66th inf. Regiment.

At 0800 hours Feb 26 1968 a heavy artillery preparation was placed in the landing zone at YB 833 277. Spending as much cash as they had. Little did they know but these gooks were dug in. Bunkers that would take anything, including 1 direct hit. There were 46 bunkers laid out in a tree line that they could hold as long as needed until they could slip away. When the 1st chopper touched ground, everything was pretty OK. Nevertheless, as soon as the 2nd chopper touched down a RPG came in hitting the motor of the chopper rendering it hopeless and shutting down the LZ. We then had 8 crewmembers and 18 infantrymen shot down in a LZ that we couldn't use again. The 26 Americans ran and jumped into a bomb crater, about 50 meters from where the advancing gooks were. Grizzly gets a gun ship to fly over them giving as much support as they can. The gun ship takes 2 hits from a RPG and is crippled to a point where they have to leave the battle. About 100 meters away there was another spot for the dust off choppers to use as a LZ. We in Recon are called in to get inserted about 500 meters from that point and work our way back so as to support the trapped chopper crew and 18 of our friends from C Company. One of was Sammy Alewine. He was also stationed with Ronnie and me at Ft. Benning, Ga. He and I were given orders for Vietnam the same day. After we had been arrested by M.P.'s for being drunk and disorderly! Then a couple days later, we received our orders for Vietnam. Could that have happened? Some time in March, Sammy was wounded and sent home. I later found him on the Internet and he is doing well considering his wounds and living in Georgia by Fort Gordon. Our team gets to the edge of the clearing here we were told Choppers are down and call in artillery to drive the enemy away from their positions and give those guys still alive down there a break from the pressure the gooks were putting on them. We are working in an area where we want to make contact with those guys and extract them from this LZ and get them home.

But we also must either retrieve the weapons from the downed choppers or destroy them. At $24 Million, each we must be in a spot where we want to bring in a couple Chinooks and fly them to Dakto to be repaired. There are too many enemy troops in the immediate area for us to call in 2 more Choppers to become discarded machinery worth twenty five million dollars apiece. In addition, the lives of several more crew members of the added choppers. What we must decide is to destroy those guns on the Gunship but take the 2 machine guns off the Chopper and the Gunship then destroy both by setting their fuel tanks a blaze. After we work our way down to where the choppers are we crawl out to the Choppers and place some C4 explosives and a blasting cap with a 15-minute fuse on the fuel tanks of each chopper. We also get 4 M60 machine guns and as much ammo as we could carry. The gooks spotted us and were putting all of their firepower on us. We had a couple gun ships flying over us and one of them opens fire into the group of enemy; which detours them away from firing at us until we return to the bomb crater. We then have to get the downed Airmen and their cargo of 9 men each to follow us and leave that area as quickly as possible. We run into a couple of NVA that were out to capture us plus the 4 M60 machineguns and all the ammo they still have on them. As the enemy concentrates on the guys carrying the M60's (which I was one) we open up on them and put all 4 guns firing at the Gooks closest to us that was beginning their assault on us. We mowed them down as we were all firing in the same place, then we had to open up on the ones shooting directly at us. We quickly laid waste to the enemy and they began to hunt for cover. We now had to get all of us together and set up some protection for the choppers that were on their way to take us to safety. We were all at the new LZ and 3 Gun-ship's and 4 Huey's are on their way to pick us up.

All we had to do was stay alive for the next 15 minutes or so. We fire all 4 M 60's at once into their attempt to overrun us. The Gun-ships draw fire from the enemy and immediately return fire 100 times, of what they receive. This enables us to jump aboard the Huey's as they come in for the quick pick-up. The only person injured was one of the Infantrymen that got hurt when the Chopper went down. There were several gooks trying to put out the fire engulfing the two birds. But to no luck, as the fuel tanks all explode at once burning several of the little Bastards, We got a-that-a boy for pulling that one off. We got back to the Fire-Support-Base and are told, Good job," again we were Stars and we have to relax for the rest of the day, we will be going out again day after tomorrow. We now challenge the Artillery guys to another round of Horseshoes. We lose the first 2 games but won the last 2. We quit while we were even. We are to go out tomorrow morning about 4 A.M. So much for the rest, we will be leaving from aboard a chopper. We really don't want to run into a large amount of enemy soldiers, even 5 or 6 would be too much if they saw us first, when we don't get seen, then we have the choice to shoot or wait for another group to shoot at, sometimes the first five to ten men might be a point squad and maybe an entire Regiment may be a couple hundred meters back that we wait until they have left our area and call in artillery on them; at least where we think they are. There were no friendly troops in the area. Therefore, everyone is fair game, but we can't take on a whole herd by ourselves, lucky for us there were no troops behind the first 5 or 6 so we called in some mortars and shoot about ten rounds into the area we believed the 6 to be. Grizzly then calls he and us wants us to find then follow those 6 that we may have shot up and follow them if they were wounded. This time we will try to find where this invisible hospital is. Everyone knows they have to have at least one in the area. They lost the one they had dug into the hilltop at 1338; which is now called Firebase # 6.

After we are inserted by repelling down about 20 feet from a helicopter and stopping in a grove of some kind of fruit trees. I must say the last 10 feet of repelling I fell and twisted my bad knee. It wasn't too bad as to have to abort the mission. We are about four klicks from the FSB where we will need to keep in constant contact with the artillery. We are a little too far for the smaller mortars. Ronnie leads and we slowly move down this side of the hill that we have never gone before. While so dark, you wouldn't know exactly where you were. Looking down this finger while still darker than hell, we had to rely on our other senses to get down the last 50 meters, it was pretty scary, and we were told to get down there as soon as possible. They want us set up for an ambush before light forces its way to the jungle floor. After about ten minutes we were told to abort that mission, they now have some place else to be.

They want us to go over to the next ridgeline and set up an ambush sight, maybe we could get a clear shot at some one in charge. Maybe we won't see anything but we were told at our meeting last night that were no friendly in this area and we are to treat anyone out here with us as enemy. As soon as the sun comes up, we are on the move without any coffee or a quick smoke, which most of the guys feel they need. Chief is point and we are told to go very slowly as not to draw attention to our movements we don't want to startle any monkeys, birds or gooks. We sit up a spot within the area they have given us. We would really like a cup of coffee right now. But we can't start a fire and cold instant coffee is not a treat, to any of us. We decide we can light up a smoke as long as we keep the light up under our flop hats. Chief takes a drag off of Ronnie's cigarette and it works out fine, after 3 hours we see our first monkey. He's not very impressed with us, pays no attention to us, that is a good thing, if he had started screaming at us we would have to move to another location and any one in a hearing range would think someone is out and about and maybe send someone to find us or set up an ambush to really screw up our day.

We sit there all day and the only things around there were 5 monkeys. You watch them and you start seeing things in the way the monkeys act are like some of the guys you are on that patrol with; it's really funny. We must find a better spot to watch this trail. The area we are in has no place to hide so we go up the side of this finger and there are some of those trees with the giant buttress roots. We find a tree trunk that is big enough for us to hide behind and go off to sleep around 2200 hours. Taking turns at guard we spent a day of watching monkeys play, which is a lot better than having a company gooks walk up on us. At 0500 hours, our noisy neighbors wake us up moving about and screaming at something or someone down below them. We very slowly take a peek and we spot maybe 12 gooks moving along half heartily. We wait a couple of minutes and about 50 more show up. So it's a good thing we didn't start shooting at the first group. We wait another 10 minutes and here comes another 50 or so. After they go by and we don't think there were others, we get a hold of artillery and have them shoot-em-up about 400 meters down the road. Battalion 6 RTO gets on the horn after we call in the artillery and he wants us to tell him all about the enemy we have spotted. He wants us to tell him if they have any heavy weapons with them, we report that we have not seen anything larger than an AK47. We tell him they are still coming by as another 50 shows up. This time they are looking around for whoever called the artillery on that first bunch. This was not a good thing; we had to figure out an escape plan if needed. We now are getting the artillery rounds backing up towards us. We call in and tell them to cease fire we don't want them driving the gooks into our laps trying to miss the artillery. However, we tell them they could hit behinds us. All of a sudden, there were no more gooks walking in that area. Ronnie wants us to walk along the edge of the tree line and see if we can spot anything that would mean anything to Intelligence. After a very exciting morning we decide we would like to stroll amongst the area we just shot all to hell. We get the O.K. but are told they want us to stay one more night. We decided we want to move a little closer to the base of the hill that the FSB is on.

While moving we get a body count of 56 KIA no weapons or papers at all. We figure there were at least 200 of them fellers in that party. The size of one of their Battalions, they were moving somewhere to get ready for an assault on some Americans. Maybe we saved some ones life, doing what we do? We sit up another location about 500 meters away from the perimeter and call in with our location. We use a code instead of the correct grid. We tell them we weren't a Rebel; that becomes Y, but we were still Americans for A then we use numbers like blank, blank sunset strip. That gives them a seven then we go through the whole grid, them, and only them; know where we were. Most people back home didn't know that a few of the enemy spoke perfect English and their job was to listen to our radio transmissions then tell others what they heard. We were told to try and get all of them next time. We get credit for the 56 and that's all I guess the higher ups thought 56 wasn't a good enough number. Five of us and we get 56 and O for us. There might have been a few more, or a few less. We took a fast count and got out of there as fast as we could. What we did to those gooks was number one killed 56, or so of them plus, they knew some one had to be close by to know where they were. So we request to be picked up 500 meters due East from where we were, but no chopper at this time, they are supplying A Company with ammo and taking on wounded, We spot a patrol of about 10, we thought it might have been out looking for who-ever called the artillery on them, which would be us! Now we had to work our way back to the Fire Support Base. We came upon a dead Gook it appears he's been dead for a couple days. His body has started decomposing, mainly by bugs and wild critter is chewing on his carcass. We have run across some Americans in that condition, all we could do was take his dog tags and give the grid where he was, we also brought back his wallet, which had his ID in it.

We know we were just lucky to have our little escapade turn out as a good as could be. Maybe next time, the gooks will spread out and look for who ever directed that artillery on them. If found, there is no good to come of it. We were about 10 klicks from our artillery; so we were at the maximum range for the 105's if we needed help. Another 500 meters and we have no luck at all. We are sitting waiting for something good to happen. We looked found and found a small canvas bag with a map over lay of the area we were at. This could be a real map or it could be one made to distract us. We call it in and are told to go ahead and come in, with the map. We were told the map was correct, but it didn't indicate where the hospital was, but it did tell where a Battalion Headquarters was, and a bomber mission was called on top of it, with results we wanted.

While at the firebase 29 we get an hour or so before lights out, so we tell a couple of stories. Mick comes up with a story that I'm just not sure is the truth. I'm not saying he would lie about anything, and almost anything can and does happen out here in the jungle. Mick starts out with We were on FSB 29 when we were asked to go into an area where no American units has been before. This could be a good thing, but more than not a BAD thing as enemy troops could have this area as their safe haven since none of us has ever been there. Its triple canopy and hardly any sun light get to the jungle floor." We stop for a meal break, Mick asked, "if he should go on with the story?" Of course, you don't start something you can't finish. After it got dark we had a strong smell creep it's way into our ambush sight. We can remember when we had that same smell; it was a Tiger and we don't have a reason to believe that this not another Tiger. Possibly a mate to the one we killed a few weeks ago. All that Battalion came up with is there are Tigers out here in the thickest part of the jungle. That's not what we wanted to hear, but it makes sense.

We sit in a circle facing out ward and talk about what we are to do if it attacks and we tell the story of the last Tiger we had stalking us. Anyway, this Tiger didn't stay long. I guess he couldn't decide on which of us he wanted to have for dinner or he thought we might be hard for him to kill one of us while the other four are pumping him full of lead. We were up the next morning and even before our coffee we are told, "Some things are going to change and we should all be in to see what the changes were." Now for them to go so far as to tell us we are going to have some change; it doesn't sound good at all. What could they do to us now? How is it going to affect our situation; will it be good or bad? LBJ our President came up with a new Rule, we are not to fire at anyone until they either make an attacking motion or fire at us. Needless to say, that didn't go over well with the guys out in the field. We rather forgot we were ever told something like that and after about a week the order was changed, back to kill anyone carrying a rifle that isn't a friendly force. It made more sense and probably cost a few friendly forces to be killed, but better them than us. Has anyone ever told you War is Hell? Well it is, and anyone that says different had a cozy job somewhere that there were no big time skirmishes with the enemy at anytime. We are to come in and to bring any paper work we had found while out in the jungle. When we walk in, we head for the mess tent and grab some bread and ham with cheese. Van asked if we had any beer? We were told there was a six-pack left so we got them, they weren't ice cold but we didn't care at that point.

Van and I were to pull OP that day, that's when a couple guys go out about 75 to 100 meters down a finger from the firebase and observe any enemy activity to warn the firebase of an assault that is brewing out in the jungle. What it is an early warning of an enemy assault to some sniper sitting outside the perimeter and firing into the firebase? After we had been out there about an hour, nature was calling on me, so I went down the finger about 20 meters more and squatted to relieve my-self, when we heard the whoosh of an artillery round coming in towards us. I had just wiped myself and pulled up my pants and fell down when the shell hit close by. I was lucky, because of the way artillery round explodes, it mushrooms up then out, so if you are close enough and are flat on the ground the shrapnel will fly over you. I immediately began running up that finger towards the safety of our bunker; Van asked if I was ok? and then we called in on our radio as we were running up to cross the chopper pad and fall into the trench dug between the bunkers. We counted 9 artillery rounds chasing us up and into our bunker. Someone had to have been watching us then called in our position, so we sat out after the artillery quit and one of the guys on top of the bunker spotted two Gooks up in a tree with a radio. Grizzly called in a gunship and when it was on course to hit the tree it opened up its guns, and when we went out to look at those guys, there were a couple piles of hamburger and a beat up radio, it was a gruesome sight, but one we were happy to see. After about another hour Van and myself had to go back out there and finish our OP, it was a little scary not knowing for sure that the artillery wasn't shot before an assault was to take place. Nothing happened the rest of that day or night. We were lucky that an assault wasn't continued; we would have been vulnerable to a large-scale attack at that point, but nothing happened at that firebase the remaining two days before we went out again. Then all they had was sniper fire into the perimeter, which caused havoc for most of that day.

It just so happened that we were sent out to find anyone that was firing into the perimeter, and after two days of hearing the fire from a SKS, we headed for an area we thought they would fire from next time, and we were correct in that assumption. We crawled up to a spot where we could observe the area we thought would be the next spot to fire from, and sure enough, there were three guys sitting up in a tree so they could get a better view of the firebase. We waited until we could see anyone else coming into the area, and it didn't take long before there were a couple hundred of those lost souls preparing to assault the perimeter from the south side, which was a less protective approach because of the steep climb that needed to be done to overtake that side of the perimeter. But because we were there and could call in artillery to first box them in, then to eliminate them all together without losing a single soul, either from inside the perimeter or us out in the jungle, with those guys. It was another win-win situation for us. We were asked to go around the perimeter in a one-day mission to checkout any other potential shooting sights. We headed straight South and after six hours, we circled the perimeter, and set up three trips booby-traps using Willie peter grenades. Then we came in and reported where we had put them. By the next morning, all three of the Willie Peter grenades were set off. That told us the enemy still wanted to attack that fire-support base with a human-assault. Nevertheless, we must have changed their minds, because we didn't get attacked there at least a week after the booby-traps were set off. But the thought was always there to work on you especially at night when it's your turn to pull guard where everything appears to move or make noise as the wind blows through the area you are looking through. You don't know if you see or hear something moving around on the jungle floor or was it some animal trying to find his next meal, looking through any discarded C-ration cans left behind.

CHAPTER FIFTEEN - DIEN BIEN PHU

At the firebase, we are handed some tracts giving us some rudimentary knowledge on how the French lost their war against these same guys that we are fighting. We are told if we want some dessert; Strawberries on Pound Cake we need to read these pamphlets. We also get mail, I didn't get any this week but there is always next week. Now I'm going to read this pamphlet. The battle of Dien Bien Phu is the battle where the French lost Indo-china .It was interesting because it lets you know to what lengths the gooks will go to, where they will win this war and if we continue like the French, they surely will win. To start off the French picked the spot where they were going to defend. Ho Chin Mihn stated to the French you can kill ten of my men for every one of yours, yet even at those odds, you will lose and I will win." Late in 1953 to stop the enemies flow of supplies and reinforcements. Hopping to draw out the Viet Mihn out into a classic battle. Just like what the Americans were doing then. The French built their Base of operations at the bottom of a bowl shaped river valley. It was about 10 miles long and could only be re-supplied by air. Both by landing at the airfield or by dropping by parachute, all the enemy has to do is keep them from being re-supplied and the battle will end soon. Right now even I don't understand the French idea here, I mean building a main garrison that would be low ground and having smaller garrisons around the main one. That is inviting disaster. The main garrison was supported by a series of firebases. On near by hills that could bring down fire on an attacker. The strong points were given women's names, supposedly after the mistresses of the French commander General Christian de Castries. The French assumed their heavily fortified positions could destroy any attack. The size of the French forces swelled to 16,000 by March 1954. About 70% of that force was made up of members of the French Foreign Legion. Consisting of soldiers from French colonies in North Africa, and loyal Vietnamese. Dien Bien Phu's outlying firebases were over run within days of the initial assault. The main part of the garrison was surprised to find it's self-coming under fire from the surrounding hills. The French Artillery Commander failed at his ability to bring counter fire on the well-defended and well-camouflaged Viet Mihn batteries. The planes had to fly higher to avoid being shot down and therefore lost most of the needed supplies and ammo. They also had essential information fall into the gooks hands. General VO Nguyen Gaip was the leader of that attack. He is still alive and using the same tactics against us.

The French surrendered. We then committed our selves to taking the place of the French in the war, Khrushchev said, If you want to, go ahead and fight in the jungles of Vietnam, the French fought there for 7 years and still had to quit in the end, perhaps the Americans will be able to stick it out longer, but eventually they will have to quit also." Speaking of the French, We heard where there were 16,000 French rifles for sale, never been fired, they were dropped once. It took me a minute to figure that one out and it was pretty funny. The French are about as good an Army as the Mexicans. The only war the Mexicans ever won was against the French. Go figure. We can't even call the Alamo as a war but as a battle, Sam Houston won the war a few weeks later. The French didn't win any war that I can think of. They did help us win our independence from Great Britain. But I believe all they did was sit one of their fleets of ships in a couple of our coastal cities and keep the British out. We might not have won that war if it wasn't for their help. Why do they show us how the French lost their part of this war, if we are assuming their role and heading down the same path? Doesn't make sense, we are told the reason we were given those notes was for us to understand that these little yellow bastards will do anything they can to upset our happy little home here. Some of us see them as letting us know that the enemy will go further than we to achieve his goals will. We should reset our goals so that we can counter anything they pull on us. We just aren't as dedicated as the gooks are. I guess if we were the ones that had someone attacking what they consider part of their country, we would give it 100% also.

We can see where some of the same things that happened at Dien Bien Phu are happening at Khe Shan. In a smaller version, they try to pull that on us while we are fighting out and about here in this lovely but completely untrustworthy dark and thick jungle. You die out here and you might not get to go home if they can't find your body. You might be buried by Mother Nature and buried with nothing but your name.

Everyone pledges when they first get into a unit that they will never leave anyone dead or alive out in the jungle, they may have to go back and retrieve them but they will do that. The enemy doesn't care how many they lose, what they care about is how many of us die or go home maimed for life. They hope pubic opinion will tell us what to do as far as getting out of Vietnam just as the French had to. Surely, our Wiz kids in our government will see this and not fall for it again. How many Guerilla wars most we fight before we as a government learn that we cannot fight and win one of these wars until we learn to fight like them? Abandon all the so-called rules and strive to win that war and not give a damn what someone in a building in New York City cares about what happened. Not just a few Special

Forces units but the whole dam Army as a Terrorist Group that they must deal with. I can see us in several other wars fighting people that don't care if someone has to die. All they care about is what our public has to say to the Government."

It's time for our daily- dailies; we don't get them every day, and especially when we are out on a mission. None of us have ever caught Malaria, maybe because we take these pills when we are in a FSB. This time they have heat tabs for us, which is a good thing. We either have to eat everything cold or tear open a Claymore mine to get some C-4.The high explosive won't explode when you light it; just burn real hot. Put a detonating cap in it and let the cap explode then you will get a big bang. The army frowns on us for using it that way. Nevertheless, eating cold C-rations with cold grease in the can makes you a little more than you were. I mean when your clothes don't always fit, your hair is always dirty, and you're always in a life or death situation and scared 99.99% of the time. We want some thing to be half way good for us. Hot meals even if they are canned 5 years before I was born and basically all taste the same after awhile then a miracle happens; we are at a FSB we get a beer ration.

We get 4 beers apiece and a 6 pack of some soda, this time it was Dr. Pepper. No way to cool it, but it beats the hell out of drinking water, especially from some of these creeks and rivers. The Vietnamese people use their rivers and creeks as toilets, and if there is a village up stream, there always is that chance of finding a turd floating down river to where we might be getting some much-needed drinking water. That pisses you off and makes you want to fuck up the guy that shit in your drinking water but; what can you do? We usually don't take water unless it's a fast moving stream because of that. This was another small thing that when added to all the other things small and large that worked on your little brain every day while out in the jungle. Van and I were selected to pull OP the next day so we went to the mess tent at about 0500 hours and got some food and coffee to take with us while out about 75 meters from the perimeter to observe anything headed our way. After a couple hours I had to take a dump, I could either walk back up to the perimeter and walk over to the other side of the formation to a latrine and do my business. But that meant I had to leave Van by himself for about 15 minutes. I didn't want to do that, so instead I walked further down that finger and squatted down to do the dirty deed when a familiar sound came rushing towards me, the sound of an artillery round coming into your area, I immediately pull up my pants and hit the dirt when this 75mm round goes off a few feet from me. I'm not injured because when an artillery round, or a mortar round explodes it rises up in a mushroom formation to where if you are flat on the ground the shrapnel will miss you. I get up and run towards Van screaming that it's me coming don't shoot. Van waits to see I'm OK then he heads towards the perimeter, a total of 9 rounds followed us. When we finally get inside our bunker, we were to look out and see if we could see whoever was spotting for that artillery piece inside Cambodia.

Lula looks up into a large tree and spots an antenna sticking up through the leaves. We call into Grizzly and give the location of where we believe the forward observers were. He calls in a gunship and tells them where the antenna was. A couple of Air Force jets fly by and report they spotted them and they were going to light up their world. They make another pass to make sure they knew where to shoot, then headed toward them while firing their Gatling guns. And/or 20mm cannons. Within a few seconds, that tree was whittled down and when Van and I went back out, we had to go passed that spot. All we found was a left hand and two SKS rifles. What a demonstration of firepower that we had at our beckon calling. After that, Van and I still had to go out and pull the rest of the day at OP. But before I went, I went, if you know what I mean? We were worried that an enemy was getting ready to assault the firebase, in which case you didn't want to be out of the perimeter by 75 to 100 meters, but someone has to do it. Lucky for us, no assault.

CHAPTER SIXTEEN - HILL TRAP

Our next mission is a normal 5 man where we were supposed to try to get a prisoner. O.K. we wonder if Hadley is another lifer? He is, but he doesn't push us into doing something stupid, just so he can get some credit, this is something we talked about openly, for we needed to know this was a man that would not throw us to the lions, just so he could get some credit for orchestrating the mission, that was something that was important to us as it would mean we weren't going to do something very dangerous so he could get credit for it. Now that doesn't mean that we didn't do dangerous things out in the jungle, just walking out there with 4 other men planning on finding a large number of the enemy was dangerous. But that goes with the job. We were told that Division wants us to capture an enemy officer with maps and to turn him over to them. I guess G2 found out that a team of us was just plain stupid and need a prisoner real bad.

They are offering a reward, depending on what rank the gook is. However, our next two missions are not productive as getting a prisoner; we do capture a map, but no live gooks. We get 2

KIA's to our credit. This area is getting to be heavily populated with gooks that could be a bad thing. During one of our information meeting we are told that the gooks are building up in this area and we don't know what for at this time so would we please get a prisoner for G2. All of us say we'll try, but it's a lot more dangerous to bring in one alive. It was so much easier to shoot them and not worry about transporting them through the jungle to a place where they can be picked up by a chopper. The next 5 missions aren't fruitful as far as getting a prisoner but we are still seeing signs of a big troop build up. We don't run into any large bodies of enemy but we find large deposits of food and clothing at several spots along the trails between villages, which tells us there will be a lot more of them coming to have that much food and ammo stored. The jungle is in a constant change; each day some new vegetation grows and adds to the thickness of jungle, that is forever growing and making an area look less like a war scene. We are at fire Base 6 which we call 1338. We get some information captured from a NVA NCO. He walked in on his own so no one gets credit for him. Nevertheless, they quit pushing for us to get another one. The information was written in Vietnamese so they had it re-written in English so we can read and hopefully learn. It really hits home. The gooks have drawn plans on how to attack an American Fire Base Camp. They have on this map a diameter 250 meters, perimeter of 800 meters, a list of the howitzers and mortars and even a red cross on the map showing where our first aide station is. There also is a note written in Vietnamese but changed to English by Intelligence.

U.S. forces in Vietnam are disposed in large fixed installations, which always provide their forces as lucrative targets. Their forces were always certain that as long as the weapons hit the installation; the U.S. forces will lose equipment, and manpower. Likewise these large posts don't have sufficient forces to control the surrounding country side, which makes these attacks easier." That's that briefly. This paper goes on to say, The use of booby traps also has had a long lasting psychological impact not knowing if your next step is your last or the fact you could lose that leg. In addition, the fact that a NVA or VC could take a shot at you, killing one or two then running into a village and you can't distinguish them from noncombatants. Also the many different booby traps, most of them were of U.S, origin, dud bombs, discarded ammunition and munitions and indigenous resources such as bamboo, mud, coconuts, and venomous snakes. Doesn't sound too good for us kids now do it?

The Division is handing out papers that will give a lesson in what the gooks call NVA Hill Trap Maneuvers. Their plan is to draw American forces into a set of meat grinder battles near their supply bases and sanctuaries. They have worked this maneuver out and while it cost them, more men than whom the trap is set on. They achieve their goal of causing a large amount of body bags to be sent home It started in 1966, the maneuver sought to exploit the known battle habits of U.S. troops, by drawing them into a mountainous killing ground where a difference in depth, combined with standoff bombardments and rear attacks, would likely annihilate them. Hills and mountains throughout Vietnam were being prepared as battlefields. One of the areas where this was taking place is the tri-border, Chu Pong war zone, as it was known. They had thousands of laborers dug tunnels, trenches and caves to house fighting units and set up hospitals and Headquarters for Combat units.

Early in 1966 we had intelligence that two NVA infantry divisions were in this area. The 1st and 10th NVA infantry divisions were operating in this area and we would have to erase them from the equation. In July 1967, elements of the 66th NVA infantry regiment severely mauled the 1/12 infantry near Duc Co the 6th Battalion, 24th NVA Regiment on June 22 1967 was engaged with the 1st Brigade 101st Airborne and in a bloody battle; the gooks had destroyed A Co. 2/503. In August 1967 ARVN troops fought the 2/174th NVA infantry Regiment near Dakto. In November, the 4/503 suffered severe casualties when it assaulted a bunker line near Dakto.

Six Kilometers south of Dakto the NVA 32nd Infantry regiment was at occupied fortified positions around hills 1262 and 1338.

General Peers, Commanding Officer of the Fourth Infantry Division commented the enemy had prepared the battle field well." The gooks objectives were to draw troops into the tri border area where some units could be annihilated .If the campaign went bad; they could withdraw rapidly into either Cambodia or Laos. We as a unit weren't going to fall for the same tricks as other units fell for and almost got whipped out because they fell for the trap. To practice the Hill Trap Maneuver in prepared battle sites. Where they have dug in and are ready for what ever comes their way. The NVA 1st Infantry Division consists of the 32nd, 66th, 24th and 174th infantry regiments along with the 40th artillery regiment. This totals approximately 7,000 enemy soldiers who were spread over 900 square miles. Their positions were so far apart that they could rarely support each other. But in early Nov. 67 an element of the 173rd Airborne fought small elements of NVA's 66th infantry regiment on hill 823. In mid-November another element of the 173rd, the 2/503 was informed that the 174th Infantry was being used to cover the units withdraw of both the 32nd and 66th NVA that was pretty well beaten up. The 174th was set up on a well-fortified position on hill 875, which was thick with vegetation and a three canopy of trees, mixed in with lots of bamboo and mid height brush, which made it hard to see any enemy positions. C & D Companies of 2/503 lined up abreast facing the object area. If they ran into any enemy, they were to call in artillery and jets .The two companies fighting side by side were fighting independently and there was no overall commander on the ground with them; the Battalion Commander was not present.

The American commanders thought they could beat up the enemy with the air and artillery support then advance and take over the trench and bunker systems. Nevertheless, the 2/174 NVA not only had the American units pinned down, but also left their fortified lines in an effort to close assault the airborne troopers. Behind the front line, setting up a LZ and outpost covering their rear of the assault was using A Company. Two platoons were bringing the wounded back to the LZ. Little did they know but two Battalions of the 174th infantry regiment were observing the reserve company and were preparing to execute a hill trap maneuver in this order of attack.

The enemy would first pin down our units attacking the bunker line with heavy Machine guns causing as much causality as possible. After a few hours, the U.S. Company would be spread very thin from carrying wounded to the rear and protecting the rear. Then at the right moment, the reserve company would be hit by mortars and attacked by 1/174 INF. The attack would take them thru the reserve company and into the attacking companies and have, them kill them all. They also had another Battalion ready on a near by hill, who could be committed to attacking from a different direction to completely destroying the unit.

Four hours after the battle began the NVA 1/174 attacked the rear guard company killing or wounding most of the human beings in their wake. The enemy then wiped out the 6-man command group in hand-to-hand combat. The NVA assault drove the reserve company up into the two assaulting companies. The battered companies formed a perimeter and were attacked relentlessly for 24 hours. While supporting fire rained down on the NVA there was an accident where a pilot dropped a 250lb on the Americans killing 42 and wounding another 45 in effect destroying one whole U.S. Company. The 4/503 attempted to relieve the beat up 2/503 but they were met with volley after volley of mortar rounds. Massive amounts of machine gun and RPG's striking an all ready beat up unit. Later that night the gooks all slipped away into Laos. Although the gooks were not successful at finishing off the Hill Trap Maneuver to annihilation of the U.S., forces they did manage to gut the 173rd Airborne Brigade. Now we have to learn from these lectures that we get concerning different gook tactics and how they seem to work against us every time used.

We will be back in the bunker facing the chopper pad. What the dinks want to do is put a mine in a hole in the chopper pad and blow it up with a chopper sitting on it. We watched but because there weren't any stars or a moon out, we had to listen for anyone digging out on the chopper pad. We had 4 or 5 claymore mines aimed at where we thought they might dig at. But that night we didn't have anyone interested in blowing up a chopper. We now need to get a little sleep if we were going to spend that day and night at this FSB then head out in the morning for another adventure. The Navy Air or Air Force can't return to their carrier or air base with unexpended ordinance, before the South China Sea was the official receptacle. That a Commander named Grizzly from the vicinity of Dakto would give a target to any aircraft that had a load to drop 24/7. No appointment needed, just call on the radio and coordinates would be provided. We even had a couple Arc Lights provided to us because after the B52's were in the air and at least half way from Guam they would have to drop sometimes hundreds of bombs. When we come in the first part of our agenda is to answer questions at TOC then we can go get something to eat or what I do. Get some much-needed rest.

We might not be able to get much sleep while out playing with the shit heads. This time we are going to be out six days and nights coming in on the seventh day. That means we will have to carry another four meals. This will be between 4 and 5 more pounds to carry plus an additional canteen weighing approximately two pounds. That might not sound like very much but when you add it to the already eighty to ninety five pounds we are already carrying it does mean a lot, going up and down these mountains, being very quiet and not noticed it means a lot. It's the little things that made life miserable more than it need be; like rain, leeches, the hot humid jungle air and the little shit heads that make everyday one you had to be on your toes 24/7. We get our briefing before our little vacation as they call it. We are told that all we have to do is set up a Listening Post in an area that has electronic pause meters and that there is something out there moving around a lot and they want us to find out if it's gooks or monkeys I voted for monkeys. This area we are to sit still at is on flat ground so there is no high ground to speak of. So the extra cans of food won't make that much of a difference to us. All they are is something to fill a hole, if they also taste good that's an extra nice thing to happen. This mission starts out really nice, just before we start out, we get about 5 minutes of light rain. Enough to get you a little wet but not soaked like so many times before. The jungle is like a spring day in the mountains around LA. Calm as can be and clean looking, the rain-washed down almost everything and it smells fresh to us today. We are hoping no one will try to screw up the rest of the day for us. We are going to a place we have been by a couple of times but from a different way. We are looking for in this valley is more wheel tracks again. What Division is worried about is if the gooks have more of that gun that we found before they might be able to cause some of us to have some very ugly moments at a FSB or even out in the boonies. That first day was pretty quiet, so TOC decides to move us about 1,000 meters to the west. We find some Chieu hoi papers that have mustaches drawing on them. It's just someone being a kid out here with us kids. The next few nights nothing happens much to us. But A & B Companies are under attack at the same time but 2,000 meters apart. The NVA are holding the area between these two companies apart this way they feel they can destroy them one at a time. No one here wants this to happen so Grizzly takes over calling in artillery in between shots coming in to the TOC area. This keeps the gooks out of the corridor that joins them and will eventually allow the two companies to merge as one fighting unit. TOC gets on the horn and tells us to go to the tip of that finger that leads up to the FSB, that we will be coming in a day early. We pull our normal guard and at 2300 hours, we hear a fire fight going on heavy and strong about 5,000 meters to the south east of us. D company is under attack by what appeared to be a reinforced Company of NVA infantry with a Mortar platoon attached to it. They kept firing and receiving fire all night long. At daybreak, we got totals. 125 NVA, KIA and 27 SKS rifles captured. D company 3/12 had 48 KIA, 22 WIA and one guy missing. Towards daybreak, they had to call the mortars on top of them selves. When things like that happen, they happen so fast you don't know where you are, what's going on or even what your name is. All you want to do is hide somewhere until morning where you can see where you are. Hopefully the gooks will have moved on, as they can't hide in daylight. Day light comes and the gooks had taken the south side of D company's perimeter and are trying to capture the remaining bunkers out side of the center. They do that then taking over the center is a piece of cake. When that happens to the interior bunkers the gooks feel the Americans will surrender and they will have won this battle. They will probably have to execute any prisoners because they will have no way to hide that many people from the air. So they must end the battle with no prisoners. The people in D Company realize this, so they put up a pretty good fight. But as soon as daylight hits the tops of the bunkers D company counter attacks and with the help of A company, that was now 300 meters north of their perimeter. D company is being reinforced with A Companies fourth platoon. At 0612 hours, with A Companies support, and D Company my old company retakes their Fire Support Base and the enemy were being driven down into us. Oh goody for the five of us. With them having 125 KIA on one side of the perimeter and taking the other side there must have been a Battalion of gooks attacking. With that being fact, a couple birds are sent in to kill the remaining gooks. And they do just that. D Company also has lost 18 people KIA and have 17 WIA so that's roughly 35% of D Company as causalities. We are not in a straight line for the gooks to pass by us. But you didn't know if they have a hospital or any medical tent set up. It could be any where along the way home. Our luck is we will be sitting on top of the damn thing. When the 173rd got run off 1338 last summer little did they realize that there was a 20 bed hospital dug into the ground almost at the top of 1338 and that was the reason the gooks fought so hard in November to hold on to that. A sanctuary away from their homes in the north But TOC tells us, Just like American units there are some gooks that can not read a simple map". If they go by the way the sunsets, they might walk into us. We now get different orders. Lt. Hadley tells us he wants us to go to the scene of the battle last night, find the bloody trails and find out where their hospital is. If we can get their hospital destroyed maybe the gooks won't be so cocky as to attack us as much as before, because we will have taken away one of their sanctuaries .

As we are prodding around in amongst the dead gooks we come across one that has lost the use of both of his legs, they are still attached but his pants legs are soaked in blood and look like a couple of hamburger patties. We don't figure he will live much longer so we leave him alone. We take his weapon away and anything close to him, we trash it. About ten minutes later, we hear a scream and the wounded gook is history .We don't find a whole lot, but it's enough we get a couple KIA's and two weapons reported captured. We do find a couple pieces of paper with gook writing on them. Turn the papers over to Battalion and they have someone that can read and understand gook. After we get back, He asked us if we knew what the letter was about.

Looking back at a little recent history. For the NVA, May through Sept. 1967 was a time of great plans and furious activity as they are prepared for their upcoming offensive. The American units were on 6-20-67 C Co. 2/503 173rd moved from Dakto Air base to the base of hill 1338, 6-21-67 A Co. 2/503 set up a Night position. About half way up 1338. 6-22-67 A Co. began their way back down the slope of 1338 and were going to return to Dakto. The NVA's 24th Infantry Regiment ambushed them as they were transiting 1338 on their way back to Laos or Cambodia. MACV after a lengthy delay announced that A Co. had a body count of 475 NVA KIA. Later it was changed to 513 NVA, KIA. Survivors of that battle were in the hospital with me and they say maybe 50 to 75 NVA, They aren't the only ones doing this, maybe if they had gone back up that hill a different end might have been in Nov 67.After the gooks have killed over half of your unit that's 475 to 513 KIA for you. . Several other units claim outlandish KIA reports. Our units do it, so the press will tell Ma and Pops back home that Sonny Boy took a lot of them with him. I remember when the Recon team we were with ran into 2 dead gooks, when we reported finding them. We got credit for ambushing several gooks and for bringing in several heavy machine guns. We did find parts of what looks like an old anti-aircraft gun. But it was rusted to a point it wouldn't fire. That's what MACV and the press can do for you. I'm surprised none of us got a Silver Star for that action. I guarantee if an officer was out with us even if he had shit his pants and cried like a little girl, he would have at least gotten a Bronze Star medal but none for us enlisted men, who get medals most of the time deserve them Officers most of the time deserve them but there are so many medals given out to someone that doesn't deserve them but would look good on their Military record.

I know Col. Hendrix may disagree with me on this issue. But we have heard of it happening in many of the different combat units. I can't think of any to which I was under their command. But it has happened through many wars. My Dad told me once that Officers in WW2 would get a Bronze Star as a Good Conduct Medal. I don't know if it went that far. But I did see a Field Grade Officer lean out of a chopper door and fire a burst into the jungle below. There wasn't anyone returning fire. I guess he might have seen Ho Chi Mihn crawling around on the jungle floor? But I bet he got his CIB at that time. I may sound bitter, well at that time and place I was scared and bitter or bitter because I was so scared? I felt betrayed by those that didn't EARN their CIB as we had to earn ours; it was a thing to do with honor. Honor was a big deal to an infantryman wearing a CIB.

Every day we either are stepping into some strong shit or we listen to someone else stepping in it. Just makes you ask, Is it my turn; and my turn for what? Will I be killed, wounded, or captured? What is to happen to me, or to the next guy? Will he get killed? And will I be able to let his death bounce off me or will I absorb his death or disfigurement and have it haunt me the rest of my military life or will it tug at my soul every day for the rest of my life?" You ask yourself these same questions each and every day. This Asian war in Vietnam did change so many people, The reality that war is not fair, not every one gets the same breaks and each of the stories told might have many different endings depending on how this action affected them. I don't mean to down play anyone in what actions they or their units took in these stories. But a spade is still called a spade and the reasons for some of these actions are unbelievable if nothing else. Some of the actions not taken are difficult to understand as well why some of them weren't followed up on. Try to understand, that the person fighting this war might not have thought it a just war either. But little he could do about it. Needless or not, it was and still is a very horrible part of those two million or so men and women's lives. None of us want to be pitied. We had to be 110% aggressive to get by. One day of not being aggressive could be your last on this very green part of our earth.

We are all up and ready to move out if we must, if not we warm up some water and throw instant coffee in a cup. That was breakfast. Then every one lights a cigarette and begins to burn leeches off our bodies. I get 14 of them and I thought I was done, Charlie tells me to drop my pants and turn around, and He then spreads my ass cheeks and gets the leeches all nestled up in the crack of my ass. He then drops his and I check him, one little one, I burn it off. Nothing was said after doing this, it's something that has to be done every morning and never spoke of. You really know who your friends are. Not everyone is willing to do that for you. As we are getting ready to move out, it's not like the gooks don't know we're out here, they just don't know exactly where we are. So we have to move away from this spot as soon as we get the OK to move. Someone will come by this spot looking for any weapons or ammo left behind. Sometimes we leave a grenade in a peach can with a trip wire to it and when the wire is pulled, the grenade comes out and the pin has already been pulled. It works almost every time. We then travel about 2 K's down into the darkness of the jungle.

We stop for about 5 minutes to get our eyes adjusted to the darkness. We sure don't want to miss anything. It's almost dark down deep into this triple canopy jungle. Ronnie tells me just wait until we set up tonight out here. You can't see your hand in front of your face. Robert Antonio is a full-blooded Indian from New Mexico and he likes to pull practical jokes on you when in a FSB, he never pulls a joke on me. I think he likes me OK, it's like he is getting short and their aren't many things funny happening out here since we moved into the Dakto-Ben Het Area of Operations. He is more concerned with going home all in one piece, he already knows he won't be 100% sane but who among us will? We move very quietly in towards the FSB, not wanting to cause the guys on the perimeter to have seen or heard any of us. We don't pull guard tonight because we believe we are between the LP's and the bunker system; which someone might have seen or heard us crawl up to this spot. So when the sun comes up we call in and tell the guys on that part of the line that we are at the wire and for them not to fire or blow their Claymores on us.

We stand up and we are 20 meters from the wire and on the inside of the OP's. When we walk by the guards at the bunker where we stood up. We tell them they were lucky we weren't gooks getting ready to throw some hand grenades on them. Its no wonder some of these guys get killed when attacked, playing cards on top of a front line bunker is pretty risky, we also tell them that when we are walking in to pay attention to each of us coming in. There are five of us; anymore and they must be Gooks who like to walk in with us then play shoot-em-up after they are inside the perimeter. We heard it happened to the 1st Cavalry about 2 years ago. I tell them about the time when I was in D Company and three gooks tried to follow the LP in The Gooks didn't make it inside that time but they still try every once in awhile, what they have planed for after they get in, I don't know, but more than likely them getting in and shooting a couple of guys will make their death worth it. If for no other reason than to harass us into always being aware of the fact, you have to be sure of each aspect of our daily routine. After we get in we are told not to sneak around like that again Lt Hadley told us we could have been killed if just one of those kids we were watching on that bunker had seen or heard us moving around out there where we found the gooks. Next time there will be an article 15 if we live through the response that we receive from the guys at the bunker line. We could all get killed and it would not be a good thing. We listen to the PRC 25 and hear where a small unit is attacking C Company; about 30 gooks are hitting 1 side of their perimeter. While there is no threat of them taking over the perimeter there still are causalities. The assault only last about 10 minutes. Then the enemy slides back into the jungle with 1 platoon of C Company following close behind. Grizzly gets on the horn and tells C6 not to follow the little bastards into the jungle. What is going on is an enemy's old trick? You follow them into their jungle and they have another large unit waiting to kill you, they then encircle you and erase you from the equation. There are no second tries, you either make it the first time or you wait for the next time if you are still alive? The fact that they do this shows that we do follow them to our deaths, it's usually someone new in charge that figures he must show his ass to get the prestige that is needed.

CHAPTER SEVENTEEN - THIS ISN'T A COMICBOOK WAR

Grizzly was a Company Commander during the Korean War. He took over a line Company while still a Lt. he knows most of the tricks that are pulled on friendly units and tries his best to educate those under his command. We were young and very ignorant when it came to handling a life or death situation. We were drunk with the illusion of our invulnerability. After a while things start to build up on you, we thought nothing could happen to us. Then someone pulls a switch and then when reality sinks in you understand that these little Asian guys are trying to snatch you down into the depths of hell and have my soul haunted forever more? We call in at noon and are told to eat a fast lunch we have to get going if we are going to get to our lager in time. Now there aren't too many fast lunches in a carton of twelve meals, which includes such well-known meals as Powered eggs with a piece of bread you can toast with your bayonet holding it over a well-managed fire. Or you could go for many the best. Ham and Lima beans to which you add some

Tabasco sauce which will kill the taste of even the nastiest meal they could send you.

The sauce comes from a Care package you get from someone in the world that cares for you. We have to get back to the chore at hand. First, we must move to a different location and call in our support people, the Artillery and the mortars, and then we set up an ambush for tonight. What this means is we will get close to no sleep tonight then go out tomorrow and be alert enough that we don't walk into an ambush ourselves we can't do this every day and night it wears you out. We arrive about 100 meters from our destination and lay low for a few minutes; we are a little ahead of our arrival time. We sit and wait a few moments until we feel it's safe to go on in to the spot we are to settle in for the night. It gets dark pretty early on this side of the mountain. We set up our guard rotation and when it's my turn, I set up by a tree and I can not only check out the trail about 20 meters down from us I can also see the valley floor. This is a good thing; we have found the perfect spot to find someone down in the valley. It's far enough away that the gooks will have no idea where we are. The trail that is 20 meters down from us is a good spot. But the valley below is so much safer for the 5 of us. As I sat there in the darkness of the jungle, I wondered if someone was going to walk up on me and what would I do? I also had to think about the different noises out in the jungle while it's pouring rain; everything is making noise, the big leaves of some of the plants as the rain strikes it, plus the puddles on the ground. Then at times when the moonlight pushes through the triple canopy there are shadows, some that weren't there last time the moon shined in on the jungle floor. Was it someone sneaking up on you or was it merely a shadow?

Because you had cleared your throat half an hour ago, was it someone investigating that noise or was there no one to hear it? I still had half an hour to go on my watch, would I be able to go back to sleep when it was time to wake the next guy or would I lie awake scared to drift off to sleep? Was this one of the mistakes you don't make it on; or was this a mistake that no one heard? Everyone has told me not to make that mistake but make it I did, now was I to pay for my mistake by losing my life or the others I was responsible for while on my watch? Should I stay up with the next guy and should I tell him I was the one that lead the enemy to us, or just tell him what happened then if I could drift off to sleep? Was I just thinking too much or was I correct in my assumption, only time will tell. As the moon splits its self through the dense jungle over-growth, I spot a shadow that appears to be moving towards us, was this an enemy crawling his way to our demise or was it just a shadow? As the shadow got closer it had to be something other than a human, could it be a large monkey? My heart is pounding, I don't know if I should open up on it or let it be, hoping what ever it was it would leave us alone. I start getting the jitters thinking if it were an enemy, how many others had he brought along for the fun and games? I slowly raise my M16 and point it towards what ever is crawling towards us, now that's it is closer it's too small to be even the smallest gook, but what is it? I was just about to pull the trigger when this monkey leaps up into the safety of the trees. That was a load off my back. It was now time to wake Ronnie for his turn; I tell him of first the monkey then about my clearing my throat, and then I lie down in the puddle where I was to sleep that night. The rain was still pouring down on me when I finally drifted off. While wrapped up in a poncho liner that is soaked, you are as warm as can be, but as soon as you get up and move it from you, you actually feel a chill even when it's 70 degrees at night.

When morning came we were all soaked but still alive, we get a heat-tab going and put on some water for our morning cup, plus the usual burning off the leeches. We decide to wait a half-hour before taking off; just in case there were enemy that were trying to hang our scalps. During this time Ronnie calls in to tell everyone we were staying here for a couple more minutes after half an hour S/Sgt Magwood calls us and asked us to partake in going back the way we came from, some chopper pilot saw several gooks swarming around in that general area at first light that morning. We gather up our claymores and proceed to head back using a different path incase someone had sat up an ambush along that way we traveled yesterday. We don't run into anyone, friend or foe so we set up on a ridge overlooking a valley, where we were to watch for any activity and report it so artillery and maybe a couple of jets can rid our world of some of those trying to eliminate us.

We set up camp and chow down on some C-rations; I had beans and weenies with a shot of Tabasco with a can of fruit cocktail for dessert, almost like eating at home. We take turns either watching the trail we were sitting close to and one person to watch down into the valley, which gives two of us some knap time. When morning comes we do our rituals, hot coffee and murdering leeches, then we head out again heading towards this village up in the mountains where we suspect there has been a large enemy concentration and we need to weed them out; if they are all NVA or VC, then we need to rid ourselves of that group by calling in a couple Navy jets to level that village. But we should make sure; there were civilians in that village and we don't want to kill any of them, if possible. After we had climbed up this muddy mountain in the rain, I look at the other guys and they had a haggard look mixed in a jaded look on top of it all. What a group of misfits! But also a group of beloved comrades in arms. We traveled to the outskirts of that village and stopped to listen and watch for any signs of enemy activity. We didn't even hear or see any type of movement. We called in what we didn't see and were told, walk into the village being ever so careful," there might be an element of enemy gathering in that village, a chopper spotted a small group of armed people walking into that village, something we might not want to run into, but we must check that out.

Before we get to the village, we stop and look and listen to see if we see anything to suggest a hostile group. We see a few of the guys that were carrying weapons. We decide to look a while longer to get an idea what was going on. We then call in and were told to go ahead and while keeping a weapon on these guys, try and find out who they are. After we first stepped into the village, we first noticed the foul smell of death. Then we started to see bodies, many bodies, there were men, women, and even small children all either shot or bayoneted. We called in and reported the awful scene, Grizzly gets on the phone and tells us to be very careful; that it looks like this is either a trap for you or it was a way of changing some other villages mind on accepting the NVA as their friends. We don't find any enemy nor any weapons or extra rice, we don't know how those guys got out of the village without us noticing them, and we never heard any gun-shots nor people screaming. We find someone that speaks a little English and he tells us they killed those people a couple hours ago and returned to tell the people of the village they will always be close by, so the village needs to get some supplies from the Americans so the enemy might come back and take that from them. We leave the village and head South. That enemy wiped out that village, but why, why would they kill the old men, women and especially the little kids, even the dogs? We were told that was so they could tell the next village that if they didn't do as told, the same could happen to them, what do you think they should do? We called in to tell Mumford of what we saw, he tells us to see if there were any survivors that need medical help. We find no one that needed medical help, but a few that needed burial. It was an awful sight, that Village of the Dead. We were told that someone, an ARVN unit will be there to burn the bodies and we weren't to worry about it, it wasn't our fault. Somehow, I thought it may not have been our fault, but I surely wished we could have stopped the murdering of children and old men and women, How can these people kill their own and expect them to arraign with them in the effort to get us out of the war?

S/Sgt Mumford calls to tell us we are losing Hadley, this was in mid-June He gets promoted and sent back to A Company where he will assume the command of the company. The Captain that is there, and in charge is a lot strange, he takes naps during a mission and his men can't get him to take command of them. So now, we are getting someone to take Hadley's place.

Hadley was a good soldier and basically a good all around guy. He wanted to make the Army his career. His father was a Lifer Lt Colonel in the Army. So I guess we will miss him because we knew he was always willing to do for us. It wasn't all for him like it was before. We will get a new Lt in a couple days in the mean while Mumford hands out the orders and we are to go on another mission, when we come back in we should have a FNG as a commander, someone to train I guess, or will he know it all?

Out on our mission we talk about whom we think we will get. I hope it's an Officer that has some combat experience and doesn't want medals. I know I was like that when I first was in country but after I learned that the most important thing is to go home and next is to have all of your fingers and toes.

We set up ambushes each night we were out but we didn't have any luck getting to pull an ambush. We found out our new Lt's name. His last name is North and first name starts with a J. He goes by either John or Jack. We come in and all 5 of the teams are in to meet him and see what kind of an Officer he is.

First thing Lt. Jack or John North wants us to do is go on a platoon size patrol to find out how much we know about guerilla warfare? Sounds pretty normal to me. Now is this some guy that has spent the last 6 months being flown around in a helicopter taking reports to different Generals and reading several Sgt. Rock comic books, those comic books have been the closest thing to real live combat that this swinging dick has every seen. We go out side the perimeter and find out this guy doesn't act afraid of being out side of the perimeter, which tells us, this guy has no idea what was really out there. Every one of us is scared before we leave the perimeter. Maybe this guy should run into a little shit today. That might put some fear into him? But not too much, we don't need him pissing his drawers.

We seem to be traveling too fast for a safe journey into Uncle Ho's playground. Ronnie speaks up and tells Lt. North that we are traveling way too fast. We are not a line company and don't want any contact. Lt. North comes back with the fact we have a pretty high body contact record. We all crack up at that and tell him that if all we do is walk out here for about an hour we will have a body count even when we haven't seen nor heard a Gook all day. Hell if we do see one and kill this poor soul maybe he can get his Bronze Star and write home and tell Mom what a hero he is. Then ask Oliver his brother if he has any medals yet? He tells us Oliver isn't in country yet, and what he wants is a score too big for Oliver to get ahead when he does come into country. Then he gets real silly and wants us to go down into this valley thru a gorge where the gooks would have high ground on both sides of us. Pure stupidity as we see it. He comes up with how are we going to get any medals if we don't have some serious contact?" Sounds like me a few months ago. I tell him the easiest way for him to get some medals is to go on a one-man mission and crawl up to some gook perimeter and snatch a gook off his bunker and bring him home. North tells us that sounds very dangerous, we all agree but you would get at least one medal for attempting that, a Purple Heart, of course you might not be alive to receive such, but he would get one. He says he might give us direct orders to do such. Now we know what he is trying to do. He's trying to scare us a little. I tell him I won't go and he can go piss on him self. Now North believes that he is an officer and should be treated with the up-most respect.

We sort of laugh at that one, then we mimic him telling us what a superior officer he is and that we should respect him because he went to OCS and learned all he needs to know from a couple classes and his comic books. Colonel Hendrix told me later that Lt North was Oliver's Brother. About half an hour later, we spot some fresh sandal prints and we get credit for 1 KIA, no weapons captured. We show Lt. North and he didn't say a word, but the way we run our missions is back to the way we were before, no more crazy thinking. We try to explain that there are two wars going on out here. The war that we know for a fact and the Comic book war that MACV and other groups want the American public to believe as the truth.

In reality, there was no way we could win that war game, as we were playing at that time. The North Vietnamese could lose a thousand men to our two people. It doesn't matter to them how much they lose as long as we lose some too. In the way their government was set up, the people as a whole have no say in what happens, or how many of their young men are killed; we also should note that they also use women in combat roles. All they need is for the American public to know how many little Bobby's aren't coming home, get their congressmen to contact other congressmen, and get the Government to with draw because of the will of the people.

We come in from the Platoon size mission and have to get ready to leave again, day after tomorrow, Apache 5 and 2 left out early the next morning and we are going to leave out before noon and the other team will leave tomorrow am. On our next mission we leave out at 1000 hours and head for the bus stop as we are going to be inserted into an area that TOC tells us has had some heavy movements recorded on one of our sensors that we have out in various parts of the jungle But before we leave it's mail call again.

I'm getting letters from a girl in Nebraska that I have never met; it was nice to get those letters. She was a friend of Jon Arnes the other machine gunner in the Company. She writes like I'm some kind of Surfer boy. I have surfed before but I wasn't what was considered a Surfer, I managed to not drown the couple times I tried it. But I guess compared to a guy from Nebraska I might be a Surfer. I end up meeting her the Christmas of 1968. I went home with Tom Tanner a guy from the First Brigade LRRP's. He lived in Hastings Nebraska. Never heard from her again, I don't remember her name, so what.

Anyway, we go out to the Bus Stop and wait for our chopper that we are going to use to be inserted. The chopper pilot tells us the trees are too high there and he will have to hover for 2 minutes at most so the 5 of us can repel out of the chopper. I wasn't real good at repelling out of a chopper; I fell the last 15 feet but wasn't hurt at all. The guys got a chuckle out of that. We repel out of the chopper and we receive no enemy fire, which is a good thing. We get out there and don't see, hear, nor smell any gooks. We climb up in trees so we can see further but still nothing. We do however see many monkeys climbing up and down in the trees. After three days and nights, we get to come back in. No contact, no body count, no captured weapons. We did watch some pretty interesting monkeys swinging limb to limb and trying to piss on us every chance they got. Other than the monkeys, all we saw was some butterflies and of course the mosquitoes that are always present out in the jungle. We also ran into some land-leeches that we poured salt on and watched them die; maybe we could get some body count from that? We didn't try to claim any, which probably was a good thing. It's been a while but we came in with the goose egg, which is a very good thing as far as we are concerned, that way we don't have to count our loses, not surprising that when we report nothing, they give us the big goose egg. We do report that their sensor is more than likely picking up the movement of all of those monkeys. We rest up for a day then out we go again. This gives us a break for a few hours where we can rest up, then eat a good meal and get new socks before venturing out into Uncle Ho's den of murderers.

Before we leave out we get mail call again; I get a letter from my parents and my one brother writes a short message to tell me he might be going to Pepperdine on a Basketball Scholarship. Good for him if he can do and keep his ass out of here. We slip out into the jungle and since it rained last night and is still raining, any sandal prints have to be from this morning. This time we run into a whole bunch of sandal prints which means since it rained heavy last night these prints have be from that morning that isn't a good thing for us because there are lots of prints. There are also wheel markings the Vietnamese are bring in something big, we don't know if it's an artillery piece or anti-aircraft gun. It could be a lot of things, a hospital wagon; Festus pops off it could be a tour bus. Maybe some Rich North Vietnamese want to see where their money is being spent. That would be O.K.; we believe it's something more sinister. Like a

Quad 50 like, we had on the razorback. They could set that up next to one of our chopper pads and wait until a chopper comes in and blow it and any one close by straight to hell. Or attack us and when we fire our big guns shoot them right to hell in a hand basket. We feel we must find this weapon and get it destroyed, and pretty soon too, before they have a chance to use what ever it is. We follow the wagon tracks for about a kilometer, but still have not reached it; we get pretty close to an area that the recorders have shown as having a lot of traffic. Grizzly gets on the horn and tells us to give him a grid and he will call in an arc light that is when 3 B52's fly over and drop all of their bombs in one area.

So that's what we do .It takes close to 24 hours to get an arc light to come in, but he has one coming that the mission was scrubbed so we are to find somewhere that we can set up and hide for a few hours. We search around and find a place to hide. It's high ground surrounded by big rooted trees that we can use for a shelter. We don't find a way to hide from the rain nor the Leeches. But there probably isn't somewhere that the leeches won't find you. We open up a couple sundries and take the salt out and pour on the leeches; it works just like they were slugs back home. It would be great if we could kill Gooks this easy. We don't hear nor see or smell anything. So we are happy campers right now. After a very good night of nothing making any noise or seeing anything except rain falling down your back we even eliminated the land leeches so when morning comes we don't have to burn any of them off our young bodies. Grizzly gets on the horn at daylight and informs us that the arc light will take place at 0145 hours and to make sure we are under cover as best that we can be. We roger that and prepare for the extreme loud noise of the bomb blasts. At 0135, we don't hear nor see any bombers but we sure as hell hear the bombs exploding about 2,000 meters up this trail. We don't hear any secondary blast nor see anyone leaving or going into the area that was just bombed. That means we are to go into that area and see what is left to see. The enemy knows that we will be coming so they are making a mad dash to that spot themselves.

We hope we can get there and back before the gooks get there and set up for an ambush.

We struggle in the dense jungle to make good time. There are wait-a-minute vines and ant nest and huge spider webs to run thru. Plus the fact, we each have 50lbs or more in our rucks and we are trying not to be noticed. One of the things we have to make sure doesn't happen is the gooks are on the same side of the bombing that we are and we over take them trying to get to the bombing sight. At 0836 hours, we get to the area of destruction and there isn't much to see. Broken trees, massive holes in the ground but nothing that would let us believe that any large number of enemy troops were here when the bombing took place. We don't go out into the massive area that the bombs lay waste to. But sit at the perimeter of the explosions and watch for signs of gooks showing up to try and get one or two of us. They know from past history that we will be showing up to get that all-important body count. We sit still for about 20 minutes then decide we have been here long enough. Lt. North gets on the horn and tells us to go out into the devastated area and see what we just spent a couple million dollars on. We slowly move out into the open field. At first, we don't see a thing then after about 15 minutes we spot a couple gooks all dressed up in their kakis covered in blood. So we dig around a little by these bodies and we come up with several more. We are now getting worried about any gooks that would be heading this way to see if they could pick off one or two of us. Lt. North wants us to go up a little in the destruction and see if we can spot anything. So we go and after another 15 minutes come up on what looks like a small Howitzer and we believe its wheel is the same size as the one track mark we saw a couple of days ago. A PAK 40, a 75mm Russian gun. Now we have what they wanted us to find. We slowly move away being oh so careful now. If any gooks were headed this way, they are here by now and the best thing we could do right now is slip away unnoticed. Nine times out of ten, we can make a break-a-way like this work. We are thankful this was one of those times. When we call in What was found at sight, 1000 hours and we are going back in to be briefed on what we saw during that last mission. There are some very happy High-ranking officers waiting for us at the TOC?

They want to know what we saw and it was worth it to call in that one arc light. So now, we are to walk in and face all of these officers that were looking for a feather to put in their cap. We have blown away probably a couple hundred gooks and several heavy weapons that they had hid in that valley. There is nothing said about the rest of the damaged area there could be a lot more of these little bastards crawling around in that valley. . Everyone is pleased with what we found and we are considered heroes for a day or two. We also state that maybe there was a large number of dead bodies either buried in the millions of pounds of dirt that the bombs had flying or maybe not right where we were at. This bombsight is 200 to 300 meters wide and a mile long. We could very easily miss something especially if it was half or more buried in the bombsight. But we found the one thing they wanted us to find that little cannon. Body and weapons count to the max, good going we are told. Now we were asked to go back the next morning to see and report on more of the devastation and maybe find an entrance to that hospital we all know was somewhere close by.

This time we are dropped off along with A Company and Lt. Hadley. The line company is to secure the area and we are to search for more weapons and body count. As we look around we see how much damage was done to this valleys beautiful landscape and how we were destroying some of the most beautiful places on this earth. Not knowing for certain that any enemy was in that valley. But I guess it may save my life if that lovely valley is overcrowded with gooks. We go in and look over the area. We see where a chopper was shot down probably 2 years ago when the 173rd or 101st were up there fighting the same people that we are fighting now, The First NVA Infantry Division.

We report what we saw and are told to catch a chopper and A Company is leaving the area to go on a search and destroy mission. We will be debriefed and can sit out tomorrow from this war. We fly in and while going by the mess tent we see a couple fresh baked pies. Ronnie and I are going to try and sneak into the mess tent and maybe steal a fresh baked pie. It might be worth a Court Marshall to get a whole pie. A pie just the 5 of us to eat; that might be worth killing someone for? We wait until the cooks have gone to bed, and because a couple of them are early risers, so they can start on breakfast we have about a 2-hour window to capture a pie. We have Chief wake us so we can slowly move around the mess tent and slide inside where we find one of the cooks asleep on a cot. So Ronnie slides over to where the pies are kept and I watch to make sure we don't get caught, But we don't get caught so we hurry and the 5 of us in our bunker devour that Apple pie. All it needed to be perfect was a scoop of Vanilla Ice Cream but no luck at getting that out here! Ronnie sneaks back into the Mess Tent and sits the pie pan back on the cooling rack. Later we hear that pie was baked for someone special and he is out looking for the thief. It was someone special that ate that pie, us. We don't worry about getting caught because we leave the area and the pie pan was back on it's cooling rack so they have no witness or proof that we stole the pie. Boy was it good! After our day of rest, we get briefed as to what we found on that last mission. They believe we found and destroyed at least a company of NVA regular soldiers and 2 to 3, 75 mm guns plus what ever hand held weapons they had on them.

We were out on a mission and it appears that someone was following us. That was not a good thing. We just get that feeling you get when you know someone is watching you only this is different. Them crawling up on you could cost way too much. They could kill us all or worst yet capture us or just get our maps and radio after killing us. All the talk back at the firebase is who stole the Apple pie? The 5 of us get a chuckle out of how much is said about that pie. We have to worry about who ever it is that following what and us is it they want? Battalion 6 calls and tells us that Apache 4 was to be inserted about 1,500 meters away from us and they are going to set up a trap where our team would come thru where they were and when the gooks that were following us will get to that spot and they will have 10 instead of the 5 they were chasing. We stop at a place where it looks like some big animal has died. The flies are thicker than anything I could come up with. Trust me on that one. After they lay their eggs in the carcass of that decaying animal, they proceed to walk around our faces and spread germs. These germs will make you sick enough to really feel lousy by not enough to put you in a nice hospital bed. We try and figure a way out of us being here. Mick gets on the horn and tells Battalion that we need fire support and need it fast. We are being chased by a platoon or more of NVA and don't like our chances. Lt North gets on the horn and tells us we need body count we ask to talk to Mumford and when he gets on we tell him that he better talk some sense into North or he might not make it out here with us heathens. Mumford says he has tried talking to him but he still carries a book on tactics and that he believes everything in that book, which was written in April 1958. He also has his brother Oliver to deal with. He feels that the tactics we are using come straight out of a book he brought over with him from OCS. So it's a book about the Korean War or World War II. Either way it doesn't work for us. We really wish the Dept. of the Army would teach their new officers about Jungle fighting? Sure, they send them to a jungle school, but they aren't told what to do if you are not in the spot you thought you were and you get contact. What if your unit gets split in half? These are classic battlefield maneuvers that the gooks use very effectively. Separating units from a safe heaven. So I wanted to go back to the Recon Platoon and read some of this book that Lt. North seems to think of a Bible for all to read. Out in the thickest part of a steep mountain you can't do what you can in the flat plain that our training was based on. Now later on I believe we started to add thick and steep into our list of Things to do or not to do.

There are other human beings out here trying to take our lives from us in any way they can. We must figure a way to get to them first while playing within the rules of warfare. It would be great if all we did were sit behind a desk and push button after button to win this little Asian war. Instead, we have to come here into this unforgiving jungle that is engulfing us into its total darkness. We are to act a certain way, talk a certain way. When in fact we see these ambush each differently. I see them as a good way to get your self, killed, where as I used to think they were a great way to kill some enemies plus getting some body count while others think this ambush will help win this war. We prepare to go out on an ambush patrol; I get to carry a M60 while on this ambush patrol. Mainly because I carried one while in D Company and I knew how to use the gun and I know when and where to lay down a wall of fire so that others can get into position to end the battle very fast and to it's effect fully.

Not that every ambush works; It's basically we sit up an L ambush with my gun is in the middle of the leg of the L. I will fire from the middle to the rear of the people that we are to rip their bodies to shreds while the guys at the other end will fire down the throats of the front of their patrol gone sour. There are 10 of us on this ambush patrol, all of us at least in country 6 months. We sit through a group of monkeys playing in the treetops just as the sun is setting on the ridgeline to our west. About 2200 hours we had an enemy element in our Kill Zone. Everyone had a slight panic attack, as we are ready to start the ambush because we don't know how many there were. We blow the claymores then I start up my gun blazing on rock n roll. First hitting at the middle of the gook patrol, the enemy seemed surprised when we started this ambush. We can see them because of the flash from the machinegun illuminates the area. They still were able to return fire and come real close to ruining my week. Some gook starts out shooting towards my gun and once that starts, I had to rid myself of that little bastard or he might get a lucky shot into my body. Another gook gets in my sight and I gave him a 20 round burst in his neck and below. This guy's head rolls on the ground and his body falls on top of it. There are about 4 or 5 of them that didn't come this far. The firefight only lasts about 3 minutes and as soon as it is over and done with the killing, the smell of the burning gunpowder mixed in with the smell of fresh blood; it gets your heart to pumping faster and you get to where you don't hear the blast from your weapon. Just the rounds being fired directly at you, it makes you turn to face the aggressor and to take him out as quickly as you can. Then after the carnage is over, we immediately were out and search each one of these dead human beings for any information that will help us later down the road hopefully leading to that hospital we must find. We get 20 body counts, about 5 of them got away, but they left some pretty heavy blood trails. We call in and are told that we are to move about 500 meters due south is a spot where we can set up another killing zone. I don't like ambushes because you really don't know how many there are unless you let them all walk by you. I used to not care as long as I got the most kills, but I had mellowed a lot since then. They want us to try and ambush the gooks that will be coming back to move their dead or taking their wounded to the hospital.

We set up a perimeter and stay awake all night in case any of them comes back to try and drag any wounded away. The rest of the night was uneventful and at daylight, we start our walk in with each of us carrying an AK 47 or two. We had our proof of a body count. We got 20 of them and not one of us is wounded. It was a great ambush. We did an excellent job on that ambush. 20 of them and not a scratch on us; how can it get any better? We still want to find the place where they take their wounded, no luck this time. We walk in to the FSB and get there in time for supper and they have macaroni and cheese and a burger, not a bad meal and a small piece of peach pie. We didn't get a slice as big a slice as the apple but that would have to do. We also were given new toothbrushes and told to use salt to brush our teeth with, something that came down from Division. We also see a movie inside of the large bunker in the middle of the perimeter. It was a James Bond movie (Gold Finger) a pretty good film, but unrealistic; if Bond were out here he wouldn't last a week.

Our next mission we move further down this ridge and set up another ambush. Because of the terrain, we set up a U formation so we can have the enemy in a cross- fire. This way we can end the ambush a lot faster than the L shaped one the day before. We just have to set up facing the right way and have someone facing the other direction. The way we were set-up was to ambush someone heading into Vietnam from the border either of Cambodia or Laos. We are in an area that they thought was being used each night by some NVA coming down from the north, and we were to ambush them and kill as many as we can. It was very dark that night All day was overcastted and then it rained and we had set out trip flares at a spot that if the flares go off we open up fire in the area around the flare, as we probably won't see anyone it was so dark. We sit still and wait for someone to trip off the flares but nothing happens! It starts out raining pretty hard then we had to try and stay comfortable as we could. We still sit up all night and decide to come in and tell what we did or didn't find. That night there was no moon and the overcast sky and triple canopy kept the light from stars out of the jungle floor, so we had nothing to report.

But since nothing goes down to which we are thankful we do get rained on and still have to burn leeches from our bodies in the morning I had a cup of instant coffee and a can of fruit cocktail for breakfast, then we sit for hours watching, hoping no one will come along. The NVA seem to have either slowed down infiltrating or they are sneaking by a lot easier than before. It would be ideal if we never fired another shot at these little people who seem to want to rid themselves of us. We get comfortable just sitting and waiting for what ever came our way. If no one came, Is it because they knew where we are? They had plans for us, and it won't be pretty. Or they aren't moving today. We call in and request to move. It is denied we were to stay there, they believe that a convoy of gooks carrying supplies or looking for their dead would be coming through this area and we need to stop them from bringing in their much needed supplies. Another day goes by and no gooks so we move towards Ben Het where there had been several sightings. We head towards Ben Het

FSB and we will be patrolling that area for the next few days. These gooks were building up a large amount of soldiers and we needed to stop them.

We were to ambush them and disrupt their month by killing as many as we could. There will be no prisoners from this ambush. We set up a good ambush site about 100 meters from where some gooks were spotted by a chopper pilot but he was heading towards a dust-off so he couldn't engage them right then. We settle down to get ready for the ambush. We decide to take turns of 3 people for 3 hours get to sleep then the other 2 get 3 hours then everyone is up for sunrise.

Since nothing happens that first night. Darrel says he wishes some gooks with paper would walk into our trap so we could go in from this mission. Darrel informs us he doesn't feel good about this mission. He tells us that he doesn't know what but something makes him feel uneasy about this ambush. Fortunately, for us nothing happens and we are told to come in, we will be going out in a different location around Ben Het and maybe we will get some information as to where the hospital is. After the second non-productive ambush, we are told to walk in to Ben Het FSB, which is about 2,000 meters away. We start out headed for Ben Het when we ran across some very fresh sandal prints. We decide to call in and await new orders even when we know they are going to want us to follow and report what we come up with. After an hour or two we catch up to what looks to us to be new recruits joining in with some well-seasoned troops. Ronnie gets on the phone and tells Grizzly what we have found and asked are we to fire them up? Or maybe follow them to what may be that invisible hospital? Grizzly wants us to follow the trail until either we find the hospital or get out of range for artillery support. We will have to be very careful because of the size of the unit we will be following is probably too large for the 5 of us to handle. We get within 200 meters from these people and for a second we thought we were spotted. But we weren't so we continued to follow. The gooks travel into a canyon covered with thick brush and bamboo and tall trees. Then we lost them. There was no way for them to get out; so we figure this might be the hidden hospital we have yet to find? We call in the grid and request a bombing raid on this valley and along the sides of this canyon. Within 30 minutes here came the Navy with 4 jets loaded with 250lb. Bombs and Napalm. They drop everything in that canyon and along the sides of the mountain ridges. We are then told to go back into that area and look for anything that would lead us to where those enemy soldiers disappeared. We found no one or no weapons, they must have a cave dug into the side of one of these mountains with a removable door like the ones we were told they have their artillery set in across the fence in Laos.

CHAPTER EIGHTEEN -
A HERD, AND A LETTER

While out on a mission to the South East, we run into a much larger herd of gooks that seem to want to capture us. They don't fire at us but they keep coming. We have become the hunted. It appears that the NVA want to punish those that have done their job of causing them to have new problems and the pain that comes with not knowing if you are to live or die that night! We call in artillery and mortars both to our front and rear incase someone has set an ambush for us. We keep moving back towards the firebase we left just a couple hours ago. Grizzly gets on the phone and tells us we better keep moving away from those guys. He tells us that intelligence has told him the gooks were trying to capture a recon team and get their maps and get to question the team as to what is going on. That was enough to get a distance between those and us chasing us so we head back home. That was a very scary situation. The thought of being captured pretty much scared the daylights out of us. We figure there would be torture and a trip to Hanoi, not first class. The enemy was looking for someone in LRRP, but if we were captured, it would be second place and they would be satisfied with that. Lucky for us the artillery barrage kept them away long enough that we were able to lose them by getting as far away from the trail as we could.

We go into the firebase and are told we will be going out after tomorrow and to get as much rest as we can, we may all have to stay awake all night if what they think is out there is there. We get our mail and such; take a little time writing home to a girl and for some of us their wives. A few such as S/SGT. Mumford have kids at home that put a lot of burden on him. He doesn't want his kids to grow up Father-less. The mission starts out ugly. About the time we get outside of the perimeter, we get sniper fire. There appears to be only one of them. But he got one of us almost and the other four pinned down for about an hour. Finally, Rex gets a shot at him with his M79 grenade launcher. This gook falls out of his roost and we go over and find a grenade taped in his hand. I guess he knew wasn't going to make it and he wanted to take as many of us as he could. But we saw the grenade and hacked off his hand with a machete. We come back in the firebase and get a new mission for the next day.

We are off the next morning at 0800 hours. No sniper fire this time. That doesn't mean there weren't any gooks watching out side the perimeter. Some times, they won't shoot at five guys traveling through the jungle they will wait for a much larger unit to attack and erase from the equation. It's not worth it to die or give up their location for only five. We are happy about that. We leave out of the North side of the FSB and travel down about 200 meters where we turn to circle it then when get to the South we head out on our mission. We find several sandal tracks about 200 meters out and they look fresh, maybe last nights. We call in our findings and are told to proceed on our mission. At 1100 hours, we stop for a lunch break. A can of Beans and Weenies is what I have. After lunch, we head out towards our objective almost on the fence. I light up a cigar to help settle my nerves a little. Something doesn't feel right about this mission, but I don't know what. We are not to go over the fence, which is just about 100 meters from us. So we can observe the Gooks in what they might think as a Safe Haven. We want to spot them, then depending on their size and what they have with them call in a fire mission for the 155's and up to an Arc Light. We get to our Objective at 1405 hours and call in some 155's on our tail. That was in case someone was following us. The artillery guys fire their usual night harassment fire towards the enemy. All except where we were, they do fire pretty close to us, so the gooks won't think there are any of us guys out here. On the third day we spot, what we think was that wheeled object they had that we couldn't find. It's a small howitzer, may be a 75 mm gun. Not large enough to hit any of our fire support bases but they could use it for troop support up to a little under ten thousand or so meters. We get a grid on where this gun is and call in a fire mission without smoke. We talk to TOC and tell them what we have found and they agree with us that we might only have this one chance to get it. So we give an order of six HE rounds and two Willie-peters .We watch as the rounds hit within twenty feet of the gun then the next one side swipes it. Then the two Willy peters hit right along side. We call the artillery guys and tell them they did well. We watch with our field glass as the enemy moving around by the gun. We notice one of them is searching the area with his field glasses and they are searching for us. We must move. Chief heads out with us following, we must get as far away from our location but we also must not be seen while doing so. We call into TOC and tell them what we have seen. They tell us to get out of that area as quickly as we can, that in about an hour they will pepper this area with more 155 rounds. But to be very careful, if they have spotted us and called in our location there might be a bunch of these little Asian guys looking for us. This was what we had started so we had a little head-start on what they wanted us to do. We head out in a straight line back towards the FSB. We don't run into any more tracks or Gooks, time has taken its toll on us. We are close to walking in but it's almost pitch black when we stop out side of the perimeter that we will walk in tomorrow morning.

We call in to TOC and tell them where we are, they tell us to stay where we are and the bunker we are in front of is told where we are and that they are not to blow Clay mores nor shoot at anything right in front of them, We are only about 50 meters from the cleared area just before the wire. If we had been Gooks, we could very easily have gotten a couple shots off into this bunker before anyone noticed us. When daylight comes, we must go home. We call into TOC and tell them to tell the guys on the perimeter we will be standing up then heading home and for them not to blow their Claymores nor shoot at us. We stand up 50 meters from the dirt before the wire and only 100 meters from their bunker. We find the hole in the fence and walk in to their bunker. We were lucky that no one at this perimeter that his sight was sharp enough to locate us as we are crawling up on them. They could have put a nasty scratch or two on each of us.

We did find a rucks sack and besides some ragged clothes there was some paper. We have is what looks like a letter from one of the gooks we killed. None of us could read Vietnamese so we shrug it off as something we won't find what was said. We turn the letter to the TOC; they have an interrupter that reads Vietnamese. After we go to supper, we are asked if we knew what the letter said? None of us did and he reads it out loud so everyone can hear it. The letter starts out.

> My darling wife, it has been 3 long years since I have seen you, or hold you in my arms. How are the children? It has been so long since I have seen them. I bet they are pretty big by now. I can't wait to see you. I don't know when my time is up or how long I must suffer out here in this hot, steamy, dirty jungle, which is nothing like where we lived once. These Americans they come at us screaming and firing their weapons at anything that moves. Their bombs fall from the sky even when you don't see any planes dropping them. Our Party

member here gives us classes every week on how these Americans eat our young, and don't worship any god. They take no prisoners and if you are captured you will be thrown out of a flying helicopter to your death. I saw it happen last week. We would rather die fighting than be subjected to such a horrible type of death. I hope to see you and my sons in the up coming year. With all of my love,

Doi,

I actually shed a tear when this guy at Battalion read that to us. These people are human beings with the same fears, wants, and the never dying need to eliminate us because they were taught that we were going to give them back to the French. I think that during our Civil War if we heard that England would get us back if the South won, Oh Boy would we fight to keep that from happening. But we have to view them as less or we might start feeling compassion towards these little bastards and end up giving them a first shot. They might actually get off a burst and instead of just killing you; they get 3 or 4 of your buddies and maybe you also. What they really would like to do is get 4 or 5 of your buddies all jacked up then letting you think about what you did to get these people murdered. Well now we know why the gooks treat us like child eaters, they think we are. It doesn't change a thing in how we react to a Gook in the jungle. All we want to do is come home alive and in one piece. If I thought one minute that the next Gook that I see isn't going to try and harm me, he could keep trucking his way home.

But he thinks I'm a really bad person. Just like, we are told of the Gooks doing things to our wounded and our dead, to disrespect them. By cutting off their penises and slipping into the dead mans mouth. I've never seen that happen but I was told that before I got here and after I got here. So do you believe it or not? We are to set out looking for any wounded gooks that have left the battle sight and might lead us to a hospital on this side of the fence. There is either someone hurt real badly or a bunch of wounded gooks ahead. We move as swiftly as we dare. It's been about 800 meters since the battle site when we come across two gook bodies lying in some brush. They were all tore up. But there are other blood trails leaving this spot. We call in and tell Mumford what we found. He asks if we found any papers to send them in. All that we say is as soon as the mailman gets here we will send them to him. Just for that, second Mumford thought he was back home. It happens sometimes. We now are back on the trail of the bloody people. For the Gooks to carry someone this far he must be an officer. This must be someone important enough that they would risk their lives hauling him around. There is the possibility of it being some ones brother that is wounded. It's getting dark and the jungle is thicker as we follow these blood trails.

Then all of a sudden they are gone; no blood trails nor footprints, nor broken twigs. We call in and are told to be very careful there is liable to be a lot of gooks hiding out in this area. We come upon an area that looks like it is well traveled and just might be the one clue we are need to find this sanctuary that the gooks have here in the thick jungle. Van finds an old bandage and we follow a trail of dried up blood to the side of a hill. We sit and wait not making any sound. About 20 meters away we spot a couple gooks. They look like they are guarding something that they don't want anyone to see. We watch as a couple bushes are moving and a cave is exposed to us. It appears to be the hospital we have been looking for some time now. Ronnie gets on the horn and calls in for some flyboys to come in and destroy this little Mayo clinic that the gooks seem to have. We have to leave because there is going to be a lot of cash spread over this hill. We decide we will sneak out of this darkness that has engulfed us into the jungle. We call in with the grid of this area and are told there will be a couple million dollars spent on that area tomorrow. They have called in an arc light to strike tomorrow morning so we are to get as far away from that spot that we can.

On the way out, we run across another wounded gook. This one has a piece of shrapnel hanging out of his upper back thigh. We go up to him and he speaks English better than some of the Hill Billy's we have in our unit. He tells us that 4 hours ago we went by him as he was hiding in some thick brush. When he heard us coming back he decided to surrender. We give him a cigarette and ask who he is? He was a fricking Major in the NVA and he's an Engineer that has designed and built most of the bunkers and tunnels out here. He was drafted about three years ago and this is the first chance he has had to surrender not at a fight. He tells us he saw some gooks try to surrender and they were shot down in the heat of the battle, we believe him. You don't always have the time to secure the prisoner and you can't let him go. So usually you waste them figuring if he's dead he can't kill you. This is another example of war not being fair. When we call in this Major who just so happens to be the one that knows where the bunker systems are and how well fortified they are and where they stock pile their ammo, he tells us he doesn't know where the hospital is, but that cave we spotted was where they are hiding a couple 75mm howitzers and some ammo for them. The arc light starts early am and we watch as the entire side of that mountain is engulfed into a pile of broken trees and dirt flying in all directions. Where that cave was we couldn't be sure, but one thing we could be sure about was, they aren't going to be using those pieces of artillery nor the caves again.

We each get a promise of a seven day R&R to be taken any where in the Pacific Area of Operations. Anyway that's what my and Ronnie's orders say. Remember Ronnie was the company clerk back at Ft. Benning, he typed my orders to come to Nam and he said if we get caught what are they going to do? Send us to Vietnam?" I forge some Generals signature on them and we are off. We have to go before someone figures out that the orders are forged, that they might keep us in jail here in country or put us out in the dark jungle by ourselves, but no one is going to stop us and tell us this looks forged to him. We are going to have a grand time. On my R & R, I went to Taipei. Ronnie and I decide to leave on the next bird flying towards home. Then we decide against that neither of our families would want us to desert during a time of war and we would miss out on the parade welcoming us back, then we would have to hide the rest of our lives. So we catch the next plane out. It's going to Okinawa and we only had a couple hundred dollars between us. I guess we were quite drunk for 6 or 7 days. We really don't remember much about while we were there. I can remember going out to a beach where the Marines landed 20 some years ago. I was in Naha for 6 of the 7 days and I went sight seeing that one-day. I sent some pictures home but my Mom says she never received them. I was drunk and might not have the correct address or something on the package. We would have stayed longer but we ran out of money and the only place we could eat free was a mess hall at a Marine Air Base. And we had to show papers to eat there. We really must eat at least once a day or close to that.

So on our seventh day we were told the next plane to Vietnam was leaving in an hour and for us to be on it. Sounded like they meant it so we got aboard a C 130 headed back to Cam Rah Bay and from there back to the Camp Enari then caught a chopper to Dakto. We have a picture of each of us wearing white jeans, some sort of a robe and a large straw hat. Neither of us remembers where we purchased such finery or did we steal them? We gave them back I guess, because when we got to Pleiku, we no longer had them in our possession. I guess we had one hell of a time? Wish I remembered some of it besides the Marine mess hall at the airfield. The Marine airmen eat real well. They have a pretty good social life from what we could see. But I bet none of them could have as much fun as what we had, wish I could remember it, oh well I still have those pictures somewhere. Ronnie and I get back in time for us to go on another mission. Oh! Joy-for-joy. They want us to try and get another Gook officer. Maybe we could get an infantry officer this time. We don't worry too much about it. We weren't the John Wayne type. We were very fortunate that the last guy wanted to be captured and he spoke better English than some of the guys in some of the Line Companies. We get a hot meal and a bunch of handshakes for the capture. Then we have to go back to reality and get ready for our next mission. At the TOC, we get briefed and told we are going into a place where no American Forces have been for several months, so there might be a large herd of Gooks in the area.

The 5 of us slip out of the firebase at 0600 hours and head down a finger where there was a trail a long time ago. We find the trail. It doesn't look like any one has been down it in at least a month. It's hard to tell because the jungle grows so fast and swallows up all. We follow it a little further and we come to an old bunker system. It doesn't look like a gook unit, maybe a French mine from when they were fighting in the 1950's? Either way this place doesn't appear to have been visited by in the last couple of months if not longer. We call it in with the grid and are told it was at one time a French company size perimeter that the gooks used as a rest stop to and from the fence line. It probably hasn't been used in a couple months. It was supposedly destroyed by artillery a couple months ago. Guess they were wrong! Ronnie is in front of me by 10 meters and I have a M16, along with enough C 4 to blow up a howitzer if we run up on one. I only have two blasting caps plus enough fuse for both hour on one, or half and hour for two. But this mission we haven't run into any thing that even looks gook to us. The other team members are all carrying M16 and 1 M79. We figure to sit by this trail and observe anything that goes by. After two days and nights all we have to report is that there are about a dozen monkeys up in the trees here and a couple of large dark colored snakes, other than that not much going on. We are told to come in from the other side that we left in.

We get about 300 meters from the firebase when we turn west to try to circumvent any enemy troops in the area. We really don't need any body count today. We are going to head straight for the entrance to the firebase. While on this travel, we run into some fresh Uncle Ho's sandal prints headed up towards the firebase. We call in to let any one on the perimeter that if they hear a noise in front of them it's a 50-50 chance of being us. We creep up towards the perimeter noting this is going right up to the clearing before the wire. As we come to a clearing where we can see down into the valley to our West we see a beautiful scene of fog rising from the rivers and the hot sun shining through the fog. It's quiet impressive, most of this country I would have enjoyed to visit as a civilian.

Ronnie all of a sudden stops and points to our right where there are three NVA sitting down and watching a small group of Americans clowning around on their bunker. We get one on each side of the boys and shout Chieu hoi and these three smart gooks drop their weapons and we tell the perimeter guys not to fire at us. We finally get the gooks to come in to TOC and that's the last I heard of them. The guys on the bunkers don't realize that almost daily someone is always watching them and when they feel the need, they will take a shot or two at you if you aren't paying attention each day that you are out in the open. There never is a time when I feel totally secured while out there, either in the fire support base or out on a mission where we could walk up into an ambush that might end it all for the five of us. Maybe while playing horseshoes? You have to have some sort of an out, to keep what little bit of sanity is left.

I have seen a gook come flying out of a chopper before. If he was thrown out or slipped and fell I don't really care, he should have talked, and it's as simple as that. It might be against the Geneva Convention but who's keeping score anyway? We didn't get another leave for these guys that we captured, which is a good thing for us. We never ask to go on a mission to capture one again, we feel we were just lucky to get that prisoner and not get caught ourselves, or even killed dead. But we are going on a recon mission tomorrow. So we get a good night's sleep and a couple good meals before we as Apache 2 head south for 800 meters then west for 300 meters and we were told to call in when we get to a certain grid. We get there in about an hour and we are told to go to the base of a finger going up to a ridge that choppers had seen a number of gooks at. That could be a correct statement or it could be true; but it can't be both. They might have seen something moved and called in several gooks or they might have seen one or two and called in several. The reason I say this is because usually several gooks won't stand out in the open while a chopper is near by. But who knows anything that is always done?

Ronnie leads and we slowly move down this side of the hill that we have gone down 5 or 6 times before. You would be surprised to see how much a thick jungle can change in a few days. After we get down about 500 meters, we stop and get a couple hours sleep before going to our spot. They want us to go over to the next ridgeline and set up an ambush sight, maybe we could get a clear shot at some one in charge. Maybe we won't see anything but we were told at our meeting last night that no friendly people in this area and we are to treat anyone out here with us as enemy. As soon as the sun comes up, we are on the move. We go very slowly as not to draw attention to our movements; we don't want to startle any monkeys, birds or gooks. We sit up a spot within the area they have given us to set up in. We would really like a cup of coffee right now. Ronnie says I don't do well without a cup of coffee in the early morning". But we can't start a fire and cold instant coffee is not a treat to any of us. We decide we can light up a smoke as long as we keep the light up under our flop hats. Works out fine, after 3 hours we see our first monkey. He's not very impressed with us, pays no attention to us. That is a good thing, if he had spotted us and started screaming we would have had to leave. But he stays quiet most of the night. Off in the distance we can hear an Arc Light going off in a near-by valley. Some other Battalion must have called it in or it might have been one of those jobs where a couple of B52's got called off their target and they have this arsenal to drop before they return to Guam. When morning comes, we were told to go to a village about 1500 meters to our west and set up with the ARVN Colonel that is in command of that post. We don't have to follow his orders but if we refuse, we might accidentally get killed if probed. We let two people sleep and take turns at watching both from outside the perimeter to watching our backs as well. It's been reported that at least 60% of the ARVN's here are really either Viet Cong or North Vietnamese Regulars waiting for that moment when we let our guard down. We end up having to pull rank on the ARVN Colonel, so we can call in Artillery around the outskirts of their perimeter. Lucky for us we don't get probed and walk away from this village hopefully never to return. That was more frightening than attacking a hill full of Enemy Troops. At least while attacking you know who the enemy was.

Van is walking Point today and I'm the Tail gunner in the rear. We are in an area that was just last week controlled by the 32nd NVA Inf. Regiment and has moved to the West towards the Laotian border. But they left some people behind and we are to find them and punish them for being in our way.

Next time while the gooks are running for cover they might decide to cuddle up with us behind some large root system. Lt. Jack or John North is competing with his brother to get some rank. Why did their sibling rivalry had to have us in the equation? His brother Oliver is in the Marines. We don't want any medals that would put our lives in harms way. I just don't want to be one of his Hero's that dies so he can get credit for something I or one of the guys I was a friend with gets killed so he gets rank. Now Lt. Hadley wanted rank and he did push you to your limit but he knows when to push and when to pull. Our next mission we are supposed to try and get a prisoner. O.K. we wonder if this guy is another lifer? We find out this is a Grizzly deal. I guess G2 found out that a couple of us were just plain unintelligent and they need a prisoner real bad. They are offering a reward, depending on what rank the gook is. But our next two missions are not productive as getting a prisoner; we do capture a map, but no live gooks. We get two KIA's to our credit. This area is getting to be heavily populated with gooks that could be a bad thing. During one of our information meeting we are told that the gooks are building up in this area and we don't know what for at this time so would we please get a prisoner for G2. All of us say we'll try, but it's a lot more dangerous bring in one alive than killing him. The next 5 missions aren't fruitful as far as getting a prisoner but we are seeing signs of a big troop build up. We are at Fire Base 6, which we call 1338. We get some information captured from a NVA NCO. Re-written in English so we can read and hopefully learn. It really hits home. The gooks have drawn plans on how to attack an American Fire Base Camp. They have on this map a diameter 250 meters, perimeter of 800 meters, a list of the howitzers and mortars and even a red cross on the map showing where our first aid station is. There also is a note written in Vietnamese but changed to English by G2 U.S. forces in Vietnam are disposed in large fixed installations, which always provide our forces with lucrative targets. Our forces are always certain that as long as the weapons hit the installation, the U.S. forces will lose equipment, and manpower. Likewise these large posts don't have sufficient forces to control the surrounding country side, which makes these attacks easier." That's that in a nutshell.

This paper goes on to say, the use of booby traps also has had a long lasting affect on the psychological impact not knowing if your next step is your last. Also, the fact that a NVA or VC could take a shot at you, killing one or two then running into a village and you can't distinguish them from noncombatants. Also the many different booby traps, most of them were of U.S, origin, dud bombs, discarded ammunition and munitions and indigenous resources such as bamboo, mud, coconuts, and venomous snakes. Doesn't sound too good for us kids now do it?

The Division is handing out papers that will give a lesson in what the gooks call NVA Hill Trap Maneuvers. Their plan is to draw American forces into a set of meat grinder battles near their supply bases and sanctuaries. They have worked this maneuver out and while it cost them, more men than whom the trap is set on. They achieve their goal of causing a large amount of body bags to be sent home.

At 0800 hours, 26 Feb. 68 a heavy artillery preparation was placed in the primary landing zone at YB833 277. B Company was to take the initial assault followed by A company, it was planned to secure the landing zone located at YB832 277, and then with a defensive position, conduct limited company size operations to the northeast, northwest and south of the objective area. At 0843 hours the artillery shifted and the first lift of 5 troops with B Company, 1st Platoon Leader and B Company's Forward Observer, landed on the LZ. Forty-seconds later, as the 2nd ship went into the LZ a heavy volume of automatic weapons fire struck it; the pilot was forced to crash land, completely blocking the LZ. The 5 troops and 4 crewmen moved into a bomb crater and were engaged by approximately 25 NVA from the top of the objective 50 meters to the west. The Battalion Commander ordered gun-ships to engage this force and direct the other troop ships into an alternate LZ at YB831 279. B Company's Commander was aboard the 1st ship into this LZ and encountered no difficulty, but the 2nd ship took hits from automatic weapons fire from the wooded knoll at YB829 282. The pilot was wounded and the co-pilot flew through the LZ without landing. The Company Commander and 4 men moved into a bomb crater under enemy fire from several directions. Both groups were heavily pressed and artillery could not be employed, as the 2 were only 100 meters apart with the objective between. The artillery did fire on the wooded knoll while the gun ships had expended their ammunition at 0930 hours and returned to Dakto to re-arm. The enemy fire increased and the group with the 1st platoon leader began taking casualties, meantime a heavy artillery preparation was fired into the enemy position northwest of the alternated LZ, at 1000 hours the gun ships returned and the assault resumed, 1 hour and 17 minutes after the attack the enemy withdrew into the darkness of the thick under brush of the jungle floor. The Tet truce was violated at 1946 hours by launching a sizable mortar attack against the Peanut and hill 900 was probed throughout the night.

The attack against our Battalion on 30 Jan. 68 between 1710 and 2210 hours, FSB # 25 received more than 60 rounds of 82mm and 120mm mortar fire, which resulted in 8 causalities. At 1847 hours a total of 34 rounds impacted on the Peanut," and hill 900. On 31 Jan. the Peanut was abandoned and A and D companies moved down to the Dak Poko River to deny the

NVA a crossing site into the airfield at Dakto. At 1145 hours, a convoy was ambushed between FSB#13 and Ben Het. LTC Hendrix (Grizzly) was in his chopper directing artillery and mortar fire to break contact with about 100 to 150 NVA. We were sitting at the FSB#13 and waiting for orders, we get an order from some Lt. At Battalion ordering our recon platoon to send in a team to figure out what the enemy strength is, Mumford, good old Mumford speaks up "You already know you have a strong enemy unit that is dug in well, why do you need 5 more dead troops to prove that point?" The Lt. said he didn't look at it that way. Grizzly popped in just in time to hear Mumford give his little speech and agreed with him. But if the whole platoon went, he would O.K. that move Grizzly likes to use the recon platoon as a small light infantry company and we do a good job acting as such. But we must be able to react as a small unit in a big units fight. Back to the important facts, we still must relieve those 20 men out there stranded in an old bomb crater. The new LZ is big enough for 1 chopper to land at a time. They land and the troops dismount and they back in the air in less than 10 seconds. We have a gun ship that has reached their spot in hell. When asked what he could do? He was told that if he could hit that tree line while these choppers bring in reinforcements and much needed ammo we would be much satisfied. The enemy fire increased, as heavy automatic weapons began an attack of their own. All we could do at this point was listen in on the war going on, there was a wooded knoll where this heavy weapons fire was coming from. We had a Forward observer in a small bird flying over and directing artillery on the wooden knoll. He also called in 4 deuce mortars to a knoll on the other side of B Company, as there were a large number of gooks preparing an attack on B Company. It would nearly wipe out most of B Company.

We are all in what the enemy likes to call their Hilltop Maneuver. The same plan that they are using at Khe Shan now. Now all of B Company is on the ground, in heavy contact and needing re supplied already. While right behind B Company was A Company lead by our old platoon leader Lt. Hadley. He seems to volunteer his unit for jobs no one else wants. I only hope someday he doesn't get his wish to be at a big battle and come out on top. Big battles you stand a bigger chance of someone getting off that lucky shot that isn't lucky for you at all. At 0800 hours Feb 27 68, B Company was preparing to leave the perimeter to search the wooded knoll when 6; 82mm mortars struck the middle of their perimeter. At 0810 hours, our Recon platoon was inserted into the perimeter. At 0820 hours A Company reported heavy movement to the south near a trench line at YB 833 275, in a few seconds enemy troops were seen moving to assault the hilltop. Close artillery concentrations were immediately fired and adjusted. The FO was directing the big guns, 155 mm howitzer. A company was directing the 105mm howitzers. B Company was shuttled into the alternate LZ followed by the rest of A company. When a sufficient number of troops were on the ground from A and B Companies, our recon platoon began the assault on the crest of the hill, 3 platoons of B Company deployed on line and moved directly up the slope. Our platoon was right behind them in the assault. As we neared the crest, enemy fire increased in intensity, slowing the attack. Gun ships were called in to fire on the wooded knoll at 1130hours. B Company's 2nd platoon breached a section of the trench line and our platoon secured the area they left.. At 1232 hours, the small group that we were and the 1st platoon were relieved by the 4th platoon of A Company. Our recon platoon joined up with the remainder of B Company and basically, we would follow them to hell if we must. We had artillery now firing at the side of the hill that the gooks would be using for retreat into Laos, We come to this bunker that is larger than the others, our Apache Team starts in when we hear voices inside. Now these people are not speaking the Kings English.

So as we enter the main room there are 5 or 6 gooks all tearing up and burning paper. So we waste them and put out the fires. When Lt. Hadley walked into the bunker, he was upset that we didn't capture 1 of them alive. I told him that we couldn't tell which one of them was trying to surrender or not. Going by the way, they all raised their rifles towards us. He was happy to get all the funny papers that we saved from burning. Also, there was a PRC 25 that was on our frequency so these NVA were listening in on our conversations. Which means at least 1 of those guys spoke English? The fighting then slowed down considerably and down to where there was none.

We have secured the area we will call home this evening. We all find a place to sleep and pull guard during the night. In the early morning, we are called back to the Firebase. The adrenaline keeps your body rushing and because you are scared 24/7 it is always there. When you run low of it you fall to pieces, you actually have a hard time getting up from a position where you were lying down. The higher up in rank think that they have to push you every day and night that you are out in the bush. If they let up on you for just 1 minute that might be the minute, you need to have it all over you for your staying alive. They are trying to keep you from cracking, once that happen it's all over. You can no longer be a person to get them a body count; it's a numbers game. We have to kill 10 of them for each one of us to keep the folks back home content and satisfied that we are winning this war. They don't understand that a Guerilla type war you fight till you kill enough of their men that the Ma and dad's tell their government enough is enough. Now I don't see that happening in North Vietnam but it could very well happen back home in the world.

We are getting shelled again, only this time they are getting awfully close to several of what would be called, a major hit. Something that could change our little parts in this little Asian war. They are coming close to the Ammo dump, TOC and the Artillery placements, which are somewhere, we don't need them to hit! We get word that the TOC has been hit with a 120mm rocket and the main radio had been knocked out. We now have no communications with TOC, which is vital for our support while we are out playing soldier. Apache 2 and Apache 4 are both out on a mission. We call and tell them that they can't call Battalion for a while but they still can call in Artillery and Mortars and they can contact us to get any new instructions. This should be taken care of in an hour or 2. TOC sends a runner down to our bunkers and tells Lt. North that he needs the remaining teams to go out and find the gook FO, other wise this guy was going to rid themselves of us. That would be bad for moral, and my Mother would not like it too well. So Apache1 and Apache 5 head out looking for either 1 set of FO's or more. After a couple of minutes, the mortars are shifted to our area. That meant to us that we must have been getting close to where the FO's are. We stop and scan the treetops until we spot half a foot through the foliage. We wait a couple minutes and sure enough that guy up in that tree looks out from the leaves and branches he had concealed himself with, 3 of us open up into the tree and 1 gook rolls out while another one gets 2 shots off. Lucky for us he was left of center when he fired on us.

Then Rex hits him with a HE round from his M79. Along with this guy comes his funny papers, a radio with head set, a SKS and a pack that the radio was in. Their sharp shooting days are gone. So that we have saved this little part of the war, we can go to the nearest creek or pond and throw out our line and fish till we were content. Maybe spend a week or 2 out there with a bottle of whiskey and a box of cigars. This area was built to be lived in that way and I guess those that actually lived there lived that way until this war tore everything apart.

In April 1968, we get a Stars and Strips and in it, LBJ our President gives a speech. Tonight, I ordered our aircraft and naval vessels to make no attacks on North Vietnam, except in the area north of the DMZ where the continuing enemy buildup directly threatens allied forward positions and where the movement of their troops and supplies are clearly related to that threat. With Americans sons in the fields far away, with Americas future under challenge right here at home, with our hopes and the Worlds hopes for peace in the balance everyday, I do not believe that I should devote an hour or a day of my time to any personal partisan or to any duties other than the awesome duties of this office the Presidency of your country. Accordingly,

I shall not seek, and I will not accept the nomination of my party for another term as your President."

Well now we will be getting a new President next   year, it doesn't make a difference to me; I'll be back home in the world when we get a new Commander in Chief and out of the Army within a year, I only hope he doesn't change the   way we were selected to go to the Nam. I don't want to come back there for anytime soon.

CHAPTER NINETEEN - GILBERT LEAVES US

Some big wig officer showed up at the firebase and told us We were told we were not to fire at anyone out and about in the jungle until fired at, we dismissed that as an asinine statement, I thought about what he said for a couple of minutes then I figured I'd shoot anyone out and about in this jungle. You can't tell friend from foe, sometimes there is a mixture of both in a unit roaming out in the jungle-covered mountains. What are they going to do? Send me to Vietnam? Oh well. Xin Loi we get another radio transmission where D company is at FSB 6, which is under a siege consisting of a small company of NVA.

The group that was fighting in the Tumerong valley are now trying to escape through the pass at Tan Canh and to disappear by allowing the thick jungle to swallow them into it. While the gooks were on the run they drop an awful lot of weapons and uniforms that was so they can merge with the local people and work their way to the border of Cambodia or Laos. While on a patrol in the area east of Dakto, we pick up several SKS's a few AK47's even two handheld rocket grenade launchers and twelve RPG rounds and at least fifty clean and pressed uniforms. We get a message from TOC that they want us to come back to Dakto 2. But they want us to stop outside of Tan Canh to be a blocking force for the gooks retreating from the ARVN attack at Tumerong. TOC tells us there are several of the gooks headed our way and we will have full fire power support and we should be able to rid this earth of their evil existence, .D company is still under siege at FSB 6 and A company is sending two platoons to try and attack the gooks from the rear and by out flanking them to break the siege. . But there still is some sniper fire, which makes for a real uneasy day. The easy day happens but not without paying a huge price. D company lost thirty-five men KIA and WIA. The two platoons of A company that didn't go to the flanking action were sent to reinforce the 1/22 infantry that also was under siege. April 29 an officer of A company was captured during the attack. But both of his captures were KIA when an artillery shell struck near them while they were eating a mid day meal of rice and dried fish.

Sounded like a fishy story to us. We get air lifted back to TOC and are told by our CO, Lt Col. Jamie Hendrix The concept of employment was for light recon to locate the enemy and report, light recons are 5 men or less patrols. When we set up the ambush Mumford calls on the horn to tell us good-bye, he's going to go home, be discharged from the army and spend his remaining years fishing but no hunting. His hunting days are over, he told us he was on the hunt of all hunts while they're in Vietnam, when you go out in the jungle with 4 other guys and hunt those hunting you. There is no greater hunt. It was a sad, but happy day for us. Everyone liked Mumford, Gilbert was his first name, if anyone was to have a first name, and then Gilbert was he. We wonder whom they will send us to take Gilberts place? Right about this time I find out I made E-5, a SGT, now I monthly pay will be $378, not a whole lot seeing the dangers we come across, almost every mission. Darrel has enough rank as an E-6 but not that much time left and I don't foresee him extending to play with us another six months. We sit up an ambush knowing that unless provoked we will not be pulling off this ambush. We are very lucky, as we don't have to pull the ambush but instead watch some very funny monkeys play in the treetops. It's amazing what we find to amuse ourselves and it is a safe period of amusement for if some gooks would venture into our AO the monkeys would go nuts and alert us that someone is coming. We had been there long enough that we were old news so they are bored with us. Our Apache team goes on our mission and we get results, it starts out as we had our night position set up and before supper, we get three gooks strolling along with their rifles on their shoulders without a care in the world. I remember how I felt as we were waiting for these 3 to walk into our kill zone, my palms were sweating as were my forehead and my heart was pounding. My trigger finger almost felt as if it was cramped and I didn't know if I was going to be able to squeeze the trigger, my finger wants to shoot now but my brain tells me to wait until we know that there aren't a hundred of them behind these three kids. They can't be but fifteen years old apiece. Chief on this patrol keeps looking my way, like I'm the one to start this song and dance. Jerry (Pluto) is convinced that there is only the three of them. So we open up and the first guy is wounded but escapes the mass of flying lead that we put forth. This point man gook stumbles. Although I killed him with a second burst with my M16, one of the guys blew a claymore that pushed his mangled body on top of my rifle and me. I thought there for a minute that he was attacking me so I pulled out my bayonet and stabbed him three or four times. I roll him over and see that he has been killed dead for some time; time goes so slow when this happens. My heart was pounding twice as much when he fell on top of me. We go to the bodies and find one sheet of funny papers nothing else. Their weapons were so old I doubt any would fire. But these three kids hadn't a care in the world. Now all they have to worry about is if there is a Hell they are on their way. We only blew one claymore so we have to retrieve the others that we didn't blow then get the hell out of here as quickly as possible. We now hear monkeys and birds going Ape shit as if there was a whole herd of gooks headed our way.

We collect our things and are gone at least five minutes before we hear bugles, there might be a Battalion there now. We quickly make a booby trap of our own; I put a grenade inside an empty C-ration can with the pin pulled, then a trip wire along our way of escape. When someone trips this wire, it will pull the grenade out releasing the firing pin and in 4.5 seconds, we have dead gook ala-carte. Not good to eat, but oh boy is it great to go watch Chief is stopped for a second to inform TOC where we are and that several gooks are chasing us and we need a shield of artillery behind us. If we can just slow these boys down, we won't have to kill a bunch of them. They get one more chance to go home to momma-san. If they follow into the killing zone, they will be buried with just their names.

We are running as fast as we dare. We could be running into a group of these little guys and they may have our scalps on their tent post. Not that they would really scalp you. It's just a relative term. But I have seen where a gook has castrated a G.I. and laid his penis on his chest. Hell, they might scalp us. we run into2 other gooks at the trunk of a tree and they come out guns a blasting. We open up on the 2 of them all at once, 1 has joined his brothers. The other one runs away and we don't chase after him. The radio that these Gooks had is a Russian radio and it has several frequencies written on the side of it. This may be a piece of the Great Puzzle that Intelligence has been waiting for? There is another one up in a tree; maybe he has something that might help us to determine what these papers mean.

I had to climb that tree to retrieve some funny papers. It wasn't a good climb considering there still were enemies in the area. But it had to be done. There are a lot of things that must be done by someone. As a team leader you must decide who is the man, who do you think could get the job done the best? Now you have to worry about any other enemy that might be around, Will the guy you pick be spotted by some enemy patrol? Will he, if he spots an enemy patrol, will he open up on them? This would give your position away. Now you have 15 seconds to determine your picks. Hopefully the person you pick won't resent you picking him. Because if he believes you consider him as cannon fodder, he won't go that extra to get you home alive. After all, of this very risky business when we find nothing on the guy we climb the tree. There is too much of a risk that someone has spotted us. Which could mean they are on their way.

After we leave this area we come across a gook that is dead, he looks like some artillery round caught up with him. It ended what might have been a very hard life. This guy looks about 30 but his I.D. says 17 and the I.D. he has on him is an ARVN card. Either this guy was killed on some mission, or he wasn't supposed to be there at that spot and one of our H & I shots got him. I vote that he was a deserter from some ARVN group and was trying to make it back home. He was at the wrong place at the wrong time. He has several shrapnel wounds. We call this in and we get the body count. I often think that if I were to die out here I would like to think I would be more than a number in some officer's head that has a real skate of a job. But I guess someone has to keep score. After all, we have to know who wins this game or test, don't we? After we leave the tree fight, we run across a dead NVA soldier that was carrying a canvas brief case. We call it in and are told to open it very causality it might have a booby trap in it. We grab hold of the canvas bag and toss it against a tree, nothing happens. I open it a little, kind of real slow. I've heard too many stories about booby traps from these little yellow skinned bastards. Rex grabs it away from me and opens it to find 3 pieces of what looks like a set of what to do orders along with some funny papers with some marks on it. This could be a good thing. When we call it in, Intelligence sounds real happy that what we have sounds like some Division level orders and we are to make sure these get in, the maps inside of it may have been a plant job. Or it could be a real map with real information in it. Of course, all of these things might be possible, but why bring it up that way? Did they take that away from us just so they could find it to be a good map but they don't want us to know it? For what ever reason?

We are always wondering what is the thought behind what ever we are told to do. How do we know we are not putting our lives in Harms way for no Military assignment that would enhance our status or benefit anyone in a military situation? We don't like exposing ourselves to danger just for some Lifer Major to get his CIB for being on the radio during our massacre. Anyone that says it doesn't happen, they need to pull their heads out of their ass and smell something other than that load of shit. We have everything in our rucks and when the chopper lands for them, the 5 of us jump in. As he is arguing that us being picked up isn't in his orders. About that time, we catch a couple rounds from what sounds like an old M1 carbine. That ends the conversation and we are up and ready. The door gunner fires back at the 2 gooks we see. Both of them go on this guys notch mark on the choppers insides.

He has 32 KIA's assuming these are correct numbers? He brags on the number of kills that he has. He tells us how some of them might be civilians but they are all gooks. We ask if he has ever fired at something he has seen from along distance, without being able to know if these people were NVA, VC, and Americans on a patrol or civilians out trying to make a meal for their loved ones? He says nothing but I think he got the message. We arrive at the FSB and are told what a good leader the XO was in getting us out of danger, as the gooks were about to scalp us. We don't say a word; it wouldn't change anything except we now would have the XO and any other officers on our Asses. Maybe next time the chopper might turn up late, too late.

CHAPTER TWENTY - S/SGT MAGWOOD

We get to our bunker; turn everything over to our new Platoon S/SGT.. Magwood. And head for the mess hall tent. After we eat Lt. North comes over to where are eating and thanks us for doing our job. We tell him that's all we do, is our Job. He tells us that he also hopes this job is over and done with. But we must get off our break from the hassle of fighting a war that we ourselves don't agree with. But if you say something against any part of the war, you are a traitor in many eyes of the people that turn their head when something really bad happens. And you step up and confront these people for their actions, which are against the rules of warfare. We have had to shoot prisoners because we have no way of policing prisoners. Which could be contrived, as an unlawful act. But if we let them go, they might come back at you on a later date. We never were ordered to do such an act but we had to look at things like if we tie them up until someone else comes in to pick them up. They either get away when one of their own unties them or they become dinner for some tiger out looking for gooks tied to trees. If for some reason they get free by themselves, they come looking for you as soon as possible. Maybe even killing you dead or one of those first names of yours. A war isn't the place to talk the talk when you can't walk the walk. . Being Politically Correct isn't always the best for you out there in the triple canopy jungle infested with little people that try everyday to make your life miserable, or they would like to end your life, or maybe you become a prisoner of war for 10 years. We talk about these things all the time. I will not be captured if I can help it.

Sure, you feel like hell if you have to end someone's life. Or let them go, knowing they will probably kill someone that had a chance to live another day. That isn't a good deal either. But what are you supposed to do? We can't take them with us; if we call in a chopper to take him away we have to go also. We just gave our position away when the chopper lands. Sometimes we can't abort the mission and letting the enemy know where we are might lead to one of us if not all of us getting killed dead. We are going on another mission in the morning; we are to leave at 0530 hours while it is still dark. The people that are on LP tonight were told before we left that we would be coming out by them and further into the jungle.

They don't want anyone to see us leave. Before we get to 0500 hours, we are told that on the other side of the perimeter that they are being probed and that we should be very quiet when going out this morning. They haven't scrubbed the mission? This could get very ugly before the day even gets started. We get up to the bunker we are to leave from at 0515 hours and are calling on to the LP to remind them that we are coming out. They tell us that they haven't heard a single movement in front of them all night. We crawl out through the wire and to a spot about 10 meters from the LP's. We stand up to walk to the LP position and once there we get down as not to draw any attention toward these poor souls that, if we are attacked they will be the first to die, either by the gooks or by their own. During a human wave, assault there is so much running and shooting, screaming and sometimes the bugles. You really don't know what is happening to you or the guy on the other side of the perimeter may not know that you have movement to your front. So no one shoots us as we leave the perimeter and after passing the LP, we have a clear avenue to approach our mission. Which is for us to go close to the border at Cambodia and see what we can, and report all that we find. We get out to a point where we can start seeing where we are, because the sun is coming up. Even though the sun is pretty much up at 0730 hours this triple canopy keeps the light from reaching the ground. We go another 2,000 meters to our south then turn west towards the Cambodian border. The sun is full up and it's a little after noon when we call in the first time to get what orders there are for us. We are told to up along the Cambodian border about 250 meters from the actual fence and not to cross it at any reason. Well we say OK but different circumstances may change what we are willing to do or not to do. We go along this perimeter they have set up for us and don't see a thing going south. But when we get back on track and head North, we run into a Mortar team we see basking in the sun. Not a care in the world. We decide to screw up their sun bathing and really screw up their whole day. Rex lobs a couple grenades inside of their little country chat room they were having such a ball, and Rex had to piss in their Post Toasties. We finally have to get someone that is our enemy doing something they make impossible for us to do. Relax!! Sounds like something I could enjoy doing. But realize I will have to wait till August 25 1968 more or less. That and Jan. 23 1968 are important numbers to me. I was wounded on Jan. 23 1968 and plan on leaving this place on August 25.We don't actually see any NVA but we do see a few Viet Cong, Special Forces. They are called Dac Cong. We scare the hell out of them because the first that they know we are around is when we shoot all 5 of them. Special forces, they were a bunch of wannabe's. They are dead now and we have to figure why their Special forces would be out here in this part of the jungle? They were on Vietnam's side of the fence but only by 100 meters.

Their maps could be wrong or they were Special so maybe they couldn't read a map? We are told to come in away from the fence by at least 3,000 meters. It would be safer for us this way. We set up a pretty good hiding place. We can see 360 all around our spot and have several ways of escape in case we need it. We also have protection from mortars and artillery rounds, by a very large set of logs, which cover us from 3 sides. We are watching the sun go down, when Rex puts his finger to his mouth as if to tell us Quiet.

We get low and watch several gooks trespassing on our hill. We can't have that. But before we can react to them being here about 6 more show up then 12 more. We can't have them walk over to us, nor decide to make this their home for very long at all. We have Squatter's Rights. They can't stay here and they really can't keep coming! Before they get any closer, we get a hold of artillery and have them shoot up this hilltop. As soon as the first rounds hit some gooks start heading towards the safety of the logs that we are using for our protection and we aren't in the mood to share what we have. We throw 3 grenades' at them just as some artillery was going off. Grenades hit right at their feet and they never know if they were KBA or not. But they might think someone has spotted them to be able to call in a direct hit on them. We don't see any new NVA coming up into this knoll top. We have to make a decision as what to do when the gooks spot us? We call in requesting that we ditty maul (leave) the area.

We don't get the chance to vote on this. All 5 of us jump up and fire into the mass of human beings that die quickly and without much noise on their part. We quickly head down on another slope, after running at least a couple hundred meters. We are worn out but still alive and we were really in pretty good shape to be able to run those 200 meters with a full pack and down hill. But humping out here in this jungle makes you pretty strong and in good shape for what comes our way. None of us wants to take off again. We still have the same objective as when we started this mission. We call in and tell Battalion 6 RTO what has happened, where we are and have our plans changed? We are told that our plans have changed and we are to set up our homestead where we are and that hill we were on is going to become a target for the new gunners that have come to the 6/29 Artillery, we have a new gun crew and they would like to blow that hill away. So all through the night we hear boom, boom, booming all night long. They hit their target on their second try and totally covering that hill with craters from their shell bursting on the ground there. When the sun comes up, we are all ready to either get away from here, or make a cup of coffee. We get orders that at 0830 hours we are to meet a chopper back on that hill we blew to hell last night. I can't imagine anyone living through that barrage of Artillery. But just to make sure we call in a Willy peter round. Ronnie starts some water boiling and we had our cup of strong black coffee. Then we leave We get to the top in about 30 minutes, and there are still gooks that are alive, barely alive, but blood is still pumping through those veins and we must stop it, if for no other reason to put them out of their misery. We go through the gooks papers and we find some that are in English; I suppose to make us aware of their intentions. The first one reads; US forces in Vietnam are disposed in large fixed installations, which always provide our forces with lucrative targets. Our forces are always certain that as long as our weapons strike the installation the U.S. forces will lose equipment and manpower, likewise these large posts don't have sufficient forces to control the surrounding countryside. Which makes our attacks easier. Dien Bien Phu, the 7th of May 1954. The date of Viet Minh's and General Vo Nguyen Gaps victory over the French will repeat it's self. America is like France and we will prevail. So why are you willing to fight for a country that if you are black treats you less than a man If you are poor White Trash fighting to make your rich Politicians richer? These are like the Chieu Hoi that we send out and into known gook held areas. The Americans will fall prey to the Peoples Republic." These are papers that I assume the Vietnam writing on the other side says the same thing in Vietnamese, but the English side was meant for one more thing and us to read to think about. I sent a copy of some of the papers the enemy uses to try and convince us that we are invaders in their homeland and we are in the wrong to be here. I might give that a nod or two in the morning we wake up early, because the jungle has gotten real quiet and even the birds that usually wake us up are no longer around and that can only mean one thing. They're an awful lot of people hanging around outside our perimeter. As we are getting our first cup of coffee 6 rounds from an artillery piece hit us. More than likely it was a 75mm howitzer. Then we are getting movement to our west, then east and north. We are getting ready for the big attack; we grab extra grenades and extra M16 rounds. We get another 6 rounds from that artillery piece and the gooks start blowing the bugles and screaming into the megaphones. First, there are a couple gooks to our left then 6 in front then another 3 to the left. We are catching fire from our right now, sounds like AK 47's firing at us.

Then there are gooks to the front again we open up on them,. We fire into them and they are returning fire and hand grenades. We toss a few of our own, and then there are about 10 of them back at our right. All firing at us and screaming into those awful megaphones. First, there were a couple gooks to our left then another 3. We were catching fire from our right, sounds like AK47's . Then there were more in front of us. I look back to get another box of shells when I notice everyone's eyes are wide open and the skin on their faces appears to be stretched on like a lampshade. Now they are all in front of us firing into our bunker, making it hard on us to return fire, but we must or these little slant eyed bastards will over run our young asses and we won't know what it is to have grand children or anything worth living for. There are 4 no; 5 over to the left now there are 6 heading towards our middle. We call in mortars right up to our bunker line and after the sixth round, we raise up and continue firing into the mass of humanity, now we must fight back and push them of of their attack. Punish them for coming this way and do it in a way that they never want to mess with us again. It's a battle of will right now. Their will to take over this position and killing us all that would make head lines back home. And our will to ke these little yellow skinned bastards away from our perimetera making any that we don't kill believe that we have their number any time anywhere. We need to keep up this battle and not give way to their advances toward taking over our position and collecting our scalps. We don't believe that the Gooks actually take our scalps but several times we have come across a G.I. and his penis was cut off and dangling from his mouth.

For that they must learn to fear the 3/12 infantry of the 4th infantry Division. They must cry like little girls every time they hear of us. I can see some of the Recon Platoon up and firing into the mass of humanity that was trying to eliminate us. All of us are pumping blood very fast to our brains so that we need to slow down just a little or we fear our foreheads might burst open. We stand and advance toward the attacking enemy. Throwing them off guard because they were told we would run when they attacked. Like what the DI's told us about the enemy, as they would run from a fight with U.S. forces every time. All of us are pitching grenades at that mass and firing heart high at their advancing soldiers. We are catching fire from our left again. Now there are 8 of them right in front of us, we fire off 2 of the claymores and now the gooks are within 5 meters of the bunker next to us. We won't let that happen, so we get up behind our bunker where we can see more of what is going on and we all open up on the gooks headed for the bunker next to us. All of the gooks that had plans to be sitting in that bunker just had their plans changed by being killed dead. Then a RPG strikes the front of our bunker and another comes right behind it striking the inside. We all jump up to where we can see what is going on and first we fire in front of us then from side to side. Some of the gooks charge straight at us screaming but firing very little. We now have to counter attack them all the way down this hill we are on. We believe they are almost out of ammo and thought we would be an easy group that would wet themselves and run at the first sign of them attacking straight at us. But after maybe 30 or less minutes of this, what ever is left of these yellow bastards are running scared because we are chasing them screaming at the top of our lungs and slashing on the rear any of them that come within bayonet reach. We will take no prisoners today. The battle is complete after about an hour of hectic and mind blowing little battles that all added up to be the biggest battle I had be in. I didn't want to be in a bigger one, please don't make it happen again.

We didn't chase them too far; incase this is a trap. I know I lost about a couple lbs during this battle plus each of us lost our minds that night when you are as scared as we were, you didn't feel as if anything can save you. If you are not the victim during an attack, you are waiting your turn. That can wear you down real fast, you feel as if no matter what is done for you that you won't survive the next attack. There was this young kid from one of the line companies, he lost both of his arms and we were told he was also blind. I figure no matter what happens to me I won't be as bad off as this kid. I heard he was from Iowa out in the farm country. He will never be able to farm again, really, I can't think of much that he could do or enjoy. We did nothing rationally during the whole battle and we were so exhausted after the battle that we all slept maybe 5 minutes until some mothers son started to wake us. He thought it might be starting all over again. But no, it was only a couple wounded gooks trying to slip away. We come up to them and they show no resistance towards us and they are pretty well screwed up, might not last another hour. I go up to them and waste them. I did it to put them out of misery and so that we won't have to guard, their sorry assess. We find out later that one platoon from A Company stayed awake while the rest of us passed out. For that, I will be forever thankful. Lt. Hadley stopped by for a brief Hello; how are you? He had a very peaceful look on his face. I'm glad he is getting what he wants from this beautiful country and ugly war. We all wish he had stayed as our platoon leader but him taking a Captains place he should be have that rank soon. We must go out and get another body count. We don't know which body was from which attack and we didn't get a good body count from the first attack. We count every mother's son and come up with over 150 dead enemy and a few people we don't know whom they were because they were so badly burnt by napalm; they could be captured ARVN which the North uses as slaves to build trenches and bunker complexes. There was a whole string of dead gooks going down that side of the mountain where we chased them in our wild man frenzy. We must now collect all the weapons and ammo that we find. We are given a that a boy from Battalion; we won't be fighting for at least 3 days we have been awarded a 3 day R & R right at the FSB at Dakto. A place where we hear they have ice-cold beer; now won't that be something? Every one of us drinks until we pass out; it's not good to have an ugly hangover when it's over 110 degrees out here! There is the possibility we might get invited to a shoot out. Not a good thing to happen to us.

We get to go down to Dakto at the Brigade Firebase; as a unit and we basically drink all we can and sleep as much as we can. Your body is so tired that when we get 5 or 6 beers in you. You have no way of staying awake. We go to the NCO club and spend every dime we have on hamburgers with French fries and all the catsup I think I need on my fries. We get the beer from what is called our allotment; we are supposed to be getting a beer and soda allotment every month. But that doesn't happen, where the beer and soda goes, your guess is as good as mine. Maybe in the Black Market? anyway, that's what we were told. We get too drunk to worry about it. Then we all find a spot and pass out not to wake up for at least 8 or 9 hours, that's the most sleep I have had since arriving in country. Then we have to report in to find we are going out again. From Dakto we are headed to an artillery support base on high way 14 just south of Kontum. We are told there is a lot of Viet Cong activity here and we are here to stop it. Well the 12 days we spend there was no V.C. activity at all so our mission was a success. We imagine that after we leave the gooks will pop up again. That's why we can't fight this or any other war not stepping on anyone's toes, we spend the time on finding out who is who and make a decision right away as to who is friend and who is foe, then take what action is needed; either support them with ammo, guns, and support from the air. Those that came out as foe eliminate them. We have been told there is an awful lot of VC here. There wasn't even a sniper active in the area. It was so calm that we got too relaxed, if we would run into some gooks we might not be as sharp as before. We get orders to head back up to the Dakto Area of Operations where we are being sent to the razorback. This hill is 700 something tall plus only about 10 meters wide at its widest spot and only about 20 meters long. There is no way anyone could hit us with either artillery or mortars. A human assault would be very costly we could stand off an entire Battalion and call in jets and gun ships we could hold off many a thousand screaming sons of bitches. The only bad thing is if we go on patrol here, we have to expose ourselves for the first hour we are on this mission. Then we have to enter the dark jungle knowing well that there could be a few to many gooks waiting for us. But because we have been shooting H&I at the area, we never meet any one as we enter the jungle. We walk the ridges keeping mortar and recoilless rifle fire down to zero. If we were attacked, we have a 50 cal machine gun that will reach the ridge to the south of us and 2 m60's that could mow down anything coming up the ridgeline. Plus a couple hundred-hand grenades we could heave over the uncovered sides. We believe the gooks know this since they never tried an attack on us the month we were there. We ran our usual 3 to 5 day missions and came up with little information. But we did keep the gooks off the ridgeline so the gooks rockets didn't shoot up the encampment of American soldiers at Dakto Air Field. That was very important because it allowed the choppers and fixed winged planes to land and take off with supplies and reinforcements, and allowed us to carry to the enemy as much fire power as we could muster. We were shot at several times from the ridgeline, but they couldn't land anything on top of the razorback except one time when a machinegun was allowed to walk his rounds up to where we were, but that didn't last long. Because we called in artillery on them and ended their glory.

We sometimes talk about what we believe should be done about this Asian war. The best we could come up with is, first we pull out. Then the gooks from the North pull out taking their brother V.C. with them. Then we don't let the French in and they keep China and Russia out of this war. Then the 2 countries North and South sit down and talk things out, with no interference from any one. Give them a year to settle their differences then and only then if they cannot settle this little Asian war that has dragged several good American youngsters into an early grave. We on support of the South and either or both Russia and China go to the table to come up with an ending that benefits all involved. But somewhere there are people making money, more money than we will ever see and unless we fight in a war every 10 or so years, our economy won't prosper. It's sad but we need to be in a high dollar war every few years to keep the rich, rich and we the lower class will pay with our lives, bodies and minds. But who would care about us? Those that don't believe that theory go back to the 1950's, 40's, then 1898,1865, 1848, 1814, then the war against England. This war is to keep the Commies from taking over the world so they say. We don't know anything about that. It could be a correct statement but what are we doing? Several of us have the same belief that the real reason we are here is the all mighty dollar. The Dollar that we as Grunts never see; and we have to pay for these Dollars with some Blood and Guts. The next morning we get called into TOC and are told that we are going on a battalion size sweep of the mountain ridge from 1338 towards the south east for about 6,000 meters they think there is the Regiment head quarters of the 66th NVA infantry regiment. A line company from the 1/22 Inf. will take charge of protecting the FSB with its artillery and mortar place-ments. Our team will lead out down this ridge followed by the rest of the Recon platoon then A company then B company with C company to our left down into the valley below and the other side of a river running along the ridge line, then D company will be across a small valley on the next ridge line. The purpose of this is our team will leave out a couple hours before the rest of recon the line companies will come an hour later. This way our recon team can move at the slow pace and the rest of recon will be a little faster than us but not as fast as the line company. The last thing we were told in the meeting was to make sure we all know where everyone else was at all times. We take off pretty much like we always do.

CHAPTER TWENTY ONE - AMBUSH GONE SOAR

Then an hour later, we get a call that the rest of recon has left the nest. Then an hour later, we are told that all is good. So this mission has started. We move along at a good pace. That ridge had lots of tall trees but really not much brush. As we get further along the brush and lots of bamboo appear to our front. Now we have to slow down again. This thick bamboo you have to move slowly in because you each have to move the same bamboo so you can pass and if you have to cut it. That's like calling ahead and telling the gooks you are coming and how many of you there is. After a couple hours of doing this, we start hearing something way ahead of us cutting the bamboo. We call back to Lt. North and he tells us that everyone is on course and where he was supposed to be. We ask for the other companies to get up here in a hurry because there is at least a company headed our way.

We find a little clearing in the bamboo and set up an ambush. There are me, Lula with his M14, Van, Rex and Ronnie. We are all pretty scared because they are making the noise of a thousand gooks headed towards us. We again call in for everyone's position. Recon Platoon about 100 meters to our rear, A company 10 meters behind them. B Company attached to A company. C company tells us he is just now crossing the river and will set up a flanking position for any gooks trying to get away that way, OK good, D company called in to tell us he's about 100 meters behind where he should be, but we can still use him to be our other flank. This sounds like an American Company size traveling down this ridgeline.

We are waiting nervously for a Battalion of NVA hot shots to come busting thru that bamboo at any moment. The noise from the bamboo stops for a minute. Do they suspect that we were there? Are they preparing an all out assault on us? Why would they stop? During this time, so many questions flash in our heads. There are 5 of us with another 26 only 100 meters to our rear, we might have a couple hundred gooks coming right into our laps. This is one of the times your butt hole puckers up and your heart beats rapidly so loud you know everyone can hear it.

Then we start thinking can we hold them off until help arrives? Will they overrun us? Or will they flee down the sides for the other companies to ambush? The bamboo noise starts up again, we all start sweating and making little mumbling sounds from our gut when out from the bamboo thicket a dark skinned, bushy headed gook. We all open up on him, he goes down and the next 5 or 6 guys behind him form a line of fire so they can get him out of our firing range. We are really pumped up at this time we can't give ground to these people but with just the 5 of us it really gets to be a fast moving couple of minutes.

Then C Company on the radio, they are in contact with a battalion size force at the edge of this ridgeline. D company reports hearing the fight on the ridge and are reading themselves for a massive amount of gooks coming into this valley between us. D Company will have the high ground and we should be able to get them all. When all of a sudden from the bamboo we hear Oh my God I'm hit" in the kings English. Everything stops and we are feeling awful, because we believe, we have just ambushed an American unit; and one from our own Battalion to make it worst, We hold our fire and call C Company and D Company to ask where they were? D company is still on the other ridge but C Company is now across the river, up the slope and in contact with a battalion of NVA. We ask them to pop smoke and right in front of us comes a yellow smoke grenade. We cease-fire and tell C company they have been up this hill for sometime. When we ask their RTO, he tells us C companies 6 wanted to be the first in contact and get all the glory. Well they were first in contact but they get no glory for their actions that day. Just like Custer, it really makes me wonder what do these people think is going on out here in the jungle? Don't they grasp the fact people might die because of their screw-ups? This stops this operation right now. We are not going to go on. If there were a battalion of gooks up this way they are gone, gone, gone. C Company hates us now, especially Lula, since he was carrying something other than a M16.

They don't look at the facts. They were not where they said they were they were heading right in to us. The guy walking point was a Mexican or Hawaiian with dark skin full head of black hair, no helmet on and their CO was trying to get to the gooks first and get his boys some medals. Well he got a couple of them Purple Hearts. When bullshit like this goes on, that's what might make you want to protest your Superior officers, and that tag don't go too far out here. Superior to whom is the Question? Most of the young officers are little rich kids that spend 6 months out in the boonies then 6 months at a skate job. Some do the skate job first; some get a whole year of skate jobs. A few spend their whole year out here with us Grunts. Needless to say, Lula gives up his M 14 and now goes back to a M16, I need to get off and stay off my soapbox for a while. Here it is another day, another battle; we hope not we need to go back to the Easy life we had on the Razorback and its 3 days rest before our 1st patrol. We get about 500 meters into the jungle that has swallowed us up in it's darkness we run into 20 or so gooks So we call in mortars for support. We form a 5-man perimeter with each of us putting our claymores out in front of us with the trunk of a tree providing a safe from back blast for us. We call mortars between us and the perimeter incase the gooks are trying the hill trap move that they put on the 101st and the 173rd earlier this year. They were trying to get between our friends and us in the perimeter then crushing us with an all out attack. But when we mortared them in that area between the perimeter and us it made them go to plan B. Which was to try and lure us into the jungle further by making us believe we have them on the run. Then pull the hill trap again. But we break contact and call in artillery to try and force them back into us. No one in our unit was injured and we find 3 gooks either dead or on their way to being dead. We wait until we are sure that we can break contact and crawl back into the perimeter to safety. We call in and get some artillery to further keep them from forming a contact with us, which would keep us from going across the area before and after the fence, which has all cover removed. We would be sitting ducks otherwise. We get past the fence and we have 50 meters to go. We move as fast as we can and we do make it to the bunker directly to our front. We slide into the trench line as our perimeter opens up with small arms fire incase anyone feels like following us. We report to the command post and tell what we saw.

These gooks were all wearing old dirty clothes and were carrying packs on their backs. This tells them that we were in contact with a unit that has not been re supplied within the last couple of weeks. But there has been a lot of activity on this area so there are other gooks in the area besides these boys. We are to go out the same way tomorrow and see if they have left the area or they could still be they're waiting for us. Only this time we are taking out another team before we go out and this other team will act as a flanking motion if they are in still in the same area. 0730 hours and we start out and we get 1,000 meters out without any contact so we are told to go ahead with our mission and for the other team to come back in. We go about another 500 meters into the jungle to where we go to the right and find a trail that has been used recently. We call in and are told to put a trip flare there and to call in the grid and if that flare goes off, they will get them with some mortars. We go another 100 meters and are in contact with 1 maybe 2 snipers. Then if there's 2, there's 10 and we are neither in another bad situation where we can't go forward nor back towards the firebase. These gooks still want to put the hill trap maneuver on us. We call Magwood and tell him what is going on. We request fire support in the area between the firebase and us. We can't afford to lose that avenue of escape. We then call in some Willy peter to our front. This will burn them out of their positions and burn away some of the hiding places that they use to their advantage. After 2 rounds of Willy, peter there is no resistance to our front or the rear. We still have small pockets of gooks to our right flank. A heavy burst of firepower from us and they are gone. We must get re-supplied with ammo if we are going to finish our mission. There is a jet coming our way, one that has to drop their payload and we can't think of a better one than dropping some napalm on these little bastards.

The napalm breaks our contact and we are able to walk in and get supplied and get some much-needed rest. We go back and wait another 2 days before we can restart this mission. When we go out this time, there are no hostile forces in the area. They shot up this area pretty much all day yesterday with mortars and the napalm sure fried a bunch of them. We get out about 1,500 meters and find 3 dead gooks but there is neither weapons nor paper work on them. We go another 1,000 meters then head west towards the fence, which we are not to cross nor shoot into. We are to observe and report that's all. We have taken extra grenades and clay mores on this mission. We are to set up an ambush and kill as many as we can. We go another 3,000 meters and stop to observe and report we see no evil, hear no evil so we go another 1,000 meters to the west. We are told to find a safe place where we can observe the area without being seen ourselves. After an hour and a half, we spot a couple gooks walking down a trail that's within our view. They don't seem concerned that we might be here, so that is a good-thing. They climb a tree and have a hand held radio with them. They are trail watchers put out here to watch for us. Surprise we are already here. Before we can move, we have to waste these 2 guys before they can get on the horn and call in our position. This will be a good kill for us. The gooks will not know the next time they go out on one of these missions if we are already there waiting for them. Just like what they do to us. We can't get a clean, clear shot at both of them from where we are. So either we move or the gooks have to move.

Ronnie is going about 15 meters to our left and I'm going about 10 to the right. I signal him that I have a shot at the guy holding the radio handset and he has one on the other guy. Ronnie fires first, me half a second later. We both have kill hits and we go and search these dead ole boys for anything we can. We get 2 SKS's and some paper along with the radio. We leave a 4th Division patch on a string around both of these guys because we want these gooks to know who to fear. Now all we have to do is get back to the firebase in one piece and this is a very successful mission. We head due east then go a little to the north. We don't go back the same way we came so that we can cover more ground. We don't see anyone on the way back but we do find some footprints in the mud. A Big Cat tracks. There is another damn Tiger out here with us. Sure hope we don't run into another cat. We call in the Tiger foot prints and am told that there has been tiger sightings in a couple of the villages out here far from any large village and they also tell us there isn't a weapon that we carry that would stop a tiger .In case we look like a easy meal. Not the way I want to go. But it's nei-ther unfortunate that we don't get to pick when nor how we go. Maybe a claymore would do the job, but you'd have to get the tiger to walk into the killing zone. Good luck. We are told that tigers usually hunt at night so we should figure out which way the tiger went and go some other way. The tiger is going west so we head east and back towards our FSB. We don't come across any more tiger prints but we do find some bare feet in the mud. These footprints are probably that of some runner for the NVA, They don't all have radios usually because the radio they had broken down or the battery died. They use young boys

12 or so to run from one camp to another to tell of news and plans of attack .It started raining at about 1720 hours and we need to find a place where we can get some sleep. Tomorrow we will walk in to the perimeter of the FSB. Our guard time is spooky because we expect that tiger to come back and screw with us. But it doesn't happen. We don't hear nor see anything in the night that should worry us. Morning comes and we have a little over 2,000 meters to get back home. It's raining pretty hard now. It makes it harder to move when it rains so hard, first because the jungle floor becomes a slippery mass of mud and goop, you keep falling in the goop and you can't see as well in the torrid rain. You and a gook could walk right up on each other and neither of you would know it. Now when you start climbing up these slopes it becomes a complete mess. You can't stand up straight and every 2 steps you take you fall or at least slip to your knees.

But we must go on; it's going to be late afternoon before we get in now. But at least we were told there are clean clothes waiting for us when we get in. Also, the Cook is saving some fried chicken and potatoes for us. We are only about 200 meters out at that time. We stop and call in telling them that we are Chicago coming into St Louis, or coming from the north east in about 45 minutes. We will step out of the jungle so don't shoot at us. We walked in and much to the surprise of the line company, they didn't know exactly where we were when we stood up, as we were only about 50 meters from their bunker not an easy throw of a hand grenade. But close enough to get a good shot with a SKS. We come in report to Magwood then go find some clean and dry clothes then we head for the mess tent where we are given 3 pieces of chicken a big pile of mashed potatoes with gravy, some green beans, and a piece of cherry desert. Not a pie but it sure was good. We go to our bunker and it's nice and dry and we aren't on the line so we don't pull guard at night which means we might pull LP, which is dangerous than being out in the jungle on a mission because the enemy knows pretty much where you are because he watches as you go down to take your place at LP. Some how we don't pull that either, we get to sleep most of the night and we all wake up before sun up so we can be ready incase the gooks want to play this morning. Well no gooks and we are next to head for the mess tent and bring our breakfast here to enjoy. It's powered eggs again but it's warm and we pour Tabasco sauce on it, so it has a good taste. Real coffee, man what else could a guy want out here in the boonies? Maybe not having to always keeping your eyes and ears scanning where ever you are for that ever so present fear that is always there waiting ever so strong.

CHAPTER TWENTY-TWO - THE TAX COLLECTOR

A Company was probed during the early morning hours; no shooting just probed enough to keep you wide-awake and feeling lousy the next night while pulling your guard. They want someone, anyone to fall asleep on their guard so they can sneak in and kill a few of us.

In July 1968, General Creighton Abrams who had taken General Westmoreland's position in this little Asian War wanted to commit B52's to this area of the tri-borders but couldn't get permission from Washington. So goes this war in a little Asian country; at least the part I experienced. There are several tribes of Montegnard in this mountain terrain, The Jarai tribe is the biggest and they could care less of who is running the government in Saigon or that the Americans were there. They live in thatched huts, usually on stilts. They are willing to share anything, but their women with us. They ask nothing in return, just want to be left alone. We give them Thompson sub machine guns, grease guns and M1 carbines and ammo for such, all stock piled from WWII, and Korea. They even get the old

Pineapple hand grenades they also make some mighty fine wine from rice. They are willing to share their wine with you. They chew beechnut, which turns their teeth black, which really ruins the look of the women.

These villages are visited by the North for men to fight along side of them, the VC come along wanting taxes in the form of rice and dried fish. We come along and tell them that these people are bad and that we will protect them, but they know as soon as we leave their village the other guys will show up wanting some of what ever we gave them. Be it rice, canned goods or ammo they will take the majority of it. We visit this village for about an hour and thank them for their wine. Did I tell you, they make some mighty fine wine? The chief of this village whispers to us that a tax collector from the North will be here in a couple of hours. They don't like him because he treats their women like whores and these people didn't even know there was such a thing, until the Tax collector started taken them as whores, for his taxes. We wait outside in some brush and bamboo. When this guy comes along, he is dressed in starched uniform, spit shined boots and an AK 47 and a 7mm pistol. He goes from hut to hut bringing out something of value from each. When he gets 2 houses from the chief, we are told that the hut next to the chief lives an informer and if we are going to take out the Taxman, we might as well take him out also.

When this Taxman goes into the informers hut, we come in right behind him. We have the chief's son with us and he points out the informer to us. We take the taxman and informer along with the stuff that he had collected to give it all back. We tell the villagers to take what was theirs. While this guy is still alive, they won't jeopardize themselves or loved ones. So we take the Tax man and the informer outside of the north gate and empty a magazine in each of them. We then ask if there are any other people that need to be killed in this village? They say no. You number 1. Which is a good thing. Number 10 is a bad one. We then call in and report on how our day has gone so far. We tell that we have several papers that this guy had in his brief case

I guess you would call it a brief case. Looks like an old burlap bag to me. After we get to come in, we find that those papers we sent in from the tax collector has names in it telling who is a VC or NVA informer. They give this information to the local police who end up making several arrests. Well good now can I go home? No, but you might not have to go on another hair rising mission again. Since I made Sgt. Now, I don't have to do the ugly jobs like honey dipping. But now we are going out on a mission where they guarantee we will have contact and they want Apache 5 to go out and make contact and reinforcements will be ready to leave within 10 minutes. Ten minutes may not sound like a long time but put yourself in a predicament where you may have 30 seconds before a whole herd of gooks are cramming themselves up your ass you may agree that 2 minutes is a long time. I don't need this to be happening but it is and I shall make the best of it as I can. No use going down as a Cry Baby on either your last or next to last mission. We sit up all night while on this mission because we are being probed by a large herd of gooks.

We call in artillery and are ready now for what ever comes our way. Hopefully it won't be much. The gooks keep circling us and at one point where we are is not their focal point, they are a couple hundred meters off. But they still are close to us and there is no-way we will make it unless we can get some artillery to mop up these bastards and allow us to creep away. After a couple of hours of not being able to find us, they spread out and go hunting for us again. This time they come even closer to walking up to us, within 5 meters but 5 meters is pretty far off considering how dark it is out here. This is the scariest moment of my stay here. These little bastards are crawling all over this hilltop looking for my friends and me, they get pretty close at different times, and we almost open up on them at one point where they were going to walk right through us. We had our weapons on Rock-N-Roll but they turned right and left our area still looking for us. We get artillery shooting up this hill and after about 10 minutes, the gooks decide we are not worth them losing so many. We now feel safe but we hear someone out there still prowling around. The gooks have left someone here to catch us in case we pop out and head for a LZ. This mission has been scrubbed. We are waiting for someone to make a decision on what, where and when. We were told that we are going into some very dangerous waters. The gooks are massing in great numbers along the Tri-border area and some of Brigades LRRP's and us are getting as close to these enemy encampments to gather information on what their next move is to be. My agenda is that I am going to get my bony ass, home all safe and sound. I've been told that the ringing in my ears will stop as soon as I get away from all the shooting and such. I can't imagine what it would be like to have one or more of your limbs gone .I shutter at the thought of being blinded If I can't go home the way I was when I came to this little country I didn't want to go home. That's easy for me to say now. But time will tell if I was to go home at all! My Dad was in WWII and he told me stories about guys into Shell Shock and go nuts over things that happen in a war. Things that you wouldn't think would happen do. After you have seen humans killed or mangled beyond recognition you soon become used to the fact several of your friends didn't make it home as they were when arriving in country.

After this meeting of the minds, we get our gear loaded up and ready. The chopper will be here in 20 minutes and we are going over what we are to do while sitting on the chopper pad. We have our radio on and listen to Apache 3 in a fight for their lives. Zollman is carrying the Prc 25 and he is calling artillery and Mortars on their perimeter. They are in contact with 6 or 7 NVA. No one on our side is hit yet, but from the sounds of the gunfire, someone is going to be out of ammo real soon our mission is changed. We are to get on that chopper but it is taking us to a clearing about 500 meters from where the shoot-em-up is taking place. Our objective will be to break Apache 3 from contact and in doing so eliminate the squad or how many there were of gooks. We get dropped off and are headed to where we hope Apache 3 is. We have lost radio contact with them. We get to within hearing distance and the Apache team is firing burst of 1 to 3 rounds at a time leads us to believe they are almost out of ammo, much to our surprise no one is injured. But they are almost out of ammo. Charlie is so relieved; he is getting ready to go on his R&R next week and had a feeling that he wasn't going to live that long. I believe he was going back to Australia to get married to the girl he spent his last R&R with, he extended 6 months in country so he could go back and marry her. We get to within talking distance to them and they ask, Did we bring ammo?" We hand out the bundliros of ammo we had collected to the guys. We get into the fight by pulling a flanking motion to the gooks left, we get them in a cross fire, like the one they tried to pull on Apache 3. We all lobe grenades into where these little yellow bastards are hiding, soon after all of the fighting stops and we inch our way over to where the gooks were. We find 6 bodies and all had grenade fragments in them. So we call in for a lift off out of this battle site. We come in with Apache 3 and are told, "Good job, rest today because tomorrow you are going out on the original mission." On one of these gooks, we find a manual that is written in Vietnamese and when we come back from this mission we would like to know exactly it means. The gooks don't need an exact map since every firebase that we had been to is laid out the same, with guns aimed to cover the chopper pad, put it this way we could walk into any firebase from our Brigade and walk straight to the TOC or any other area.

We have been crawling around the jungle looking for a well hidden fortress of NVA regulars and obtain what information we can we are to give all information to Intelligence and let them decide how much money are we going to spend on these guys. We're out 2 days when we come across a trail that has been used quiet a bit, we slow down and follow this trail until we find a spot to set up our little camp. We put out our Claymores and trip flares and get ready for the jungle night to begin. All of a sudden, we hear monkeys going crazy around us. There is a large element of enemy soldiers surrounding us and we have to find a way out. There must be a lot of them; we can hear them moving all around us. They are talking so they aren't afraid of us as we are of them. We are all trying to keep a level head on to get out of this circumstance and not get shot up or captured. We are scared to death that one of us will sneeze or cough anything that will draw attention to our sorry Asses, the gooks know we are in the general area, but not exactly where by listening to our radio transmissions. Darrel gets on the phone and calls in artillery and mortars all around our scared little group, that wants no part in what is about to happen. The gooks are closing in and tighten their hold on us. We were going to have to spend the night out there, it's getting late and there isn't a LZ anywhere close to us and we don't believe the gooks would allow us the time to cut out a LZ in this brush and bamboo stretch of jungle. We can't get killed dead today, it's 2 days till my 20th birthday which makes it July 26 1968.

The gooks are having a hard time locating us and we aren't obliged to showing them where we were, as long as we can keep from being discovered we will be OK. We go through most of the night with them still trying to locate us, they start out heading right at us then for some reason they turn left, and go real slow as they are wanting to find us. Talk about being scared, we thought we might be either captured or killed that night. They came back around in about an hour and if they would keep going straight, they would run into us, not that we were wanting that to happen. There is no way the five of us could have won a shoot-out with the number of enemy that we had looking for us. The next morning, we still hear the monkeys going ape over the gooks being there and pestering them. Darrell gets the 5 of us together and try to figure how we can get out of this circumstance without getting hurt in any way. Here we are the 5 of us, it just doesn't look good for us. Van and Jerry decide they might know a way to get out of here. They think that if they take off running down a finger and have already called in mortars on the area we will be transcending we can get away. We talk this over and as a last resort we may have to do this but if we run into a large body of NVA and if they decide they want a fight we won't stand a chance. We keep firing artillery at the enemy when they are seen, but little that we know that this is a regiment sized until that is limping home after several battles with some of us Americans. Most of the next day we spend hiding and trying to figure a way out of that circumstance we figure we were destine to. The next night we get another probe from the gooks. They don't know exactly where we are or how many of us there was. They probably want to get across the fence as soon as they can. But they have the 5 of us in their way.

We decide it's best for us to move as far away as we can to confuse them in anyway we can. We decide to set up a couple booby traps of white phosphorus grenades that we saw go off during the night and we heard some screaming from that area where we had planted the Willy Pete grenades. We all feel better because if we had not moved we would be the ones screaming. The loud noise from these fried little people stops after we hear a couple well-placed rounds from a SKS Russian Rifle. All of this time we have been in contact with Battalion 6 and he has told us we will be picked up today just as soon as we can find and get to a LZ for the chopper to land and pick us up. But we still have to deal with these enemy soldiers that are looking forward to wearing our scalps and collect the fifty-dollar apiece bounty they have placed on our flop hats. That's a lot of money for one of those people. We have to not run into any of them while we are moving. Talk about something that leaves you shitless, that night was such. We had no idea what we were up against until Grizzly gets on the phone and tells us Apache team you are in some deep do-do. It appears you are surrounded by a regiment of the NVA's 1st Infantry Division and they are trying to crawl up your rear end, we will stop them with all the artillery, mortars and any Navy jets, I can muster up for you, hang in there I just wanted you to know what was going on." Enemy troops are all around us cutting away the tall grass and bamboo trying their best to locate us. We figure they know we are a small unit; otherwise, they wouldn't leave themselves to being located by a much larger unit. After an hour or two, we get the news we wanted to hear, .we get a chopper to head our way, but they first had a gunship spray the area of the LZ. Then

Grizzly has to tell us the chopper has been called away, they have a mechanical problem and have to return to the airport at Dakto. They fire some high explosive rounds into that area and along the path, we will have to run through. Maybe later in the day we will be picked up? Jerry then decided we should again hide out until the enemy moved on, not finding us and them out in the open during day-light hours, we didn't think they would stay long. After about another hour the enemy gave up hope of finding us, and moved on towards the border with Cambodia, they didn't want to spend another day bombarded by artillery and mortars.

Darrel later tells me he was scared more on that last hill; than he was the whole time they were attacking hill 1338, which is saying something. We travel another 100 meters away and call in artillery on their bony Asses. We are scared, I believe that was the scariest I have ever been in my life what happen next I have no idea, but Rex and Darrel both jump this guy and send him well on his way to hell with a cutthroat? The Gooks left someone to watch for us, and then we believe he was to call and report where we were. After this takes place, we start out heading for our pick up point. We wait for first light and sure enough, here comes B Company 3/12 to take our place. As soon as the gooks have noticed that, a line company is about to be on their ass they head for the fence and maybe that hospital that everyone is so certain is around here. We get on the first chopper that lands and First SGT. Ben Reynolds from Ft. Benning is on that chopper and he had a gung ho picture on his face.

After we land I get to our bunker and I get some well deserved rest. I'm told I won't be going out on any more missions because I'm so short. So I stay in while everyone except Apache 5 is out trying to find that hospital that I'm beginning to wonder if it's really there?

CHAPTER TWENTY THREE - ONE MAN SHORT

S/SGT. Magwood Calls me into his bunker. He wants me to do something stupid, all of the teams are out except Apache 5. He had a mission for them, but they are 1 man short. Would I be willing to go on a 5-day mission going into the Southeast of where we are now? It would be just to walk around the perimeter 2 to 3 klicks away from the safety of the perimeter, I thought about it and decided I was supposed to go, it was still my job to make sure the others could go home as I would shortly after that mission. It would give me one more chance to help find that illusive hospital.

I wished that I could have slept that night before starting out on my last mission; I lie there and sweat most of the night away. I couldn't stop worrying if I had made the correct choice at going on that mission or not, I could have said no and I probably would not have been on that mission, especially since the mission last month was so hair rising and scared the hell out of the 5 of us. I didn't want to be out there just so Lt North could out do his brother Oliver again. Oliver wasn't even in Vietnam at that time. What they had as a contest I had no idea. I could be at Division Headquarters getting my ticket to the Freedom Bird heading home. But I made the decision, now I have to live by my word. I go and meet with the same guys my last mission was with, Apache 5. I told them I decided to go, because it was the right thing to do. We start getting all of our stuff that we need to take on this little mission Southeast of FSB 29. I tell Sgt. Magwood and Lt. North that I will go on this mission but have already turned my M16 in and don't have a weapon to carry; this was on purpose, because without a weapon I can't go on another mission. But I am given a M79. And all the rounds I can carry, 40 or so. So I am going out fully armed and that's the only way to go on a mission, you might not have enough food or water but your skinny little ass better be carrying enough ammo including hand grenades. Which I had 9 frag, 2 Willie-peter and 3 different smoke grenades. I figure it this way if I don't go out with them and if something happens to them I will feel responsible for their injuries or death, because if I had been there it might have made a difference. Here's hoping I won't need to use this Bloop Tube to cover our ass. Here's hoping all is well and I get to go home with my mind at ease. We went out about 3 klicks and headed North towards a group of hills that we should reach on our third day. The rain is coming down, not hard but steady a typical monsoon rain, after an hour of dragging ourselves up and down these small hilltops we rest for an hour, eating a cold meal, soon we take off again, until we come to our spot to spend the night.

Parrish goes to one side of the hill while the rest of us. We call in artillery that night not only around us but also up on the hilltop we are to spend the next night at, also along the trail we will follow tomorrow. When morning comes we burn some leeches then have a hot cup of coffee, then we head out towards our next objective, which was another low hilltop about 3 klicks away. It rained pretty much through out the night and it doesn't look like it's going to let up any now. When we head out along side of this trail we start noticing foot prints and sandal prints, this tells us some of the villagers are probably walking along side of the enemy. It looks like 5 or 6 with sandals and 4 or 5 barefoot. When we call in with our discovery, we were told to follow the tracks at a slow pace, and see if we can't find a hospital along the way. When we stop for our evening meal, we set up an ambush in case someone is following us, we sit there for a couple hours and when no one seems to be following us, we head out toward our next accommodations out in Uncle Ho's Jungle Hotel. The accommodations won't be as nice as those on my R&R in Taipei where I had one hell of a time. I stayed drunk most of the time, until the guy that ran the hotel told me " Let me take you to see the sights of my country, plus he took me where I had 3 Sharkskin suits made for me under $100 for all three. Then the next night I went out hunting for women again.

We set up for the night and call in our support groups to keep us safe incase some mothers son walks up on us and wants to play tag. All goes well like I want it to, on my last mission. Next morning the sun is up and we have hot water brewing some strong coffee before we head out to a hilltop where we could see across the valley to Firebase 29, the place we left from. First thing we do is call in some mortars along the trail we will be following, then a couple artillery rounds on top of the hill we will be at later in the day. Then a couple rounds on a hill we won't be going to, so the enemy won't be able to figure out where we were going to set up that evening. We listened to a battle-taking place four thousand meters to the Southwest of us. It appears to be at least a Regiment size force and they have been in close combat for about three hours, which is strange for a battle to last that long. The enemy regimental size force leaves the battle and heads West, towards Cambodia and us. They probably would not risk being spotted and drug through a meat grinder again. It has rained for days and our feet were pretty much like prunes and starting to crack and bleed. About noon we arrived at our next place to camp at, the rain seizes, a welcome sight. Parrish goes up front to watch and Van goes back to make sure no one was following us.

Darrell and Rex and I took off our boots and wrung out our socks waiting for them to dry. Rex starts a heat tab ready to cook some C-Rations when Jerry opens up with his M16, a startling sound especially, when 4 or 5 AK47's open up on him. Darrell and I put our socks on and slide into our boots without tying the laces. I immediately start firing M79 grenades up into the air where they will come down approximately 20 to 30 meters down that trail. My heart is racing and I'm panting, I need to calm down and figure out what we were to do. This could be that Regiment that was in the fight yesterday, and they probably won't want another battle unless they knew we were but 5. Then it wouldn't be a battle, they could simply overrun us and then head straight for the border.

Rex also has put on his boots and has crawled up to where Parrish was to give him support fire. Darrel immediately calls in artillery to stop a frontal attack if that occurs, it's always easier to stop an assault before it starts, then to wait until you are almost overran. The enemy is moving on 3 sides of us and we estimate at least 30 of them. Why they don't just overrun us and kill us all we don't know, unless they think there are more of us than the 5. We call in all the support we can; the 155's, 105's, four deuce and 81 mortars and request a couple jets to bomb these little bastards that are more than likely going to add our scalps to their collection. With all of the air support, and artillery, and mortars we still have less than a 50-50 chance if they decide to rush with more than 20, we are now in a situation where one mistake could very well be your last mistake. We start figuring what we are going to do in case they rush us, which is a strong possibility, in my minds eye I could see them all charging at once firing their fully automatic AK's and completely overrunning us, but for whatever reason they don't, and for that we were thankful, the only reason we figure they don't overrun us was, they were the guys that had had the big battle last night, and they were pretty well beaten-up. Why did I stay on and go on this mission, I know I thought it was my job, but was it? I could have gone home and no one would think any less of me, and they probably don't think any more of me for staying. It's what I think, and had to live with the rest of my life, hopefully longer than that day.

Once they figure out that there are only 5 of us, we figure we won't have time to go by any plans if they assault us with more than 20 people. Why did I have to be there in that predicament? Why did I say yes, I would go on this mission? The only answer I can come up with is, because it's my job to do these things Until I get on that Freedom Bird my job is to go on these missions and pull my weight incase of enemy contact. These 4 other men don't deserve to have me wimp out on them at this time. It's going to be hard enough fighting them off with 5 let alone with someone crying like a little girl. Grizzly gets up in his chopper to figure out a plan to get us in and safe. He radios us to say "It appears Apache team that you are surrounded on three sides by what appears to be the 40th Reinforced Artillery regiment from the First NVA Infantry Division." Not the same enemy unit that screwed with us 2 weeks ago from the First Infantry Division of the NVA that was from the 66th Infantry Regiment but still part of the First Infantry Division.

This mission was supposed to be my swan song. We only have 5 men and probably not enough ammo to kill each and every one of them. Why don't they attack? We have to keep them guessing as to how many and what weapons we have up here. We either have to hit a Home run or we strike out. There will be no second chances; no calling time out, this is it. We are going to have to live or die by instinct. This little knoll has become a bastion for us. Do we have enough ammo, enough grenades, water, and food, do we have enough Intestinal stamina? If so we might be able to hold these little bastards off, we might not have to, we could get relieved from our post, have a massive air strike all around us, and maybe even the gooks get tired and walk away. My mind is going a million miles per second and everything adds up to those guys rushing us as soon as someone gets close enough to our perimeter to figure out there are only 5 of us. Van and I say to the rest we are going over to the other side of this finger to try and find a way out of here. We will be back if it looks good. If it was a wrong decision, we might not make it back! That would upset Mother if her little boy doesn't make it. Xin Loi, after we get about 25 meters down that finger we sit down, look and listen. We don't hear nor see anyone so we creep along down about 40 meters when we come across 5 Gooks just as surprised to see us, as we are to see them. Van opens up with his M16 and 2 of them drop, I fire my M79 and the shell goes about killing the remaining 3, now that was a trick shot, it hit one guy in the back and then the shell slammed into a tree not far from where these 3 guys were and the blast killed all of them.

To this day, I tell that story; it was amazing. We can't go down that way we tell Darrel; nothing else was said. After another 30 minutes, I get the shakes. Why did I agree to go on this mission? Especially after what the last one was like? Why am I not on my way to Enari, I'm so worried about making that fatal mistake, staying on to go with Apache 5 on this mission could be that one great last mistake that I have made, or someone else makes it, then it is out of my control. What is in my control is how I handle any and all adversity, I mustn't show that I am afraid, I don't want the other guys thinking they have to go an extra mile for me to make it home or not, it's not their fault I was there. All I need is for each of them to want to make it back and in one piece for themselves. We are a team and not just a word to use loosely, if one of us quits we all quit and if that happens we are all killed dead. It's getting late I pull first guard. Darrel comes up with an idea. We light up a whole pack of cigarettes to make the gooks think we are more than 5. All we need is for them to be off guard this one night. We might not be able to do this again, so tomorrow we have to do something even if it's wrong.

Parrish is the guy I'm to wake up after my guard, I accept him. He has really stood up well considering the circumstances, where you feel something tearing at your guts thrashing your very soul, him being the New Guy on this mission, you really don't know what to expect from a New Guy. Sometimes you believe you may not make it, but you grab your boots pull your socks up and get ready for what might be the day that establishes the way you live out your life. That gut wrenching force that makes or breaks your ability to stand tall and do what must be done for your very existence. Although I have never experienced it; I feel like a small deer being taken down by a huge alligator and being thrashed around and around under water and hoping it will hurry up and let me die, so I can have that peace.

But that isn't what's happening. I must keep looking out into where the firing would come from and deal with what must be done by the 5 of us! The question must be asked, Do you have what it takes to keep your head in a frenzy of an all out assault, by a superior force, and can you still fight on even as the battle would seem to be lost? Again, there will be no prisoners today. Just before sun up Darrel wakes us before the shelling starts up again. We are going to get 105, 155; howitzers and mortars fired right up to where we are. There is so much confusion you don't know if some were running at you or away from you and in the dark jungle, even in the morning sun, because of the triple canopy, you can't really see who it is that's shooting at you, but you can't let him kill you, or any of your men. At one time I saw an American that was so scared, the platoon Sgt. shot the guy that was nuts without killing him, and together with the rest of his platoon they pushed the enemy down and out of their perimeter. The gooks might over run our position; it happens all the time because when 300 gooks attack you they attack one bunker with usually 4 guys in it and they are given the duty to repel the enemy back with all of this noise, then the gooks add to it by screaming Yankee Die, G.I. Die and blowing their bugles. At nighttime when you can't see anything or anyone except the flashes from their muzzle you have to shoot back at anyone shooting in your direction. We call for all the shelling we can get. This is it; they are going to overrun our position, like we have a position. We get our heads down and call in the mortars on top of us. All of a sudden the bugles stop, no more screaming into those damn bullhorns. Maybe we held them off;

maybe they decide it wasn't worth their losses compared to their gain. Both ways we are alive, alive and no one is wounded. I raise my head high enough to see three maybe four of the little bastards walking around trying to draw our fire.

I found an AK47 lying on the ground about 20 meters from our location. I had gone there by myself, hoping to find a way out. I picked up the AK along with 5 magazines. It gives us a little more firepower than we had before. When the sun comes up we experience another bugle attack, they don't really attack us, but blow their bugles to make us scared, I put the selector switch on my new weapon on rock n roll and decide if they run up on me I'll have to kill as many as I can before they get me. We all decided we weren't going to be captured and put in a hellhole until this war was over. The gooks must not know where we were because they were firing their weapons into the different clumps of bamboo and small brush. We get a reality real quick when a B40 rocket comes busting in on us. It doesn't come close to any of us, but it sure scared the hell out of me.

The Recon Platoon Sergeant, S/SGT. Magwood gets on the horn and was surprised when he called and got an answer from us. He said from all the noise he heard that morning maybe our scalps would be hanging from some medicine pole. The gooks have a completely different way at looking at death then what we do. If you die for your cause you died a good death, if 30 of them die so that one American machine is disabled it was a good death, if they take out some people with it, it's icing on the cake. As it is, we all 5 made it through the night, through the attack and mortar attack upon ourselves. The 5 of us were as frighten to the up-most level, our concerns were but one, to live another day, then tomorrow the same, it's August 14 1968 at 0650 hours and the sun comes up like any other day. Raining and hot, we start the day like all others. First, we burn leeches off ourselves. We don't feel like eating but some good strong coffee sure sounds good. Parrish makes enough for each of us can have a little bit of the espresso strength coffee. I hope at this time that we will be rescued and be safe the remaindered of time I have left. I hope that going on this mission is not that mistake that would cause me to be killed or maimed. We are told if we can hold out until 1100 hours a line company will relieve us. We tell them that they need to keep these bastards off our backs by shooting artillery into their rank and file, while they are assaulting us. Then we could probably keep them from wearing our scalps on their poles. I keep firing the M79 into the air causing a light mortar barrage to keep these people from getting together on what to do about us. I have about 20 rounds left and I feel I need to save as many as I can for when the assault begins.

The enemy was trying to make their way across the fence into Cambodia or Laos when we got in their way. We were told it looks like a bunch of ants crawling up towards us. This is a very expensive piece of property that we have already put the down payment on, and some Company is going to make the rest of the payments, maybe the whole lump sum. The choppers are going to leave Firebase 29 at 11am and we will be able to see them leave. We are told that when the choppers arrive that we are to get on the first one ASAP. Grizzly gets on the horn and tells us to keep very low a Navy jet is going to drop a load of napalm on top of the gooks then another jet is to drop 2, 250lb bombs further down the slope. Right after that is when the choppers will be in. This way when the napalm goes off it will fry anyone up that high on the slope and anyone lower than that will stay in the area the 2 bombs will be dropped. So we grab everything we have and get ready for the exchange of human bodies, which could end up Cannon Fodder. I sure hoped not. We think that whoever is coming they may need all the luck in the world. We may have taken all the luck out of the barrel, there might not be any good luck left, I really hope just a little more. Get us safely home and I know it sounds horrible but who ever is coming to save us, I hope they get here to take our place before we are all killed dead. The 2 jets drop their payload and we are off to the races to get close to where that first chopper is landing. Van and I are on the left side and the other 3 on the right side of this bird from heaven, taking us out of hell's grasp. It's A Company coming to our rescue.

The first guy out of the chopper is Lt. Leo Hadley our old platoon leader. He shakes Van's hand and looks me square in the eyes. He has the look of death in his eyes. Lt. Hadley is an eager, impulsive officer who is anxious to tie into the enemy; he pushed his men hard, but never too hard. We feel these people that have come to relieve us were lucky to have Hadley as their CO. The pilot shouts that if we are going, we better hurry, and get aboard, he's taking off now. Van and I both jump into the chopper on our side and the other 3 were already aboard, as we are flying away Van asks "Did you see that look in Hadley's eyes, it looked all hallow and like you could look down into his soul." I tell him "it was the look of death staring back at us". Part of me wanted to stay with Hadley and protect him, as we believe he may have given up his life so that we might live ours. Van tells me "LT Hadley didn't want to be there." I tell him "Leo Hadley didn't want to be there, but LT Leo Hadley the soldier knew he must." He was a dam good soldier. Maybe the enemy will move on now that there are more troops there now?

Within a couple minutes we are at the firebase and some of A company is still there getting ready to hop aboard and meet up with the rest of their company. Nothing happens to the guys on the ground so we figure the gooks have left the area and all A company will do is chase them back into Cambodia or Laos. We were tired and hungry therefore we headed straight to the mess tent for a quick recharging of our human batteries. As we sat at our bunker by the pad eating our lunch, we could look out past the chopper pad towards that hilltop we had left but a few moments ago. At last feeling safe, and that those left behind had put themselves in harms way in the simple step taking our place on that hilltop. As we were again looking out over the chopper pad we saw then heard the rocket impacting on the poor souls that had taken our place.

We all prayed that the one projectile was all that was heading their way. A hope that was suddenly replaced with our acknowledging those that had taken our place, may have given the highest price one could spend to save us. Then we saw five rockets all landing in the area we had just left, Lt Hadley gets on the phone and tells, Grizzly, We're receiving in-coming!" Then he goes off the air for a couple minutes, and then comes back on with "Grizzly" and that was the last we heard from one of the men that took our place. We hear no more from that knoll for around 2 minutes except for more rockets striking and then some one gets on the phone and asked if they could be escorted off the hill. The rocket attack was over and they were afraid that there might be a human assault coming and they were unorganized and that they might not be able to hold that hill top if the enemy wanted to kick them off of it. Grizzly recalls he got on his chopper and went and directed the remaining men of A company to a safe spot, because he can fly right over where the remainder of A Company is, he directs them off of that knoll, and to a hill where they can be extracted. It took 2 days before someone could go out and retrieve the bodies of those that gave all, so that we might live another day. Leo Hadley had given all, so that we might live long enough to tell his story. I know you may think this story was about me. It wasn't. It was all about a group of men, like so many other men who give up all, so that some of us can go on to I hope, better things. At least we can hope they didn't suffer, when we heard that Hadley was one of those that were killed, my heart sunk. We were there just an hour ago and we might have been all killed if it hadn't been for Hadley and the 14 others that gave their all that the 5 of us might have not made it. As I kiss my wife and children good night, I realize that if it had not for those 15 men, none of us would live the life we have today. We put all of the bodies in body bags and set them back on the chopper pad so we could load them up and get them out of sight, out of thought, but that sight has never left my mind. Hadley had so many holes in his young body. To this day, I still feel that I was the one that was supposed to have those holes in my body. All of us feel that way. The irony of it all was that Lt. Hadley had four weeks to go until he could have gone home. I believe he was from Manhattan, Kansas. I wish that I had gone there to talk to his relatives to remind them that he was a great man and that these 5 men have their lives because he gave up his in their place .I found out later that Col. Jamie Hendrix did just that. I contacted Hadley's Sister, Linda and she gave me copies of some of Hadley's letters home. I told her of the brave Leo Hadley and how we realize he took our place on that small hilltop. She told me Leo wouldn't want us to feel guilty about him taking our place, he was just doing his job, a job that he truly loved.

About a week later I got on my last chopper ride and headed for Dakto, then a convoy to Camp Enari where. I filled out some papers, put on a khaki uniform, and received my Purple Heart, Army Commendation Medal and other ribbons. While waiting for my exit from the war I run into 2 guys I went to High School with. Jack Moore and John Phillips, My Junior year I went to school in Decatur, Illinois. They were on the basketball team along with my cousin Jack Sunderlik who was an all area sports figure at SDHS and on their way to the same unit, together I believe. Sure hope they make it for the whole year, without getting hurt, or killed dead In some ways having a friend over there is great, just as long as he doesn't get hurt real bad, or killed dead on the spot. It is a million times worse if the one hurt had a chance to get by with the injury, but because you were there, it made it possible for him to be maimed for life. This you will carry to your grave. I found out later that they both were alive. After I also learned, that Lt North's brother wasn't even in Vietnam while Jack was there. They still kept score.

When I changed planes in San Francisco, I was spit on my some black lady that asked me " Why did I get to come home when her boy didn't?" I couldn't answer that then, or now. I was home for a couple weeks I received a letter from Rex. He tells me, a sniper killed Mike Faulkner while he was on a mission two weeks ago, and that he thought I might like to know. It was a sniper that fled, after firing that fatal shot. I lived only a few miles from Mike's parents and I had a fight with-in myself as should I go, or not. I decided that I would not go. Because if his loved ones would ask me the question I ask myself each day, as the sun rises in the East, why did I get to come home and their son Michael did not? It is a question that I have tried to answer. But I still don't have an answer that I accept; maybe it's just bad luck? Never did find that hospital we looked a year for, maybe it wasn't there? I will always remember August 14, 1968 as the day I started a new, very lucky life. We will never forget those that took our place on that day, there is no way that we should. Every day that I'm alive, I will have to thank those 14 and LT Hadley for doing their duty and taking our place on that little hilltop where I left my soul and ever since have been trying to grow a new one.

The letter from Colonel Jamie R. Hendrix dated 2006 Feb. 17

Dear Mike,

Thank you for your letter about your service with the Recon Platoon of the 3rd Bn, 12th Inf.; and your kind remarks about 1st Lt. Leo Hadley (which I obviously agree) and me.

When I came through 4th Div. HQ in late Oct. 67, on the way to Dakto to assume command of the 3/12th, I met Lt Hadley who was serving as an Asst. Public Affairs Officer. He impressed me very favorably and I "recruited" him to come to the 3/12th if he could get released from Div. HQ. One day toward the end of the Battle of Dakto in Dec., Lt. Hadley reported for duty! I assigned him to A company, as a Rifle Platoon Leader. He distinguished himself in his very first action, earning a Silver Star and a Purple Heart!

I used the Recon Platoon as a ready action force," or as a "light" (very light) fifth rifle Co. I tried to maintain it as near full strength as possible (never possible!) and manned it with good soldiers and my best Platoon Leader. So shortly, after Lt Hadley returned to duty, I gave him the Recon Platoon where he excelled.

I took a personal interest in Leo Hadley, probably because he reminded me of myself when I was a Rifle Platoon Leader and a Rifle Co Commander (also as a Lt) in the Korean War. He had informed me that he had decided to make the Army a career, which influenced me to offer him command of Co A, because he was a better leader than a captain on my staff, and it would help his career. I was surprised when he almost turned it down, because he felt such loyalty to you guys in Recon! Then I informed him that I was going to make the move anyway, and he agreed!" he knew it was a good career move, but he still hated to leave Recon.

When he relieved you guys on 14 Aug, they had not even had time to dig in when they were hit by recoilless rifle fire from the vicinity of the Cambodian border. I was watching the relief from on top of the TOC, when Leo called me on the radio. He only said: Grizzly we are receiving incoming" (which I could see) when he went off the air. In a minute or two, he came back and I could tell he was seriously wounded from the sound of his voice. I could see the rounds impacting on his position, and he only got out my call sign "Grizzly" The irony was that he would have rotated home in just two more weeks. I immediately called for my helicopter and directed the withdrawal of the survivors carrying the wounded. We recovered the bodies two days later.

After I retired, I visited Leo's Mother and sister in Manhattan, Kansas (his Father ,an Army LTC , was already dead.) I then visited Leo's grave in the Post cemetery at Ft. Riley, Kansas, where Leo is buried beside his father. In his last action, Leo received another Silver Star and Purple Heart posthumously. I also visited the Wall" in Washington, and the only name I touched was Leo L Hadley. I was too overcome with emotion to look up the other 121 who died under my command in the 3/12th. Mike, although I went to Vietnam four times, I will always consider my year in command of the 3rd Battalion, 12th Infantry as the highlight of my career. To have had the honor and privilege of leading such outstanding soldiers as you and Leo Hadley epitomized under such trying conditions- was more than I could have hoped for. I only wish that I could have told all of you that in person.

Thank you for your dedicated service to our country.

Respectfully,
Jamie R. Hendrix
Colonel, Infantry (retired)

P.S. I like the patch   "GRIZZY"

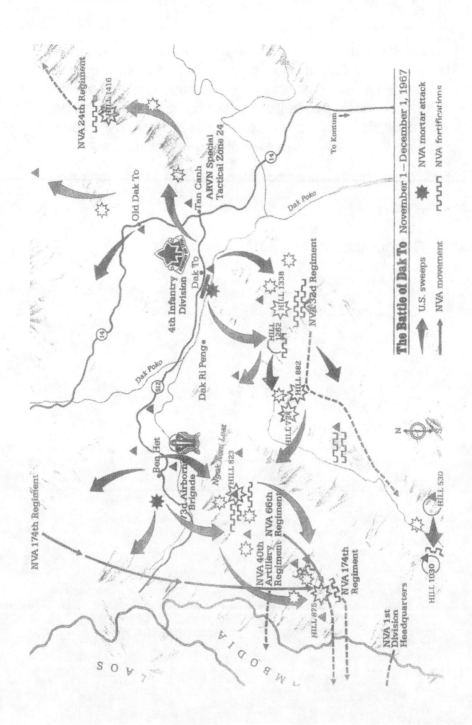

The Battle of Dak To November 1 – December 1, 1967

ME WITH SKULL ON HEAD

Some of the Guys from Recon

me coming in from mission

LT. HADLEY. 1st silverstar

SAFE-CONDUCT PASS TO BE HONORED BY ALL VIETNAMESE GOVERNMENT AGENCIES AND ALLIED FORCES

Đây là một tấm Giấy Thông Hành có giá trị với tất cả cơ quan Quân Chính Việt - Nam Cộng - Hòa và lực lượng Đồng - Minh.

№ 301289 E

An ARVN soldier "opens his arms" to an NLF soldier on one side of the leaflet.

ĐÂY TẤM GIẤY THÔNG HÀNH CÓ GIÁ TRỊ VỚI TẤT CẢ CƠ - QUAN QUÂN CHÍNH · VIỆT - NAM CỘNG - HÒA VÀ LỰC - LƯỢNG ĐỒNG - MINH.

SAFE-CONDUCT PASS TO BE HONORED BY ALL VIETNAMESE GOVERNMENT AGENCIES AND ALLIED FORCES

The other side assures safe passage to the pass holder.

PATCH I DESIGNED 1968
BEFORE LEAVING VIETNAM

Group getting our beer RAtion

GLOSSARY OF TERMS

AGENT Orange - Highly toxic defoliant sprayed on vegetation and us

AK47- Automatic weapon of NVA

ARVN- Army of the Republic of Vietnam (South)

Base camp- Brigade or Division-size headquarters

Bird- any aircraft usually a helicopter

Body bags- plastic bags used for retrieval of dead bodies on the battlefield

Bush- an infantry term for out in the field

Bust-caps- term for firing rapidly at an enemy

C-4- plastic explosive, can be used to heat your meals or blow a LZ.

Chieu hoi- a voluntary surrender from the NVA or VC

CIB- Combat Infantry Badge (Badge of Honor)

C-rations- canned food usually older than you were (1945 and older)

Claymore- antipersonnel mine carried by infantry, defense of perimeter

CO- commanding officer

Deros-Date eligible to return from overseas

Dust-off- medical evacuation helicopters

Fire fight- exchange of small arms fire with the enemy.

Hooch-a simply constructed dwelling

K-bar- combat knife

KIA-killed in action

Killed dead- an infantry term when killed in action

Lifer-a career military person (some were good)

LP- forward Listening Post (used at night)

LZ- landing zone

M14- wood stocked rifle 7.62 rounds; US forces quit using in 1966

MIA-missing in action

M16-standard weapon of American forces after 1966

M79- single barreled grenade launcher used by US Forces (40 mm)

NCO-Noncommissioned officer

NVA-North Vietnamese Army

Point- the forward man or element on a combat mission

Poncho liner-Nylon insert used as a blanket

Recon- a small scout patrol to search for enemy activity

RTO-Radio Telephone Operator

Sapper-NVA commando caring explosives to blow up bridges bunkers ECT.

SP pack-cellophane packet containing cigarettes and salt & pepper

SKS- a rifle used by the enemy could be fully automatic by selector switch

VC- Viet Cong, we didn't see much of them

Wasted-killed dead

WIA-wounded in action

Those that have made this story what it is.

Colonel Jamie Hendrix
commanding officer 3/12th Inf.4th Infantry Division

Lt. Leo Hadley
commanding officer A Co., also our old platoon leader, Recon

Lt. E Joe Jones
2nd platoon leader B Co. 3/12

Lt. Edwin Hines Aug 14 was his 21st Birthday
4th Div. HQ

Lt. J North
Platoon Leader recon, Col Hendrix is the one that told me he
was Oliver's brother

S/SGT Gilbert Mumford
Platoon SGT recon

S/SGT Magwood
Platoon SGT recon

Ronnie Baker
team leader recon

Van Brown
team member recon

Mick Cole
team member recon

Mike Lula
team leader recon

Jerry Parrish, I think his first name was Jerry,
he wasn't a first name yet when I left
team member recon

Darrel Stewart
team leader recon

Robert (Chief) Antonio- walked point
team member recon

Charlie Zollman
team member recon. He extended so he could go back to
Australia and get married, she got to the states then disappeared.

Mike Faulkner
team member recon. killed just after I left Vietnam

Pluto, Jerry or Jerome was his first name;
Pluto was a nickname from home
team member recon

Keith Wynn
team member recon

Galen (Festus) Cartright
team member recon, crazy?

Bill (Big Reb) Watkins
team member recon. wounded on hill 1338

Steve (Little Reb) Moore
team member recon. died from cancer (agent orange)

Mike Moomey
team member, author, recon (diabetes agent orange)

Little Beaver
team member recon

Dempsey
team member recon

Thornton
team member recon

Ron Brown
team member recon

Sammy Alewine
C Co 3/12th

Tom
D Co 3/12th

Pete Graham
My asst gunner D Co 3/12th

Jon Arnes
Other Machine gunner D Co 3/12th, he went to 9th

And a few more that I'm sorry but I don't remember your names there may be a couple of the names that may not be the correct name but I put them as I remembered. You probably don't remember me either. But, I made it home I hope you did also.

Group getting our beer Ration

LaVergne, TN USA
22 July 2010

190441LV00001B/60/P